STUART MASQUES
AND THE RENAISSANCE STAGE

A Glory and Cloud Machines at Turin (Seventeenth Century)
Biblioteca Nazionale, Turin.

STUART MASQUES
AND THE RENAISSANCE STAGE

BY

ALLARDYCE NICOLL M.A.

PROFESSOR OF THE HISTORY OF DRAMA AND DRAMATIC CRITICISM IN
YALE UNIVERSITY
AUTHOR OF "THE DEVELOPMENT OF THE THEATRE" "BRITISH DRAMA"
"MASKS MIMES AND MIRACLES" "THE THEORY OF DRAMA"
"FILM AND THEATRE" ETC.

WITH ONE HUNDRED AND NINETY-SEVEN
ILLUSTRATIONS

Published by Benjamin Blom, Inc.
New York 1968

Printed in U.S.A. by

NOBLE OFFSET PRINTERS, INC.

NEW YORK 3, N. Y.

THIS VOLUME,
DEVOTED TO A STUDY OF THE STAGING
OF THE STUART MASQUES PRODUCED AT
WHITEHALL UNDER THE SUPERVISION OF
THE LORDS CHAMBERLAIN TO KING JAMES I
AND KING CHARLES I, IS RESPECTFULLY
DEDICATED TO

The Right Honourable the EARL OF CROMER
G.C.B., G.C.I.E., G.C.V.O., P.C.
LORD CHAMBERLAIN TO HIS MAJESTY
KING GEORGE VI

PREFACE

UCH has been written concerning the masques presented at court during the sixteenth and seventeenth centuries, but no attempt has hitherto been made to present a comprehensive and detailed survey of their staging. My endeavour in this book is to examine the work of Inigo Jones and his fellow 'architects' in the light of contemporary Italian theatre practice for the purpose of determining—so far as such a determination is possible—the precise methods employed in the production of these royal entertainments. Naturally, in this task I owe much to previous studies, in particular the work of Rudolf Brotanek, Paul Reyher, Enid Welsford, Percy Simpson, W. J. Lawrence, and Lily B. Campbell; but I trust that I have been able, by special attention devoted to one single aspect of Renaissance theatrical activity, to add to the results of their researches.

In the preparation of *Stuart Masques and the Renaissance Stage* I have been greatly aided by the resources of the recently established Theatrical Collection of Yale University, instituted by a grant from the Rockefeller Foundation. In connexion with the work of gathering material for this collection I was enabled to make a complete photographic record of the Inigo Jones designs preserved at Chatsworth, as well as the exceedingly informative drawings of contemporary Turin ballets. Thousands of other Renaissance sketches have been similarly photographed for the collection by Mr George Kernodle, Mr Stanley McCandless, Mr John M'Dowell, and Mr Clark Mendum. Most of the prints used for the illustrations here were made by Mr Mendum. Of these illustrations all but about half a dozen have never hitherto been reproduced.

The stage directions from masque libretti are for the most part quoted from the original quartos; for masques by D'Avenant and Jonson, however, I have used the folios of their works, except in a few instances where the quarto provides material not printed in the folio text. In quoting these stage directions I have modified the original punctuation and modernized the use of *u* and *v*.

For permission to make use of the Inigo Jones designs I wish to thank his Grace the Duke of Devonshire; in obtaining access to these I owe much to the kind co-operation of Mr Francis Thompson, librarian at Chatsworth. I am indebted for much courteous assistance to the authorities of the British Museum, the Bodleian Library, and Yale University Library. Mr Allan H. Bright, of Barton Court, Colwall, kindly put at my disposal his comprehensive collection of emblem books, thus considerably facilitating my work in that field. My thanks are due as well to the many Continental libraries—notably the Biblioteca Nazionale of Turin, the Uffizi and the Biblioteca Nazionale of Florence—where permission was granted for the copying of original designs and engravings.

A. N.

CONTENTS

11

ILLUSTRATIONS

14

ILLUSTRATIONS

ILLUSTRATIONS

I

THIS INSUBSTANTIAL PAGEANT

PROSPERO has frequently been treated by the commentators as a symbol—a symbol of Christianity, of civilization, of William Shakespeare himself. Whatever truth may rest in these speculations, of one thing we may be assured: in that scene wherein he celebrates the betrothal of his daughter to young Ferdinand his actions make him thoroughly representative of the princely ideal which animated his age. If he had had human courtiers to do his bidding he would unquestionably have caused them to present some show allegorically bearing upon this special occasion, just as dukes in Milan, princes in Florence, and kings in England made glorious their courts by wedding entertainments and masquing revelry. Not having such human servants in his command, Prospero summons to his aid Ariel's spirit troop. Before the wondering eyes of Miranda and Ferdinand come forth Iris and Ceres and Juno. A band of nymphs, the Naiads with "sedgèd crowns," dance in company with some country reapers, celebrating thus the royal and happy occasion.

Suddenly, in the midst of these revels, harshly breathes rumour of rebellion, and Prospero, dismissing his airy wraiths, finds occasion to utter what are perhaps the most famous lines in the entire Shakespearian canon, likening life to this show which had passed away, dreaming that the gorgeous palaces, the solemn temples, the cloud-capped towers, even the great globe itself, would one day dissolve and vanish into nothingness.

Reading that speech to-day, we endeavour to interpret it in terms of the palaces and temples known to us; in our minds hover vague impressions of solid buildings with, superimposed upon them, an image of the world's orb, which, for its very vastness, we cannot, try how we may, succeed in making concrete. Not so, perhaps, did Shakespeare conceive it, or his contemporaries interpret its significance. The commonly accepted date for the composition of *The Tempest* is 1610–11; six years earlier, with Samuel Daniel's *The Vision of the Twelve Goddesses* and Ben Jonson's *The Masque of Blackness*, was inaugurated that rich and nobly foolish line of courtly entertainments which made magnificent the reigns of James and Charles. That Shakespeare himself, as a prominent member of the King's company of actors and thus attached to the royal service, would have been granted the opportunity of witnessing some at least of these entertainments seems likely, and the likelihood strengthens almost to certainty when we observe that the whole imagery of Prospero's speech, together with the masque from which it springs, is based on revels which had already charmed Stuart eyes at Whitehall. Ceres and Juno had appeared in *The Vision of the Twelve Goddesses*. Nymphs, called naiads, were footing it in the same author's *Tethys' Festival*, and their companions, the reapers, gave a "country dance" in the anonymous *Four Seasons*.[1]

Were this all, we need have experienced no surprise. That Shakespeare, designing a short insert for his comedy, might seek for material in the likeliest available places is readily understandable; in any event, Ceres, Iris, Juno, and the nymphs were all very commonplace figures of Renaissance imagining, and no masques were necessary for their invention. The immediate source, indeed, of

---

[1] For the contractions used in citing the titles of the various masques and for their dating see the list given at pp. 215–218. The precise occasion when *Four Seasons* was presented is not known; it may be later than the *première* of *The Tempest*. In any case, the examples given here are to be regarded as merely typical of the kind of scenes shown in the early masques.

the dramatist's characters matters little, and assuredly can never be precisely determined. When, however, we find that all the images employed by Prospero in his following speech correspond to other elements introduced into these very masques, the identity in mythological characters assumes a fresh interest. Towers, palaces, temples, and the globe are mentioned in Prospero's oration. One of the scenes of *Tethys' Festival* displayed a marvellous palace wrought of pillars seemingly

Fig. 1. KING OBERON'S PALACE IN "OBERON" (1611)
Inigo Jones. Chatsworth (*Designs*, No. 43). Copyright of his Grace the Duke of Devonshire.

made of burnished gold, and in *Oberon* appeared "a bright and glorious *Palace*, whose gates and walls were transparent" (Fig. 1). Glorious and gorgeous were these, yet insubstantial too, for in a moment they vanished from sight, giving place to new wonders and seeming as though they never had been. Somnus, the spirit of that sleep by which Shakespeare saw all our lives surrounded, awaking in the cave of *The Vision of the Twelve Goddesses*, waved his wand "and so made them seem to see there a Temple"—the Temple of Peace. The suddenness of its appearance, its creation out of dream, its airy quality—all these are reminiscent of the scene introduced into *The Tempest*. Of clouds Inigo Jones, the great artificer of such things, was enamoured, and oftentimes his soaring towers had their tops hidden within the canvas frames of the theatrical heaven, "cloud-capped" literally and more materially than the towers of reality. Most significant of all, a globe, or μικροκόσμος, painted to show the countries of the world, was one of the admired novelties devised for *Hymenæi*. "This stood, or rather hung (for no *Axell* was seene to support it), and, turning softly," disappeared before men's gaze. Maybe in Shakespeare's mind as he penned those famous lines for Prospero was an image, not abstract and vague of this earth we tread on, but concrete and exact of a sphere in a masque, turning and vanishing.

Fig. 2. A Cloud Scene
Inigo Jones. Chatsworth (*Designs*, No. 384). Copyright of his Grace the Duke of Devonshire.

Hymenæi perhaps gives us the real clue to the source of the dramatist's imagery. Those haunting final words—

> like this insubstantial pageant faded,
> Leave not a rack behind—

find a direct echo in Jonson's own description of his spectacular entertainment. "The upper part of the *Scene*," he writes, "which was all of Clouds, and made artificially to swell and ride like the *Racke*, began to open." The rack of the sky may be a natural thing, but for Jonson and Shakespeare it could also apply to that last, that slowly passing wisp of painted canvas over the stage heavens which, once gone, left naught of the scene remaining save a dying memory. Of this, one may imagine, Shakespeare thought; from this came to him his vision of the world when all the seemingly substantial things of our universe should begin to shift and change their forms as easily and as miraculously as the scenic fabrics conceived and built by the skilful hand of Inigo Jones. For the masque there was no lowering of a curtain that the scene-shifters might alter the setting unseen by the audience. 'Suddenly' is a word we meet with frequently in the descriptive accounts, and there can be no doubt but that the artist's main endeavour was to secure so swift a passing away of the existing set and so rapid an appearance of its successor that spectators should fail to observe the means whereby the one was made to transform itself into the other. "The *Alterations of Scenes*," remarked Francis Bacon,[1] to whom these toys were dear, "so it be quietly and without Noise, are Things of great Beauty and Pleasure: For they feed and relieve the Eye before it be full of the same Object."

Further might we proceed in an examination of the playwright's indebtedness to the masquing devices of his time, seeing the genesis of Ariel in those "spirites of the ayre . . . making musique" who surrounded Juno when the clouds parted in *Hymenæi*, even suggesting that Prospero's kingdom was based on the "Island floating on a calme water" which moved forward in Jonson's *Beauty*, but that field has already been surveyed and need not here be further traversed.[2] Sufficient be it to observe that if these conjectures are justified the scenic artistry of Inigo Jones, first to develop such arts in England, served to stir the imagination of one whom we recognize as the greatest dramatist of all time.

THE BODY AND SOUL OF MASQUE

Prospero's lines, dealing with the transitoriness and evanescence of lovely forms, bear with them a pathetic melancholy, and just such a melancholy pervades many of the descriptions penned by the authors of these masquing entertainments. That such beauty, produced of so much labour, should have no power to remain and to claim permanence might provoke none other than thoughts of sadness. "The honor and splendor of these *spectacles*," wrote Ben Jonson, "was such in the performance as, could those houres have lasted, this of mine now had been a most unprofitable worke"; and again, "Onely the envie was that it lasted not still, or (now it is past) cannot by imagination, much lesse description, be recovered to a part of that *spirit* it had in the gliding by." The sadness arises from the recognition that no human endeavour could lengthen by a jot the passing hour or snatch from it one moment to hold and to preserve. The performance over, dead was the beauty and vanished the grace.

Vanished because, whatever lyric lovelinesses Jonson or Shirley contributed to the masque and whatever grandiloquent claims the former made to poetic pre-eminence, this kind of show owed its very life to visually exquisite presentation. With somewhat sour grace Daniel recognized that the "pompe and splendor of the sight takes up all the intention without regard what is spoken"; even though it irked him, thus in his first masque, *The Vision of the Twelve Goddesses*, he was compelled to

---

[1] *A Harmony of the Essays*, ed. Edward Arber (1871), p. 539.

[2] The relationship between the masque in *The Tempest* and contemporary entertainments is discussed in Enid Welsford, *The Court Masque* (Cambridge, 1927). This book deals mainly with the literary qualities of the Stuart productions, although there is in it an acute and painstaking examination of early ballet. The entire subject is examined also by Paul Reyher, *Les Masques anglais* (Paris, 1909), and by Rudolf Brotanek, *Die englischen Maskenspiele* (Vienna, 1902). Mary S. Steele, *Plays and Masques at Court* (New Haven, Connecticut, 1926), gives a chronological list of productions, with notes. Surveys of masque development appear in Sir E. K. Chambers, *The Elizabethan Stage* (Oxford, 1923), and C. H. Herford and Percy Simpson, *The Works of Ben Jonson* (Oxford, 1925). Mary Sullivan, *The Court Masques of James I* (New York, 1913), deals largely with the social and political significance of these shows. A bibliographical *List of Masques* (1902) has been prepared by W. W. Greg. Among other studies of special significance are Ashley H. Thorndike's *Shakespeare's Theater* (New York, 1916) and the same author's essay, *Influence of the Court-Masques on the Drama, 1608-15* (Publ. of the Modern Language Association of America*, xv (1900), 114-120). W. J. Lawrence has a special study on *The Mounting of the Carolan Masques* (*The Elizabethan Playhouse*, Stratford, 1912), together with other individual essays referred to later. *Italian Prototypes of the Masque and Dumb Show* (*P.M.L.A.A.*, xvii (1907), 140-156) are discussed by John W. Cunliffe. Edward J. Dent deals with the musical element in his *Foundations of English Opera* (Cambridge, 1928), pp. 18-42.

speak the truth.   Dekker might grumble that, while "the soule that should give life and a tongue" to such things was breathed "out of Writers pens," yet "the limnes of it ly at the hard-handed mercy of Mychanitiens," and Jonson contrast the spirit of poetry with the physical properties of the scenery; but the fact remains that audiences derived their impressions not so much from the words spoken or sung as from the glorious settings and the scintillating costumes.   "In these things," wrote Daniel in a later masque, "the only life consists in shew; the arte and invention of the Architect gives the greatest grace and is of most importance."

That Jonson quarrelled bitterly with Inigo Jones on this score is a fact well known, and maybe even now it is difficult and dangerous to take sides with one or the other.   For Jonson verse was the soul of masque and Jones's scenes merely "the bodily part"; this was the source of their difference, and the angry outbreak of 1631 was merely the result of divergent opinions established at the beginning of their collaboration.   Collaboration, indeed, was hardly what Jonson aimed at; one might almost say that it was precisely this at which he rebelled.   At the start, in *Blackness* and *Beauty*, all the descriptions stress his own contribution.   Everything was "my invention."   The success of Jones's settings, however, soon compelled a change.   In *Queens* a specific note had to be introduced informing the reader that the "device" of the witches' attire, together "with the invention and *architecture* of the whole *scene* and *machine*, . . . was Master Iones his," while in 1631 the aged poet found that his name had to be placed, ignominiously, with that of the architect on the title-page of *Love's Triumph*.

Jones became for Jonson "the greatest villain in the world" simply because he refused to bow to his judgment concerning the relative values of their work.   No doubt in this quarrel there were personal grievances; but the break between the two collaborators was symbolic of an ageless conflict between the scene-designer and the playwright.   Observing that in the masque all eyes were intent upon the settings and the costumes, Inigo Jones claimed that he had the right to as much credit as had the poet; Jonson, impatient and sceptical concerning the value of any art save his own, glanced angrily at the esteem won by a man who, in his eyes, was little more than a master-craftsman, a petty architect.

> Mr Surveyour, you that first beganne
> From thirty pound, in pipkins, to the man
> You are: from them leap'd forth an Architect,
> Able to talk of Euclide, and correct
> Both him and Archimede; damne Archytas,
> The Noblest Inginere that ever was;
> Control Ctesibius, over-beareing us
> With mistooke names out of Vitruvius;
> Drawne Aristotle on us, and thence showne
> How much *Architectonice* is your owne;
> Whether the building of the Stage or Scene
> Or making of the properties it meane,
> Vizors or Anticks; or it comprehend
> Something your Sur-ship doth not yet intend—
> By all your titles and whole stile at once
> Of Tireman, Mounte-bank and Justice Jones,
> I doe salute you.[1]

So Jonson wrote, setting down in candid terms the opinion he had formed of his adversary and fellow-artist, and as he wrote he found his bitterness welling up within him.

---

[1] This poem is in the British Museum (MS. Harl. 4955); printed in *The Poems of Ben Jonson*, ed. B. H. Newdigate (Oxford, 1936), pp. 295–296.

What makes your wretchedness to bray so loud
In Towne and Court?   Are you growne rich and proud?
Your trappings will not change you, Change your mind;
No velvet sheath you weare will alter kind. . . .
What is the cause you pomp it soe, I aske.
And all men eccho, You have made a masque!
I chime that too, and I have mett with those
That doe cry up the Machine and the showes,
The Majesty of Juno in the cloudes,
And peering forth of Iris in the shroudes. . . .
          O showes, showes, mighty showes!
The eloquence of Masques!   What need of prose
Or verse, or sense, t'express immortall you?

The result of these reflections was that he came to determine that "Painting and Carpentry are the soule of Masque," instead of poetry, as it ought to be.   The world was out of joint, and in this "money-got, mechanic age" there could be no hope of virtue from this form of artistic expression. Money and fame alike passed to his rival.   True, he tried to rise above it all, to demonstrate his own superiority, but not all his protestations can conceal the deep-felt anger of his heart.

I am too fatt to envy, hee too leane
To be worth envy.   Hence-forth I doe meane
To pitty him, as smileing at his feate
Of Lanterne-Lerrey, with fuliginous heate
Whirling his whimseys, by a subtilty
Suck'd from the veines of shop-phylosophy. . . .
O wise Surveyor, wiser Architect,
But wisest Inigo, who can reflect
On the new priming of thy old signe-Posts,
Reviving, with fresh colours, the pale ghosts
Of thy dead standards; or with miracle see
Thy twice conceiv'd, thrice paid-for Imag'rie
And not fall downe before it and confesse
Allmighty Architecture, who no lesse
A Goddess is then painted cloth, Dele-boards,
Vermilion, Lake or Cinnopar affords
Expression for, with that unbounded line
Aym'd at in thy Omnipotent *Designe*!
What Poesy ere was painted on a Wall
That may compare with thee?

To Shakespeare these things were marvels from which he wrought some of his most beautiful lines; to Jonson they were merely annoyance and vexation of spirit.   Such is the measure of difference between these two authors, and in their difference each stands representative of an ideal recognizable beyond their own land and age.

The scurrilities which Jonson heaped on this "Mime" and the burlesque portraits of him that he inserted into his later plays need not concern us, for they relate mainly to the personal antagonism between the two men, and in any case have been dealt with fully elsewhere.   Significant for our purpose only are the fundamental principles underlying that antagonism.   In Jonson's defence many things may be said, but in one particular respect his argument fails.   Between the masque and the kind of drama which was produced in the public theatre he made no distinction, with the result that standards fitted for *Hamlet* and *Volpone* were imposed on *Chloridia* and *Oberon*.   When a great comedy or a tragedy instinct with metaphysical reasoning is burdened and made embarrassed with

24

scenic panoply and the encumbrance of pompous clothes we may agree that the essential spirit of the theatre has been betrayed, but in another light must we view the masque. Here, as in the popular emblem literature of the age, the visual and the auditory have to meet in harmony if complete expression is to be secured; the picture addressed to the eyes has as much importance as the dialogue spoken or sung. While, therefore, we may legitimately deplore the frequent way in which over-rich designing has been used to crush dramatic masterpieces, it is open for us at the same time to condemn Jonson for his failure to accept the conditions inherent in the art of masque-manufacture. For a bare stage, a poet's burning words, and an actor's passion we may pine without thereby rendering ourselves completely oblivious to values inherent in another theatrical realm, where 'lantern-lerry,' painting, and carpentry hold equal place with lyric song and the words of wit— a smaller realm, perhaps, and of secondary importance, yet worthy of our attention.

THE MASQUING SHOW

Poetry lives, as Jonson vociferated, but the art of the scene-designer and the producer dies soon. Are these spectacles, then, which once charmed so many eyes, which were so clear a symbol of their age, which inspired the imagination even of a Shakespeare, gone as utterly as Prospero's visions? Must we accept them as purely transitory things and so dismiss them from our minds? Undoubtedly in seeking an answer to such a question we must confess that these revels at Whitehall can never be resummoned for our delectation; the canvas frames of the scenery are irretrievably lost, and the rich costumes become mere crumbling dust. One chance alone remains—that we may so reconstruct the forms of the masque as imaginatively to place ourselves amid the thronging courtiers of that bygone age, or else in fancy work back-stage among Jones's marvellous "machines."

Such an imaginative reconstruction, of course, implies much effort and demands the utilization of many diverse, often seemingly trivial, scraps of information. The descriptions provided by the masque authors, invaluable as they may be, are by themselves inadequate, partly because some writers, like Jonson, objecting to the predominance of the physical show, insufficiently outlined the nature of the spectacle, and partly because mere words, however brilliantly manipulated and penned with no matter what technical assurance, could never hope to express fully things conceived of in terms of another art. The descriptions will aid us certainly—indeed, from them must we start; but other sources of knowledge will have to be brought into association with them before we can hope to transmute their verbal forms into imaginatively visual shapes, and thus interpret their sentences aright. Clearly for this purpose it is necessary to have something conceived of in the same way as the settings themselves, something that speaks directly to the eye.

Happily, partial, if not complete, assistance of the kind is available for us in the collection of designs executed by Inigo Jones for various masques performed between 1606 and 1640.[1] These designs, many of them showing progressive stages in the invention of a costume or of a set, are invaluable, and from a study of them alone may we hope to reach any remotely adequate conception of what appeared before the eyes of James, Charles, and their courtiers. Not, however, that they tell us all; indeed, if we treat them solely as designs we shall not do them justice. A scenic artist's sketch is at best nothing but the basis for a setting, and to interpret it, to translate its vague terms into actual stage proportions, demands more than simple æsthetic appreciation. A canvas or a mural painting is complete in itself; its destiny is achieved when it leaves the painter's hands. Not so a scenic design, which exists for an ultimate purpose not yet realized when it itself is completed;

---

[1] This collection, now in the possession of the Duke of Devonshire at Chatsworth, has been ably catalogued and described by Percy Simpson and C. F. Bell in *Designs by Inigo Jones for Masques and Plays at Court* (Oxford, 1924). The catalogue is cited here as *Designs*. It includes fifty-one plates of reproductions.

its intent must always presuppose the creation of some other thing guided by its directions. To judge these designs rightly, therefore, we must know the precise methods by which the artist intended his primal conception to become transmogrified into the theatrical scene. Valuable as Jones's drawings are, they prove virtually useless if independently considered; knowledge alone of stage mechanics during the seventeenth century can make them yield their secrets.

So far as England is concerned, unfortunately, such knowledge is not fully obtainable, but by good fortune, although no theatrical artist of London left behind him a book of technical instructions relating to the stage practice of his time, cognate material, eminently serviceable, exists elsewhere, and may legitimately be applied to the English theatre. We are aware, from many scattered indications, that basically the means employed in the presentation of the masques at the English court were the same as those employed during the same period in the production of Italian *intermezzi* and operas. Because of Jones's debt, both in method and in conception, to Continental examples, an interpretation of his work in the light of Italian procedure is amply justifiable, and from such a process of interpretation we may hope to reach at least some fairly adequate understanding of the appeal made by these shows on which vast sums were expended from the royal treasury and concerning attendance at which dignified ambassadors wrangled and intrigued.

Our obvious task, therefore, must be so to co-ordinate our knowledge of masque descriptions, of specific designs for those masques, and of Italian stage practice as to enable us, if we desire, to reproduce exactly the appearance which these productions assumed in seventeenth-century London. We require to know, not merely that a cloud descended, but by what mechanical process it was thus made to descend; when we see allusion to the rising of a curtain we must discover the means by which that curtain was manipulated. It behoves us, by combining an accurate investigation into the *minutiæ* of technical method with an imaginative appreciation of the problems confronting those who were responsible for the productions, to make ourselves thoroughly acquainted, as it were, with the regular routine of the seventeenth-century director, scenic artist, and stage-hand.

The information demanded is not over-hard to obtain, but so far it has been only slightly applied in the manner suggested. For earlier practice there is the section on the stage included by Sebastiano Serlio in his *Architettura* of 1545,[1] interesting and suggestive, but unhappily very brief and for the most part general in its account of stage and set. More elaborate is the *Pratica di fabricar scene e machine ne' teatri* of Nicola Sabbatini.[2] Although issued in 1638, at a time when the English court masque was about to vanish with the monarchy supporting it, Sabbatini's work almost certainly represents, not the latest and most progressive in contemporary stage method, but rather the older,

---

[1] This appears in *Il secondo libro di Perspettiva*, separately published. The Italian text has been reprinted by Sir E. K. Chambers in his *Elizabethan Stage*, iv, 353–365. A translation from a Dutch version was issued in London in 1611. Serlio's essay is important because it forms the first attempt to establish the principles of the Renaissance stage, and because, as a result, it exercised a tremendous influence on later theatrical effort. Unfortunately, the *Spectacula* of Pellegrino Prisciano, addressed to Duke Ercole d'Este about 1500 (manuscript in Biblioteca Estense, Modena) deals entirely with classical effort, and so does not serve our purposes here. The significance of Serlio's work and that of other writers on theatrical procedure has, of course, been recognized. Lily B. Campbell's *Scenes and Machines in the Renaissance* (Cambridge, 1923) is an important volume which, while manifestly not professing to be exhaustive and neglecting many salient aspects of the Italian theatre, is a useful survey of some at least of the problems involved. The Italian material too has been utilized in several studies by W. J. Lawrence, in Paul Reyher's section on the *mise en scène* (pp. 332–333), and in S. W. Holsboer's *L'Histoire de la mise en scène dans le théâtre français de 1600 à 1657* (Paris, 1933). Theories concerning perspective scenery during the sixteenth and seventeenth centuries are outlined in Günter Schöne, *Die Entwicklung der Perspektivbühne von Serlio bis Galli-Bibiena nach den Perspektivbüchern* (*Theatergeschichtliche Forschungen*, No. 43, Leipzig, 1933). Most of these are neglected here since they deal only with the method of securing perspective effects, and not with the practical problems of building the sets or the machines. In a volume shortly to be published under the editorship of George Kernodle and John McDowell the writings of Serlio, Sabbatini, and Furttenbach will appear in translation with critical commentary. It may be noted here that all three authors seem to be describing stage practice which had already been established some years before the appearance of their respective studies; we know certainly that many of Sabbatini's devices were old-fashioned by the time he set them down in his chapters.

[2] The first book appeared in 1637, but it is the second book, added to the edition of Ravenna in 1638, that gives us the most important information. The entire text has been issued in facsimile under the editorship of W. Flemming (Weimar, 1926). The footnote references to Sabbatini's work allude to book and chapter.

tried procedure, much of which had been invented and applied in the preceding century. On Sabbatini we must most rely, but besides his comprehensive treatise are several others, among which may be especially mentioned here the various writings of Joseph Furttenbach.[1] These and further studies noted later may aid us in rounding out our mental picture of the masque performances. Serlio's short paragraphs and Sabbatini's longer chapters have frequently been referred to, while occasionally a footnote has called attention to some other author's work, but only few historians have sought by careful examination of their contents to learn from them the exact operations involved in the presentation of Italian *intermezzi*, and, in spite of the attention devoted to the masque in general, and to Jonson's masques in particular, no comprehensive effort has been made to explore in detail the corresponding stage method in England.

With the end in view of determining those operations and methods let us enter Whitehall.

---

[1] This German architect, born in 1591 at Leutkirch, lived for several years (1610–20) in Italy. His *Neues Itinerarium Italiæ* (Ulm, 1627) contains several notes on the stage; much richer material appears in his *Architectura civilis* (Ulm, 1628), *Architectura recreationis* (Augsburg, 1640), and *Mannhafter Kunstspiegel* (Augsburg, 1663). There is an analytical study of his works by A. A. Gvozdev, Иосиф Фуртенбах и оформление спектаклях на рубеже xvi–xvii веков (*O Teatre*, iii (Leningrad, 1929), pp. 103–152).

II

THE BANQUETING HOUSE

ROYAL PATRONAGE

WHITEHALL gives us the appropriate start.
This is no common theatre we approach, but a royal banqueting hall which for the space of a few nights will house a magnificent spectacle. The King or the Queen is the focus of attention, the cynosure of all eyes, the prime mover in these affairs.

It behoves the high
For their own sakes to do things worthily,

declares Jonson in *Cynthia's Revels*, and this comment might readily be taken as the fitting motto for the entire series of court masques. "Princes of sweet and humane natures," says Sir William D'Avenant in his *Britannia Triumphans*, "have ever . . . presented spectacles and personal representations, to recreate their spirits wasted in grave affairs of State and for the entertainment of their nobility, ladies and courts." These things were, to use the words Samuel Daniel employs in *Tethys' Festival*, "Complements of State, both to shew magnificence and to celebrate the feasts to our greatest respects," "the necessary complements requisit for State and Greatness." [1] Even Jonson, while decrying the "bodies" of such entertainments, found it necessary to aver that it rightly became "the most royall *Princes* and greatest *persons*" to be "studious of riches and magnificence in the outward celebration or shew."

Through these entertainments, lavishly ornate in their embellishments, a monarch displayed to an admiring world his mighty magnanimity. Meanness and avarice by this action he thrust aside, and demonstrated to all the liberality which was a sign of his princely nature. "The more money," wrote Serlio, "that is spent on things of this sort, the more deserving are they of praise, for, in truth, they are to be associated with magnanimous princes and noble lords to whom ugly Parsimony is an evil stranger." All this proud and vital flourishing of theatrical art was, then, the work of rulers whose greatness of soul became manifest in their generous support of artistic talent. Their patronage, again to use Serlio's words, "put Avarice to shame," and the less enduring were the efforts the greater glory reflected upon them. In the *Dialoghi* of Leone di Somi [2] there is described a wondrous setting, "enriched with so many reliefs, embellished by such admirable architecture, with such variety of lovely inventions," erected at the expense of the Duke of Mantua in the year 1561. This was of "lath and plaster," but, remarks one of the interlocutors in the dialogue, "All the greater was Duke Guglielmo's magnanimity in spending so many thousands of ducats on that marvellous set and then destroying it when it had served its immediate purpose."

Italian comments of this kind serve to provide the light in which Whitehall's entertainments are to be viewed. When we translate seventeenth-century money into modern terms we must remain startled at the sums laid out, not for some rich show intended by a long run to liquidate the initial expenditure, but for a production given before privileged guests only, and then performed merely

---

[1] The last phrase appears in *The Vision of the Twelve Goddesses*.

[2] These, preserved in a manuscript at the Biblioteca Palatina, Parma, were written about 1565. A translation is given in *The Development of the Theatre* (second edition, 1937).

28

once or twice. In 1618 James, by no means the most financially reckless of monarchs, devoted £4000, a sum to be valued now at about £40,000, on a single production, while in 1633 the Inns of Court, preparing a vast entertainment which was virtually an answer to William Prynne's *Histrio-mastix*, succeeded in spending over £21,000, or £200,000 in our money.[1] If the King were the host his liberal nature was demonstrated by this expenditure; if the hosts were his subjects, no doubt could remain concerning their loyalty and essential nobility of nature.

COURTLY TOYS

The theatre thus supported—of Italian *intermezzi* and of English masques alike—was a courtly toy, admired with a kind of childish interest. "These Things are but Toyes," says Bacon at the start of his essay on *Masques and Triumphs*—with his familiar incisiveness placing them for all time.[2] Celio Malespini, the novelist, has a rather amusing story illustrating this in his *Ducento Novelle*.[3] It relates to the festivities arranged in connexion with the marriage at Mantua of Duke Guglielmo and Eleanora of Austria. To ensure the most magnificent and the most princely spectacle, Leone Aretino, famous sculptor and architect, was dispatched from Milan that he might take charge of the arrangements. Finding himself pressed for time, this gentleman in turn sent for his close friend, Malespini himself, to whom was entrusted the onerous and at times even dangerous task of supervising the affairs of "Hell," the under-stage machinery and effects. Their joint labours are interestingly described for us, and entertainingly we are made acquainted with their several trials and difficulties. Of these the chief of all was the fact that their work was constantly receiving interruption through the importunities of curious visitors from court, who, heedless of the time they wasted, demanded to see how things were getting on and insisted upon personally conducted tours of the work. "Truly," says Malespini,

> this occasioned much trial to these two men, for they had to go round with the visitors and explain everything in detail to them. At last Aretino became so fed up with the whole affair that he left this business to Malespini, who, in turn, got so sick of it that, whenever he saw anyone approaching, he would run and hide till the visitor had gone, in order not to be compelled to repeat once more the same story he had already repeated a million times.

The theatre, we must remember, like all the art of that time, was merely part of an embellishment to a courtly existence in which the Grand Style reigned, and the artists, although admired and welcomed, were definitely retainers. For the palace halls the painters executed their lavish canvases and frescoes; to delight royal tastes they, and their colleagues the sculptors and architects, could abandon their more important works of art and devote their energy to devising toys for the delectation of their masters.

How close the theatre was to ordinary court routine is demonstrated by the intimate connexion between the performance of plays or of masques and the elaborate banquets which have given this age pre-eminence in the art of feasting. Leone di Somi's dialogues end with an elaborate description of such a feast. At the court of Mantua a drama had been presented, and immediately after, almost as though it were part of the same show, came a pastoral banquet. For it his Excellency the Duke

> had got built in a great hall two orders of square rustic columns, evenly spaced and bearing vaulted arches. Although it was winter-time, these were all covered with green boughs. Thus were formed

---

[1] A. W. Green, *The Inns of Court and Early English Drama* (New Haven, Connecticut, 1931), p. 126. The modern equivalents given here are approximate only. It is, of course, impossible to relate exactly the value of money in different periods; see A. V. Judges, *A Note on Prices in Shakespeare's Time*, in *A Companion to Shakespeare Studies*, ed. Harley Granville-Barker and G. B. Harrison (Cambridge, 1934), pp. 382–384.

[2] *A Harmony of the Essays*, ed. Edward Arber (1871), p. 539.   [3] Venice, 1609. Parte II, novella xi.

two lovely, long, and leafy loggias with diverse festoons of fruits and flowers, some artificial (since it was out of their season), some real. Within the columns (which were hollow) there had been concealed many lamps, which, shining forth from shades made of coloured glass and skilfully placed, illuminated the whole room in a delightful way; still greater splendour was provided by several great globes filled with water, cleverly set in the middle of each archway. Above these, lamps had been placed in such number that each arch seemed lit up by a blazing sun. Indeed, it seemed brighter than at high noon. Between the two loggias was a space of about ten cubits; it was considerably higher than the two loggias and was entirely roofed with a blue sky set with stars and having a magnificent great moon in the middle. The rays from this moon fell on a deliciously set table which stretched the whole length of the open space, and on which was spread a rich supper of diverse fruits—mostly artificial sugar fruits or else real fruits preserved in sugar.

The play over, an Orpheus, attended by shepherds and shepherdesses, summoned the guests to this feast, and when all were seated the various courses were ushered in with groups of men dressed to represent hunters and the like, each of whom presented his meats to the lord "with many witty remarks," music, and verses.

Such dramatic banquets were beloved in this age. Vasari [1] tells how Giovan Francesco Rustico once gathered a party of friends and seated them in a great and cunningly illuminated cauldron; how a tree with many branches was made to rise from their midst, with divers viands hanging on its boughs. On another occasion he describes the assembling of guests, who are startled by the entry of Ceres. This lady explains that she is seeking her daughter Proserpine, who had been rapt away by Pluto and begs the company "to follow her to hell." After a discussion they agree, and

enter into a rather dark room, the door of which was a huge serpent's mouth covering the entire wall. Ceres asks the barking Cerberus if her lost daughter has come there, and on hearing that she has says she wishes to have her back again. Pluto replies that he will not give her up and invites all the company to the wedding. This invitation is accepted, and all enter through the serpent's mouth full of teeth which, being set on hinges, opens and closes on each pair. They then find themselves in a large round room illuminated by one very small light in the middle which gives so faint a glow that they can scarcely see each other. They are led to their places at the black-draped tables by a hideous devil holding a fork, and Pluto orders that, in honour of his wedding, the pains of hell should cease during their visit, an order immediately carried out. . . . The dishes of this infernal feast were all of animals of the most horrid appearance, but diverse delicacies were placed underneath. . . . Instead of fruits and sweets, dead men's bones followed, . . . but they were of sugar. The banquet over, Pluto declared that he would retire with Proserpine and that the damned should once again suffer their torments. Suddenly the light was extinguished, and there were heard deep rumblings, cries, and exclamations of horror and fear. In the midst of the darkness, illuminated by a small candle, appeared the figure of Baja, one of the guests, condemned by Pluto to hell because of his always having represented in his fireworks the seven deadly sins and the affairs of hell. While all were looking at this and listening to the wailing voices which accompanied it, the gloomy device was removed, lights were brought in, and in its place was seen a royal and munificent scene, decent servants bearing in the remains of a magnificent banquet. At the end came a ship full of various sweets; its masters, taking their goods, gradually led the guests to the upper rooms, where there was a stage excellently appointed on which was performed a much-admired comedy, *Filogenia*. At dawn all returned light-heartedly to their homes. [2]

So clearly, indeed, was feasting allied to the dramatic performance in those days that Joseph Furttenbach, [3] that German architect whose writings bore northward knowledge of the Italian

[1] *Vite de' più eccellenti pittori, scultori, e architetti* (Milan, 1811), xiii, 111, 118–120.

[2] For the account of another interesting theatrical banquet see Domenico Gnoli, *Il Teatro capitolino del 1513* (*Nuova Antologia*, cclxix (1930), 419–420).

[3] *Mannhafter Kunstspiegel*, pp. 113–114, 255–260.

scenic styles, designed a special hall with not one, but four separate stages, in the midst of which was a semicircular table set on a revolving platform. On occasion seats might be placed on the floor and a performance given at one of the 'theatres,' but, remarks Furttenbach, "if one wishes to present a truly princely banquet," then four troupes of actors are to be engaged and entertainments

Fig. 3. A Royal Banquet and Entertainment at Turin, 1645
("Il Dono del re dell' Alpi")
Biblioteca Nazionale, Turin.

given between or during the courses of the meal, the table with the guests being turned on a pivot as circumstances should demand.

Precisely similar links between the banquet and the stage entertainment manifest themselves in the Stuart court. Each masque was followed by a feast where the guests, noble as they might be, scrambled lustily for the sweetmeats furnished by the royal treasury. Beyond this practice, ample indication is there of the close alliance between masque and banquet. Frequently the king or the queen came directly from dinner to witness the spectacle, or else that spectacle became a kind of cabaret show to entertain them in the course of eating. "After dinner," Jonson writes in his description of the entertainment presented before their Majesties at Theobalds, the King and Queen entered the gallery, where "there was seene nothing but a traverse of white acrosse the room, which sodainely drawne discovered a gloomie obscure place"—the setting for the first scene of the performance. Campion's *Caversham Masque* started with an outdoor playlet, and continued, immediately after supper, with the entry of those persons who had previously, out of doors, greeted the royal party. Perhaps the most striking instance is that of Jonson's *Love's Welcome*, where "His Majesty being set at Dinner, Music: The Passions, Doubt and Love, enter with the Affections, Joy, Delight, etc., and sing this song," while "after dinner" the persons of the masque proper make their appearance.

THE MASQUING HALL

The entire production was bound up in strictest intimacy with court procedure, and naturally the centre about which it moved was the king. The 'theatre' in which the masques were performed was simply a hall of state, specially adorned for the occasion, prepared so that the auditorium where royalty was seated came to possess a richness hardly less elaborate than that of the stage spectacles themselves. Typical is the description given us by a contemporary of the so-called Teatro Mediceo, created out of a *salon* in the Uffizi at Florence. Bernardo Buontalenti was the architect and the year 1585.[1] The particular hall selected measured 142 feet in length, 52 feet in width, and 36 feet in height. Over the original level flooring was placed, for the better accommodating of the guests, a sloping platform to serve as a stage. Buontalenti, we are informed,

made this hall into a theatre by erecting six tiers of seats which went right round the walls up to the stage, which occupied 30 feet of the room's length. In the very midst of this great hall, 45 feet from the stage, was a platform set one and a half feet above the floor level. . . . It was 18 feet broad and of equal depth, sloping downward till at the end farthest from the stage it came to the level of the floor. Between the tiers of seats and this platform designed for the prince the hall was filled with benches so that all the surrounding crowd, without anyone's being impeded, could easily be accommodated. On this platform, all covered with crimson velvet embroidered in gold and draped with magnificent velvet curtains, were set the princes and princesses on rich and splendid chairs, upholstered in fine cloth-of-gold. At the foot of the tiers, which were covered with precious tapestry and painted to resemble stone-work, as were also the steps leading to the stage, were twenty-four pyramids set at equal distances from each other. These pyramids were painted skilfully to resemble stone and bronze. . . . At the top of each was a vase so exquisitely painted that you would have sworn it made of serpentine marble: in these vases were set torches of white wax which, as they burned up, illuminated the entire hall. . . . On the rich and embellished tiers was a row of pilasters a trifle more than one and a half feet in height, so brilliantly painted by the artist that they seemed of finest marble; this row of pilasters, encircling the whole theatre, made a most lovely balcony. Among them at equal distances from each other were ten fountains, likewise painted in semblance of finest marble and adorned with burnished gold; upon every one of them was the figure of a child, some painted to look like marble, others like bronze, so that all might see they came from a master's hand. From the pilasters rose a row of flowering myrtles, which also encircled the theatre. Above all were seen the tops of diverse leafy plants, bearing a great variety of fruits, some just ripening, others fully ripe, others still as yet in flower. In among these plants you could see diverse animals, such as hares, rabbits, and so on, constructed in such a way that they seemed to move and run about; and upon the trees all kinds of birds, some having their wings spread for flight, others perched on branches ready to sing, and others still seen in the air as if they had been lured to flight by the songs of those perched on the branches. Naught was needed save movement and the sweet melody of the song itself: for the rest, Nature, in the opinion of the onlookers, had been bettered by Art. . . . In fine, it may be said that this whole balustrade represented a garden lovelier and more charming than anyone had ever seen or imagined.

Such embellishment of the auditorium may not always have been so elaborate, but de' Rossi's account of Buontalenti's achievements differs not overmuch from the words in which a Venetian

[1] Bastiano de' Rossi, *Descrizione del magnificentiss. apparato e de' maravigliosi intermedi fatti per la comedia, rappresentata in Firenze nelle felicissime Nozze degl' Illustrissimi ed Eccellentissimi Signori Il Signor Don Cesare d' Este, e la Signora Donna Virginia Medici* (Florence, 1585).

visitor cast his admiration of the Banqueting House at Whitehall. This gentleman, Orazio Busino, chaplain to the Venetian ambassador, had been invited to attend Jonson's *Pleasure reconciled to Virtue* in 1618. Before the curtain was drawn to reveal the scene he amused himself by looking around the hall. This place, he wrote,

> is fitted up like a theatre, with well-secured boxes all round. The stage is at one end, and his Majesty's chair under an ample canopy. Near him are stools for the foreign ambassadors. . . . Whilst waiting for the King we amused ourselves admiring the decorations and beauty of the house, with its two orders of columns, one above the other, their distance from the wall equalling the breadth of the passage, that

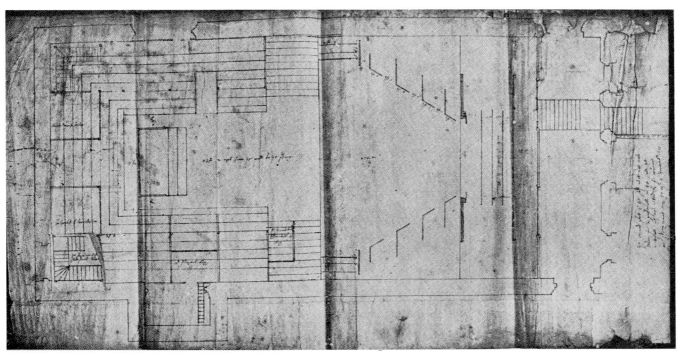

Fig. 4. GROUND-PLAN OF THE AUDITORIUM AND STAGE FOR "FLORIMÈNE" (1635)
Inigo Jones. British Museum (Lansdowne MS. 1171, *ff.* 5*b*, 6).

> of the second row being upheld by Doric pillars, while above these rise Ionic columns supporting the roof. The whole is of wood, including even the shafts, which are carved and gilt with much skill. From the roof of these hang festoons and angels in relief with two rows of lights.[1]

This building described by Busino was the old Banqueting House of Queen Elizabeth, originally built in 1581, as it had been reconstructed for the production of masques in the year 1606. Here most of the entertainments in this kind were presented up to the time of its destruction by fire on January 12, 1619. A new Banqueting House was erected by Inigo Jones in 1622, a hall still to be viewed, although turned now to far other than its original uses. This served for most of the masques produced between the year of its opening and 1637, when, fearful of damage to the painted ceiling, Charles commanded Jones to design a "Great new Masking Room"; there were performed *Britannia Triumphans*, *Luminalia*, and *Salmacida Spolia*. One other place was occasionally used for these shows—the Great Hall. Here appeared *Lord Hay's Masque* in 1613, as well as a few others prepared during the period (1619–22) when the new Banqueting House was a-building. Of these

[1] Sir E. K. Chambers, *The Elizabethan Stage*, i, 202–203.

halls the "Masking Room" was the largest, being 112 feet long and 57 wide, with a height of 59 feet; the Great Hall was only 89 feet long and 39 feet wide (Fig. 78).

THE AUDITORIUM

All such theatres, it will be realized, were princely *salons*, and in approaching any masque performance we must endeavour fully to appreciate the rich ornaments which graced each interior. We must envisage, too, the eager concourse of socially distinguished guests—"the favoured ones who are invited," as Busino describes them—the boxes filled "with most noble and richly arrayed ladies" attended by their lords hardly less colourful in their attire. These, gathered in expectation, had to wait until the king made his formal entry and took his seat under the "ample canopy." This seat was in the most privileged position, set upon the 'state,' none other than that platform prepared by Buontalenti for his Florentine festivities of 1585. In the English masques frequent allusion was made to the state, but nowhere do we find of it any detailed description. That it was placed at the level of the scene's "horizon" Jonson informs us in *Blackness*, and that it abutted on to the "dancing place" [1] is clear from Campion's notes to *Lord Hay's Masque*. This location is clearly marked in the ground plan for *Florimène* in 1635 (Fig. 4). The platform there was eleven feet wide; it had two broad steps in front and a railing round the back and sides. Such a position was determined by the point of distance, for from that location alone did the perspective scene assume its true proportions and cheat the eye by means of cunningly painted vistas. How important this was may be realized from the account of a Latin comedy given at Oxford in 1605.[2] The Vice-Chancellor had set "the chair of Estate" for the King "so . . . that the auditory could see but his cheek only"—it was, in fact, in the approved position; but to this objections were made. The matter was debated in solemn council, and

> in the end, the place was removed, and sett in the midst of the Hall, but too far from the stage, viz. 28 foote, so that there were many long speeches delivered which neither the King nor any near him could well see or understand.

As the Vice-Chancellor had pointed out, "by the art perspective the King" would have "beholden all better than if he sat" in the alternative position provided for him.

From the approved position, explains Sabbatini,[3] "all the scenery will appear better than from any other place in the hall"—words which are almost the same as those employed by the Vice-Chancellor. In shape, the state must have taken the form of a canopied platform, palisaded about "so that the crowd of guests (who on such occasions are wont to show but scant discretion) cannot come near to injure it." [4]

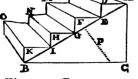

Fig. 5. PLAN FOR SCAFFOLDING IN A HALL THEATRE (1638)

Nicolà Sabbatini, *Pratica di fabricar scene e machine.*

For the guests Busino declares that there were "boxes," and the same word is used by Inigo Jones for two enclosures towards the rear of the auditorium in his plan for *Florimène* (Fig. 4). Formal boxes of modern theatrical type no doubt they were not—probably nothing more than sections of the hall, separated by columns; at any rate, the usual accommodation, both in Italy and in England, took the form of steps, or *gradi*, commonly called 'degrees' or 'tiers,' raised on wooden frameworks. In describing the performance of *Somerset's Masque* Campion remarked that the portion of the hall immediately opposite the stage "was Theatred with Pillars, Scaffolds and all things answerable to the sides of the Roome," referring certainly to seating arrangements of the kind alluded to above. Over thirty years later, too, for Shirley's

---

[1] *Infra*, p. 35.   [2] J. Nichols, *The Progresses of James the First* (1828), i, 530.   [3] i, 34.   [4] *Id.*

The Triumph of Peace the audience was accommodated similarly, "on the degrees prepared for that purpose."

Since the auditorium was but temporarily put to use as a playhouse, obviously great care had to be taken to see that neither the floors nor the walls were damaged in the erection of the scaffolding. To this subject Sabbatini devotes some considerable attention,[1] explaining that the desired result might be obtained by making a set of triangular frames composed of stout beams (Fig. 5). These, joined by longer boards, could then be placed against the walls, thus providing the basis for the series of steps which were to form the bench-like seats. By this means, he comments, "the tiers are constructed firmly and securely, yet so as to injure in no wise the floor or walls of the hall."

THE DANCING PLACE

Immediately in front of the state, between it and the stage, stretched the 'dancing place,' in itself one of the most important provisions for the evening's entertainment. The masque was not just another theatrical performance; it had grown out of a kind of elaborate charade—groups of disguised dancers suddenly intruding into a festive assembly, selecting partners, and inviting them to grace the floor. To the very end the masque retained this essential core of its being, and consequently an opportunity had to be provided for permitting the performers to spread outward, beyond whatever was built of a stage frame, into the body of the auditorium. Habitually the masquers descended, and with selected guests footed it upon the 'dancing place'; while frequently, in the very course of the masque action, characters were made to move downward and approach the royal throne. Such practice, it is true, was more common in early masques where 'dispersed scenery' was employed,[2] but the practice was not unknown even when, as, for example, in *Tethys' Festival*, which had a "tree of Victory" represented by "a bay erected at the right side of the state, upon a little mount there raised," a formal 'picture-frame' arch enclosed the stage proper. Four Squires approach the presence in *Somerset's Masque*; Primavera persuades the gods in *Flowers* to do likewise. Other examples are numerous. Of them perhaps the most interesting is that in Townsend's *Tempe Restored*, where Harmony, with the whole chorus, "goes up to the State and sings," while her companions, the Influences of the Stars, "fall into their daunce, which being past they are placed on the degrees by the Lords and Ladies where they sitt to see the *Masque*." Later the Queen, who had been interpreting one of the characters, descended to join the King on the state and to watch the rest of the action.

There was thus a free space immediately in front of the stage utilizable either for the dancing with which all the masques concluded or for the occasional movement of performers during the course of the entertainment itself. Regularly this space was carpeted. "In the middle of the theatre," wrote Busino in his account, "there appeared a fine and spacious area carpeted all over with green cloth." For the cloth used and for the labour of nailing it to the floor workmen's accounts are still extant.[3] Naturally, this space could not have served its purpose without the provision of some means of easy descent from the stage level. Here in London, as in Ferrara and Florence, steps or sloping platforms were built to join the acting area to the auditorium. The simple stairways, commonly double, seem to have been those usually prepared; their presence is indicated in a few at least of Jones's designs (Figs. 12, 16, 36).[4] Occasionally, however, there were variations. "An Ovall staire downe into the roome" was erected for D'Avenant's *Britannia Triumphans*, while Campion in *Lord Hay's Masque* had "a broade descent to the dauncing place," evidently in the form of a wide ramp.[5]

---

[1] i, 35.   [2] *Infra*, p. 56.   [3] P. Reyher, p. 358.
[4] In addition to these see *Designs*, Nos. 193 (Pl. XXIII), 243 (Pl. XXVIII).   [5] P. Reyher, pp. 358–359.

STUART MASQUES AND THE RENAISSANCE STAGE

THE STAGE

The stage proper was always raised at "the lower end of the hall," a platform of fair size fit to accommodate the throngs of elaborately costumed actors. In 1605 a platform set on wheels, 40 feet square, was constructed for *Blackness*.[1] Later in the century evidence is forthcoming to show that a width of about 40 feet and a depth of 28 feet were the common proportions.[2] Such allowed, in *Flowers*, the introduction of a great bowl, raised 9 feet above the stage level and 24 feet "in circuit" and of an arbour 33 feet long and 21 feet high.

Apparently the average depth of the stage in front was 6 feet. Four feet is mentioned as the height of the platform in *Blackness*, but here there was a kind of double stage; *Salmacida Spolia*, the last of the Stuart masques, had a stage 7 feet high at the front and 8 feet at the back, and 7 feet likewise was the height of the platform in *The Triumph of Peace*. These figures, however, seem to have been exceptional. At any rate, a depth of 6 feet is recorded for Carew's *Cælum Britannicum*, D'Avenant's *The Temple of Love*, and the same author's *The Triumphs of the Prince d'Amour*. In endeavouring to envisage this theatre we must, of course, remember that six feet was six feet and nothing more; the fact that the entire platform was built up on the level floor of a hall prohibited any use of a deep below-stage area. Most of the operations conducted underneath the acting level must have entailed backbreaking work. Here again the English practice differed in no essential wise from the Italian. Sabbatini, in giving his practical directions for the building of the platform, suggests 4 feet as a minimum height, and recommends a slope of about half an inch in the foot towards the back; with a stage of 6 feet in front and a depth of 28 feet this would give a height of 7 feet 2 inches at the rear wall. A height of 5 feet rising to 7 was advised by Furttenbach,[3] who found corroboration from Giulio Troili.[4] The latter declared that the stage front should be about 5 feet, "rising towards the back a ninth part of its length." "If," he adds, "the stage front is less than 5 feet, experience shows that a tenth, eleventh or twelfth part is sufficient elevation."

It is important to note here that the stage plans extant from the hand of Inigo Jones indicate that his stage was divided into two portions, in a manner fundamentally similar to that suggested in contemporary Italian designs. A glance at Fig. 4 will show that there is a front acting area bordered by wings; this is marked off clearly from a rear area which houses the back-shutters and the back-cloth. A precisely similar arrangement is shown in the later plan for *Salmacida Spolia* (Fig. 78). What has not hitherto been sufficiently realized is that Italian theatrical practice habitually utilized a kind of inner stage, basically of the same character. A still existent example may be seen in the Teatro Farnese, at Parma, where a second brick 'proscenium' divides the forestage from the rear. Fig. 6 shows clearly the divisions that are created there.[5] Amplest indication of the purposes to which this rear space could be put is given in Furttenbach's instructions.[6] He specifically calls for a back pit, 12 feet deep, immediately behind the forward acting area; this was to be "laid with strong but light planks left un-nailed so that they might easily be removed." Sometimes (with the board-

---

[1] P. Reyher, p. 358.

[2] Dimensions of 40 feet by 27 are recorded for Shirley's *The Triumph of Peace* and of 42 feet by 28 for D'Avenant's *Salmacida Spolia*. The stage for *Florimène* was 23 feet deep.

[3] *Mannhafter Kunstspiegel*, p. 114. In his *Architectura civilis*, p. 12, he speaks of 4½ feet, but this stage seems to have been an exceptionally simple one.

[4] *Paradossi per pratticare la prospettiva* (Bologna, 1683), p. 110.

[5] These divisions may be related, too, to the perspective vista revealed through the central doorway of the Teatro Olimpico, at Vicenza. For the construction of the Teatro Farnese see Glauco Lombardi, *L'armonia del Teatro Farnese* (*Aurea Parma*, ii (1913), 117–125), *Il Teatro Farnesiano di Parma* (*Archivio storico per le provincie Parmensi*, N.S., ix (1909), 1–51). These present more exact and fuller material than the earlier studies—Paolo Donati, *Descrizione del Gran Teatro Farnesiano di Parma* (Parma, 1817), and Pietro de Lama, *Opuscoli letterari* (Bologna, 1818), i, 193; ii, 146. Marcello Buttiglij presents some interesting contemporary records in his *Descrittione dell' apparato fatto per honorare la prima e solenne entrata* (Parma, 1629).

[6] *Mannhafter Kunstspiegel*, p. 115; *Architectura civilis*, p. 28.

ing down) this could serve for specially deep scenes; serve for the introduction of various startling effects. this rear stage and the inner stage of the Elizabethan public theatre seems proved by the plan for *Candy Restored* (Fig. 111),[1] where the wings at the front lead the eye back to what is indicated as the "scene itself."

Within the restricted space provided between the hall floor and the stage boards was prepared all that series of rich and surprising machines which so delighted contemporaries. The most ambitious effects were attained in spite of these limitations. In *Cælum Britannicum* a rock began to rise, "which by little and little grew to be a huge mountain that covered all the Scæne," with, seated upon it, "the three Kingdomes of *England*, *Scotland* and *Ireland*, all richly attired in regal habits"; no wonder need be experienced that such a "strange spectacle gave great cause of admiration, but especially how so huge a machine, and of that great height, could come from under the Stage, which was but six foot high." Concerning this, more must be said hereafter.

Both Sabbatini[2] and Furttenbach[3] counsel the erection of a kind of separate stage front, taking shape as a parapet placed at a distance of from 1 to 10 feet before the acting platform. By this means there was formed a pit (corresponding to our orchestral pit) separating the audience from the performers. Its uses were various. First, it served as a convenient receptacle for a falling curtain;[4] perhaps that was its original purpose, but besides this service it provided a space for musicians and light for below-stage workers. In those days of lamps and candles safe illumination for these nether regions must have been hard to come by, and this device of a stage-floor unboarded at the front may well have proved welcome. Of it, however, the English masque had perforce to remain innocent, owing to the necessity of giving free access from the upper to the lower level. It seems likely that the open spaces shown in some early stage designs[5] were devised to supply, by compensating 'windows,' the light thus denied to the workers of the windlasses and the traps. In England the stage-front had to be attached to the scaffolding of

sometimes (with the boards removed) it could That there may be some connexion between

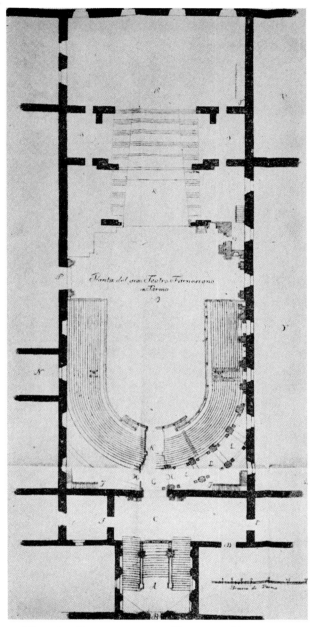

Fig. 6. PLAN OF THE TEATRO FARNESE
AT PARMA
Paoli Donati Parmigiano, *Descrizione del Gran Teatro Farnesiano di Parma* (Parma, 1817).

---

[1] *Infra*, pp. 151–153.   [2] i, 3.   [3] *Mannhafter Kunstspiegel*, p. 115; *Architectura civilis*, p. 12.   [4] *Infra*, p. 40.
[5] These appear in Serlio's comic and tragic sets (*The Development of the Theatre*, Figs. 79, 80) and in the stage prepared for a production at Siena in 1565 (*id.*, Fig. 83).

the platform itself, but it is to be observed that fundamentally this attached stage-front at Whitehall was treated precisely as the Italian stage parapet is treated. Sabbatini [1] points out that the latter might be painted in various ways—the most common being the simulation of brickwork or stone. "The basement" of the stage built for Shirley's *The Triumph of Peace* was similarly "painted in rusticke work," while several of Jones's designs display fictional stone facings (Fig. 14). [2]

Traps have been mentioned above. Of these, we can remain in no doubt, there were plenty. Some may have been small, but the descriptions make it clear that occasionally there were demanded large openings permitting the ascent or descent of numerous persons. From ancient times, of course, the value of such devices had been recognized, and in thus making use of them the masques were introducing nothing new; all that we may say is that trap-work was probably more frequent in these court entertainments, and certainly more elaborate, than it was in the public playhouse. Once again information regarding procedure may be derived from Sabbatini. [3] The simplest trap-door consisted of two flaps opening downward, with a stout bar to secure them when closed. When the trap was a large one, however, means had to be provided for raising and lowering the huge pieces of boarding forming each of the flaps; this means consisted of a series of props, each hinged to the under-side of the door, manipulated by a group of men working in unison. "Great care," remarks Sabbatini, "should be taken to engage persons experienced in this business, and trust-worthy, so that the movements will go smoothly."

THE AUDIENCE

The state, the tiers, and the stage thus were built and set in place, a task necessitating the services of many workers. On the back of one of Jones's sketches for *Britannia Triumphans* [4] the artist has jotted down some notes on this subject, from which it appears that twenty men were "on the roofe" and twelve "on the windows"; eight men were needed for "making reddy the boardes," and another twelve were occupied "on yᵉ bourding yᵉ flower" (floor); the "degrees and galleries" took the services of twenty men, and there were ten men at each end of the passages. In this case, "the scene" had "to bee all tiled ouer," and for this purpose eight tilers were employed. In the preliminary work, and quite apart from the construction of the scenery, a crew of some hundred skilled artisans was required. When these men had completed their tasks and when the furniture of the stage had been prepared, the audience was summoned to the hall, and there the guests were shown, not without confusion, to their appointed places. In England it was the Lord Chamberlain who superintended these arrangements, just such a dignified and "discreet person" as Sabbatini advises should be chosen for this office. [5] Discretion was required because of the careful grading of the spectators and because of the lack of reserved seats. Ambassadors were apt to stand upon ceremony and demand places near the state, while for the courtiers in attendance a strict order of precedence had to be observed. No evidence exists to show whether at Whitehall a common Italian practice was observed of separating the women from the men; Sabbatini records this, and suggests a further division whereby the younger and prettier among the former should be placed on the lowest benches facing the stage, so that the actors, viewing this serried rank of beauty, might be encouraged and inspired to perform with added vigour and vitality. As early as 1502 there is indication of such differentiation between the sexes in Italy; when Isabella Gonzaga attended the Ferrarese performances given in honour of the marriage of her brother and Lucrezia Borgia she noted that the tiers, or *gradi*, had barriers marking off the men's seats from those of the women. [6] Over a century and a half later the same practice was observed in the theatre of the Accademia

[1] i, 31.　　　[2] *Designs*, Nos. 67 (Pl. X), 193 (Pl. XXIII).　　　[3] ii, 17.　　　[4] *Designs*, No. 286.

[5] i, 40.　　　[6] Alessandro D'Ancona, *Origini del teatro italiano* (Milan, 1891), ii, 383.

degli Immobili.[1]   So far as the men were concerned, "the cultured people of taste" were "set on the floor of the hall, as near the middle as possible, in the second and third rows," while the less important guests were apportioned places higher up or at the sides, whence the view of the perspective scenery was bound to be less satisfactory and less pleasing.

THE CURTAIN

Seated thus, and glittering in resplendent clothes which showed bravely in the light of the torches and the candles, the audience eagerly awaited the rising (or the dropping) of the curtain.   This curtain, both in Italy and in England, extended across one end of the hall, concealing the stage and all its wonders.   Concerning its appearance and manipulation there are many matters of interest. During the early years of the Stuart masque it was frequently known as the 'traverse,' [2] a word of some considerable antiquity.   The traverse was no new thing in court entertainments.   In sixteenth-century pageants it had been commonly employed to reveal the actors; [3] in 1565, for the performance of an Elizabethan masque, the Revels Office was called upon to provide "a vayne of sarsnett drawn vpp and downe" before the performers.[4]   Fundamentally, all that happened in the seventeenth century was that what had originally been used only to conceal and suddenly to discover a group of performers came to be employed for the concealing and discovering of a stage set.

Frequently, during the earlier years of James's reign at least, it formed part of the scenic display, being painted as if it were part of a setting.   Thus in 1604 a masque (now not extant) was, according to Carleton,

> brought in by a magicien of China.   There was a heaven built at the lower end of the hall, owt of which our magicien came downe, and after he had made a long sleepy speech to the King of the nature of the cuntry from whence he came, comparing it with owrs for strength and plenty, he sayde he had broughte in cloudes certain Indian and China Knights to see the magnificency of this court.   And thereuppon a travers was drawne.[5]

Clearly, from the reference to "a heaven," this traverse must have been painted to represent clouds. The following year, in *Blackness*, the first scene was "a *Landtschap* consisting of small woods, and here and there a void place fill'd with huntings"; this, in a contemporary manuscript account of the performance, was described as "a downeright cloth, strayned for the scene," which opened "in manner of a curtine." [6]   Clouds were painted on the "double veil," or curtain, used in Campion's *Lord Hay's Masque* in 1607.   "A curtaine . . . in which the *Night* was painted" concealed the setting for *Beauty*, and a similar device appeared in *Tethys' Festival*, where "on the Travers which served as a curtaine for the first Scene was figured a darke cloude, interser[t] with certaine sparkling starres."   More elaborate effects were aimed at in *Flowers*, in which

> at the entrance of the *King*, at the lower end of the Banquetting house appeared a *Travers* painted in *Perspective*, like the wall of a Cittie with battlements, over which were seene the Tops of houses.   In the middle whereof was a great gate and on either side a Temple . . . in either of which opened a little gate.

The gates thus described were practical, and out of them entered Inverno, Primavera, and other characters.   A kindred structural effect is suggested in *Pleasure reconciled to Virtue*, which had, according to Busino, "a large curtain . . . painted to represent a tent of gold cloth with broad fringe." [7]

---

[1] *Descrizione della presa d'Argo* (Florence, 1658), pp. 7–8.
[2] The word appears in several descriptions of masques between 1604 and 1615 (see *infra*).
[3] P. Reyher, p. 362.
[4] Sir E. K. Chambers, *The Elizabethan Stage*, i, 181.   [5] *Id.*, iii, 279.   [6] *Id.*, iii, 375.   [7] M. Sullivan, p. 114.

These perspectively painted curtains were no doubt taken from Italy; interesting parallels appear in a number of engravings illustrative of performances there, and Furttenbach, who based all his work upon what he had seen during his Italian journeyings, devotes considerable space to a discussion of what he calls the *fuora*, obviously curtains painted in a similar manner.[1] The only difference between them and Jones's traverses is that they were obviously intended to form sets for a series of *intermezzi*, and so in a way were illustrative of the action to follow rather than initial flat scenes. It is to be observed, however, that a similar device was employed in the production of French ballets, and possibly from this source Jones took his immediate inspiration.[2]

It seems that in England, as the years progressed, preference was given to a curtain either plain-coloured or painted decoratively. At any rate, Carew's *Cælum Britannicum* in 1634 presented not a perspective front, but a curtain coloured "watchet[3] and a pale yellow in panes." Here it had come to be merely a means of concealing the main set from the eyes of the spectators, and that, after all, was the primary function of the curtain even when it had a secondary function as a flat setting.

Neither kind of front curtain was employed during the period to conceal a change of scene. For that reason in the earliest masques of James's reign its manipulation could be of the simplest. There it was dropped down from above, to fall immediately in front of the stage. One may well wonder how such a large piece of cloth, rumpled up from its descent, was prevented from interfering with the downward movement of the masquers into the dancing place. Possibly attendants (not noted in the descriptions) were employed to drag it to the side or at least to clear it away from the steps. Distinct references to a "falling" curtain occur in *Blackness*, *Lords* (where "the sodaine fall of a curtaine" is mentioned), and *Pleasure reconciled to Virtue*, in which, according to Busino, "a large curtain dropped." These seem specific enough, although a slight element of doubt enters in by reason of the fact that in a manuscript of the first the curtain is said to have opened, not fallen ("which openinge in manner of a curtaine"). The use of the word "openinge" suggests a second method of operation, technically described as 'drawn.' Between 1606, when the "scene" was "drawn" in Jonson's *Hymenæi*, and 1615, when "a travers was drawne at yᵉ lower end of the hall" for *Browne's Masque*, there were some dozen allusions to this method of revealing the scene; presumably the "travers" which "slyded away" in Marston's *Huntingdon Masque* was of the same kind. What was the usual procedure between 1615 and the thirties of the century we cannot tell, but certainly from 1631 onward the prevailing practice was to draw the curtain, not to the sides, but upward, and from the expressions used it would seem that every means was sought to make it rise as rapidly as possible. 'Flying up' is the usual phrase adopted, and where the less arresting 'drawn up' is substituted, commonly is added the adverbial 'suddenly.'

All of this evidence corresponds precisely to what we know of Italian practice. The falling curtain, a relic from Roman times, had been in operation from the beginning of the sixteenth century, and, according to Sabbatini, still was employed in the seventeenth.[4] Since it was the universal desire of all stage architects in those days to display the scene with as startling a suddenness as possible, it was perhaps best calculated for their purposes, besides being the simplest to rig and control. All that they required was a pair of pulleys attached to a beam in the roof of the hall. Cords, fastened to the topmost ends of the curtain, were passed through these and thence drawn down to the floor level, where they were held by a couple of stage-hands. When these men at a given signal let go, naturally the curtain fell by its own weight. Possibly it was these stage-hands who removed it so as to clear a space for the masquers.

---

[1] *Mannhafter Kunstspiegel*, p. 258; *Architectura recreationis*, pp. 59–60.
[2] H. Prunières, *Le Ballet de cour en France avant Benserade et Lully* (Paris, 1914), p. 147.
[3] *Infra*, p. 159.
[4] i, 37. W. J. Lawrence has an essay on *The Story of a Peculiar Stage Curtain* in *The Elizabethan Playhouse*, i, 109–121; in this he quotes from Ariosto to show the use of such a curtain at Ferrara in 1515. See also *The Development of the Theatre*, pp. 103–104.

On the second method—drawing the curtain—Sabbatini maintains silence, but unquestionably the traverse hung upon a rod and pulled to the sides had been known for many years, and it may be presumed that such was the device employed in several masques before 1615. A good example is provided by a miniature showing a performance of a pastoral by Louis Papon at Montbrison in 1588. There the rods, the curtains, and the attendants are clearly shown (Fig. 7).[1] The chief defect of this type of manipulation was that there could not be the sudden and startling view of a stage setting, so instantaneously appearing as to suggest wizardry on the part of the 'architect.' The emotion of wonder constantly was aimed at in the Renaissance playhouse, and many are the allusions to it in Italian writings. To increase the wonder a definite and deliberate delay before the curtain was removed was regular practice, and to this was added the sounding of trumpets or other loud instruments when the long-expected moment finally arrived. At Ferrara in 1613 military bugle-calls were used for the performance of Ongaro's *L'Alceo*,[2] and at the same city in 1632 "the curtain disappeared at the third trumpet call" when Francesco Guitti's *La Contesa* was performed;[3] a kindred practice was still in regular use at Turin in the middle of the century. *Il Tobacco* (1650) had "a thrice-sounded consort of trumpets" when "the curtain disappeared like a cloud and the scene was discovered";[4] "military trumpets" heralded the disappearance of the great curtain in *L'Educatione d'Achille* the same year. Just such a period of expectation followed by startling music is alluded to frequently in England.[5] "When the king is set," runs the manuscript account of *Queens*,

Fig. 7. STAGE SET FOR A PASTORAL AT MONTBRISON (1588)

British Museum (MS. Harl. 4325) (miniature in *Pastourelle sur la victoire*).

---

[1] Sylvia L. England, *An Unrecognized Document in the History of French Renaissance Staging* (*The Library*, xvi (1935), 232–235).

[2] Antonio Ongaro, *L'Alceo* (Ferrara, 1614), p. 14.   [3] *La Contesa* (Ferrara, 1632), p. 9.

[4] The Turin ballets referred to in this book were those produced before the court of Savoy between 1640 and 1660. Special 'books' of these were prepared by the ducal secretary and adorned with numerous illustrations. About a dozen of these books are preserved at Turin in the Biblioteca Nazionale and the Biblioteca Reale. A complete photographic record of their contents is included in the Yale University Theatrical Collection. Although containing valuable material for the study of seventeenth-century staging, they seem to have been entirely neglected by historians of the theatre. The performances themselves were recorded in C. F. Ménestrier, *Des Représentations en musique anciennes et modernes* (Paris, 1681), and in F. Mugier, *Le théâtre en Savoie* (*Mémoires et documents publiés par la Société Savoisienne d'histoire et d'archéologie*, xxvi (1887), 117–124).

[5] It would appear that the sounding of trumpets before the production of plays in the public theatres may be related to this common Italian practice.

"and the full expectation of the spectacle raised, there shall be hearde a strange murmur with a kinde of hollowe and infernall musike when suddenly an orcus or poeticall Hell is discovere'd." Similar phraseology is employed in Jonson's *Love freed from Ignorance*—"So soone as the Kings Maiestie was set, and in expectation, there was heard a strange Musique of wilde Instruments"—and in his *Love Restored*—"The King and court being seated, and in expectation," the curtain was drawn. Sometimes, for a similar reason, the scene itself was allowed to remain unpeopled by actors; "the eye first of all" was "entertayned" by a view of a seascape in Campion's *Somerset's Masque* before the action began; in Jonson's *Chloridia* "the spectators . . . fed their eyes with the delights" of a landscape for some silent minutes; "the Spectators . . . entertained their eyes a while with the beauty and variety" of a scene in Shirley's *The Triumph of Peace*; a "strange prospect detain'd the eyes of the Spectators some time" in Carew's *Cœlum Britannicum*; and in D'Avenant's *The Triumphs of the Prince d'Amour* a setting was permitted to continue "a while in prospect." The "rapture of the beholders," as Jonson phrases it in *Hymenæi*, was ever aimed at; to excite "the admiring spectators"[1] was their object, and among their means was the suitable manipulation of the curtain.

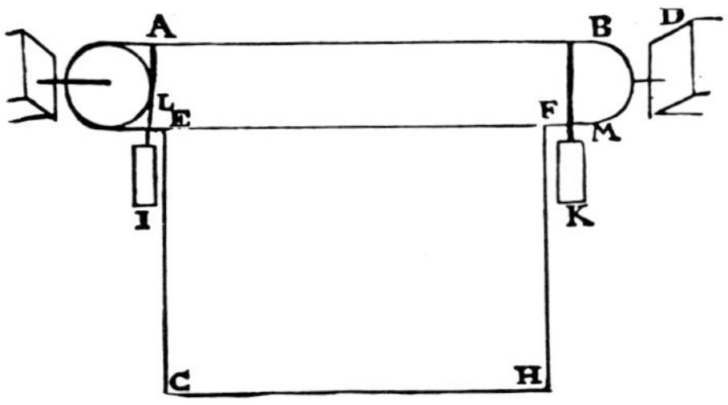

Fig. 8. CONTROL FOR A RISING CURTAIN (1638)

Nicolà Sabbatini. Diagram in *Pratica di fabricar scene e machine.*

If the second method was unsatisfactory, the third—raising the curtain upward—when carried out in the Renaissance manner, possessed the advantages of the first and added the further benefit that the curtain might be lowered when desired at the close of the entertainment. True, the only record of such a lowering is to be found in *Richmond*, but it may well be that every instance of its employment may not have been specially noted. The rising curtain had been known in Italy since the sixteenth century, and the specific manner of operation finds a full description in Sabbatini's book. In order to secure a real 'flying up,' a large cylinder was constructed, its diameter one-third the height of the scene opening (Fig. 8); this was fixed in pivots set in blocks of wood attached to the side walls of the hall. On the cylinder the curtain was nailed, and at its outside edges were placed a couple of counterweights attached to ropes wound round the drum.[2] At a given signal the counterweights were released, and the curtain consequently was caused to ascend rapidly. The utilization of this cylinder was, in Sabbatini's opinion, advisable, for by the first method there was danger lest, through inadvertence, one part of the curtain might fall before the other—"a thing which arouses distaste in the spectators since they lose that sense of wonder" which came from its "sudden and co-ordinated" vanishing. On the other hand, he noted that mishaps might occur even with the use of the more elaborate mechanism, and counselled that two men should stand on guard "to obviate any accident or tumult such as may result from deliberate malice or carelessness or indiscretion" on the part of the audience.

Presumably of such a kind was the type of curtain operated by Inigo Jones during the last decades of the Stuart masque. On occasion, perhaps, the cylinders were set in front of the stage itself; at any rate, in Kynaston's *Corona Minervæ*, "a Curtaine being drawne, there is discovered a Frontispiece." The word "drawne" is used here, but the upward moving curtain had become so fully established by the thirties of the century that the verb may be suspected to be a variant for the

---

[1] Chapman's *Middle Temple Masque.*

[2] W. J. Lawrence, *Pre-Restoration Stage Studies* (1927), p. 170, denies that there was knowledge at this time of the principles of counter-weighing, and gives as a first reference to it a passage relating to the Parisian theatre in 1673. Federico Zuccaro in *Il Passagio per Italia* (Bologna, 1608; section "La Dimora di Parma," p. 27), describing the performance of a play at Mantua in 1608, refers to the raising of the "great curtain" to the sound of a trumpet; this, he states, "was brought in an instant from the stage to the roof of the hall by means of huge counterweights" (*per grandissimi contrapesi*).

commoner 'flies up.' W. J. Lawrence has commented upon the fact that in Webb's plans for *Salmacida Spolia* (Figs. 78, 79) "only a meagre space of 18 inches intervened between the proscenium arch and the first pair of wings," and hence argues that for the production "the curtain was not situated behind the proscenium." [1] This, however, is not necessarily so. "The roofe of ye sceane" is duly marked in the cross-section; below this come the "pieces of Clouds which came downe from ye roofe." The 'roof' indicated here cannot have been the ceiling of the hall, for it descends sharply downward, and, if we assume that the true ceiling was flat, there must have been a space towards the front of about five feet between the two. For bunched *tableaux* curtains the space between the sky borders and the proscenium frame would not have been sufficient, but clearly, with a cylinder set on high, even so meagre a space as 18 inches would have been enough to permit the passage of a cloth drawn vertically upward.

So far comment has been devoted only to those curtains which were in one piece, but it is to be observed that, in addition to such, Jones made a few early experiments in the use of double curtains, the two parts being removed separately at different moments during the performance. Thus in Campion's *Lord Hay's Masque* there were two "veils" placed in front of the stage; at the sounding of some music "the vale on the right hand was withdrawne and the ascent of the hill with the bower of *Flora* was discovered," while later, at the conclusion of a song, "the whole veil" was "sodainly drawne." The same year Marston's *Huntingdon Masque* had a "traverse" that "slided away," with a second traverse "drawn before the masquers" which "sank down" when "the cornets were winded." The last record apparently of a kindred scheme occurs in Beaumont's *Inner Temple*, where a "first traverse was drawn and the lower descent of the mountain discovered," followed by the drawing of "the second traverse" and the resultant revealing of "the higher ascent of the mountain."

Many instances have been given of music used to herald the curtain fall or rise, and similar flourishes were introduced to accompany scenic changes within the shows themselves. The true explanation of this practice may lie in Sabbatini's remarks wherein he describes the "tricks" which could be employed to distract the attention of the audience while a change of scene was being effected. A "confidential person" might be "sent to the rear of the hall and, at the proper time, feign to have a noisy quarrel with another person in the know"; some one might "pretend that the beams of the tiers were breaking," although, as could be expected, this device was likely to "occasion much disturbance"; and, lastly, "the sounding of a trumpet, drum or other instrument might draw attention from the stage." Records of this use of music are numerous in England. "The cornets were winded" in the *Huntingdon Masque* for the revealing of a scene; "solemne musique" accompanied the "breaking forth" of a bright sky in *Hue and Cry after Cupid*, and "a lowd and full musique" attended the breaking of the rock; the infernal music at the beginning of *Queens* was followed later by the "sound of lowd musique as if many instruments had made one blast" when the scene disappeared and the House of Fame took its place; in *Tethys' Festival* the goddess and her nymphs appeared in a new scene "at the sound of a loud and fuller musique," while the third setting was shown as "the lowde musique soundes"; "a double consort exprest by severall instruments" served a similar purpose in *Lords*; "lowd Musicke" was played for the drawing of the traverse in *Flowers* and "againe sounded" for a scene change; there was "lowd musique," too, in *Mercury Vindicated*, *Pan's Anniversary*, and *Golden Age*; Apollo, Mercury, the Muses, and Harmony in *Neptune's Triumph* gave a musical accompaniment to the moving forward of the island. Occasionally other sound effects were tried, as when in *The Triumph of Peace* "there is heard a great noyse and confusion of voyces within, some crying they will come in, others knock 'em downe, call the rest of the Guard; then a cracke is heard in the workes, as if there were some danger by some piece of the Machines falling."

---

[1] *The Elizabethan Playhouse*, i, 119.

The positions occupied by these instrumentalists and singers were various. Sometimes they were clad in rich clothes and appeared on the stage or in an elaborate cloud machine. The musicians in *Hue and Cry after Cupid* were "attir'd in yellow, with wreathes of *marioram* and veiles like HYMENS priests." In *Somerset's Masque* "Harmony with nine Musitians more" came on stage "in long Taffata robes and caps of Tinsell, with Garlands guilt." "The whole Musicke was discovered" in *Pleasure reconciled to Virtue*, "sitting at the foot of the Mountaine," and in *Tempe Restored* "Harmony comes foorth attended by a *Chorus* of Musique." A "discovery" seems to have been the most frequent method of presenting them, but occasionally they were concealed behind some portion of the scenery. Thus the "consort music" was "placed in the *cupola*" of the temple "out of sight" in *The Vision of the Twelve Goddesses*, although other instrumentalists were revealed on the mountain. In *Lord Hay's Masque* they sat on the right hand of the dancing place, and "on either side of the room" in *Lords*.

THE PROSCENIUM ARCH

With the music contributed by these persons the scenes changed and the curtain was removed. The presence of a curtain generally, if not universally, implies the framing of the stage by means of a proscenium arch, and such an arch, specially constructed for the occasion, seems to have been the almost regular accompaniment of all the masques superintended by Inigo Jones. The development of this picture-frame forms a story of great interest, but one so complex as to prohibit any full treatment of it here. It may be sufficient to say that, although a frame, often in the shape of a triumphal arch, had been known in pageants and even in theatrical representations from the earlier part of the sixteenth century, its regular employment in the playhouse was singularly slow in becoming established. Of it neither Serlio nor Sabbatini says anything, both assuming that the front wings of their sets would provide masking for the rest of the scene. Virtually, of course, these wings, associated with a valance, or 'teaser,' did provide a framework, and it seems reasonable to conclude that the familiar proscenium of to-day arose from a combination of several elements, the most important being the pageant arch, the central opening in theatres of the Roman type, and the wings and valance of the perspective stage. Thus Sabbatini [1] describes "the completion of the front part of the heavens . . . by making an artificial festoon of leaves and fruit," with the arms of the prince or some other *impresa* in the middle, or else by having "a piece of cloth simulating brocade sprinkled with gold, in hanging folds and golden tassels," perhaps accompanied by "figures painted at the corners." Valances of a similar kind are referred to in the technical discussions of Furttenbach, and, as will be seen, they were definitely recommended by Ingegnieri for the purpose, not of masking, but of lighting the stage. [2]

Perhaps it might not be wrong to say that the prehistory of the proscenium arch gave rise to a double convention, so that not infrequently a single show presented a complete and an incomplete frame at the same time. That is what is implied when in the Turin *L'Educatione d'Achille* (1650) we are told that "one sees a noble scene between two proscenia," the first being a unified rectangular masking for the entire set and the other a half-frame composed of side-wings representing the walls of a formal garden topped by balustrades and stone ornaments (Fig. 9).

The development of Jones's use of the masking frame may easily be studied from the extant evidence. At first there is only a tentative approach, but by the time when *Salmacida Spolia* gave a final flourish to the court entertainment the conception had arisen of a surrounding border to a picture. "And indeed," says Townsend, [3] "these showes are nothing else but pictures with Light and Motion." The most primitive form is to be seen in Jonson's *Hymenæi* and *Hue and Cry after Cupid*.

[1] i, 32.   [2] *Infra*, p. 134.   [3] *Tempe Restored*.

The former had two statues, representing Hercules and Atlas, which supported the heavens rising above the great globe forming the setting. For the latter there

> were erected two *pilasters*, chardg'd with spoiles and *trophees* of *love* and his *mother*, . . . amongst which were old and young persons figur'd, bound with *roses*, the wedding garments, rocks and spindles, hearts transfixt with arrowes, others flaming, *virgins* girdles, gyrlonds and worlds of such-like; all wrought round and bold: and overhead two personages, *triumph* and Victorie, in flying postures and twise so big as the life, in place of the arch, and holding a gyrlond of *myrtle* for the key. All which, with the *pillars*, seem'd to be of burnished gold and emboss'd out of the metall.

Fig. 9. Proscenium Frame and Setting for "L'Educatione d'Achille" (Turin, 1650)
Biblioteca Nazionale, Turin.

That the upper figures were not joined to the lower seems implied by the phrase "in place of the arch," yet that phrase itself undoubtedly suggests that an arching frame was already in 1608 no unknown feature in the court theatre.

From that time onward we are provided with many elaborate descriptions which amply serve to bring before us the appearance of these proscenia. Daniel's *Tethys' Festival* in 1610 has various such "adornments":

> First, on eyther side stood a great statue of twelve foot high, representing *Neptune* and *Nereus*. *Neptune* holding a Trident, with an Anchor made to it, and this Mot: *His artibus*, . . . *Nereus* holding out a golden fish in a net, with the word *Industria*. . . . These Sea-gods stood on pedestals and were al of gold. Behinde them were two pillasters, on which hung compartments with other devises, and these bore up a rich Freeze wherein were figures of tenne foote long of Flouds and Nymphes, with a number of naked children, dallying with a draperie which they seemed to holde up that the Scene might be seene and the ends thereof fell downe in foldes by the pillasters. In the midst was a compartment, with this

inscription, *Tethyos Epinicia*, TETHYS feasts of triumph. This was supported with two winged boyes, and all the worke was done with that force and boldnesse on the gold and silver as the figures seemed round and not painted.

The likeness here to contemporary Italian designs is immediately apparent—the painted figures, the falling drapery, the central *impresa*. This *impresa*, which Sabbatini said might be the arms of the prince, commonly in England took the form of the masque title, set in the midst of what technically was named the 'compartment.'

Fig. 10. PROSCENIUM FRAME AND SETTING FOR GELONE (TURIN, 1656)
Giovenale Boetto.

The "Arch Tryumphall, passing beautifull, which enclosed the whole" setting of *Somerset's Masque* seems to revert to an earlier tradition. A clear "Arch Triumphall," too, graced Jonson's *Lovers made Men* in 1617. On its top sat

> HVMANITIE, placed in figure . . . with her lap of flowers, scattering them with her right hand and holding a golden chaine in her left hand, to shew both the freedome and the bond of Courtesie, with this inscription, SUPER OMNIA VULTVS. On the two sides of the Arch, CHEEREFULNES and READINES, her servants. CHEEREFULNES in a loose flowing garment, filling out wine from an antique piece of plate with this word, *Adsit lætitiæ dator*. READINES a winged Mayd, with two flaming lights in her hands, and her word, *Amor addidit alas*.

Whether Jonson's *Neptune's Triumph* was intended to have a formal frieze or not is uncertain; the description merely declares that "all that is discovered of a *Scene* are two erected Pillars, dedicated to *Neptune*, with this inscription upon the one, NEP. RED., on the other, SEC. IOV." [1] By the thirties

[1] The earliest English design we have for a proscenium is that which accompanies a French pastoral in 1626: *Designs*, No. 67 (Pl. X).

of the century these arches had become technically known as 'ornaments,' an appropriate name, for ornaments indeed they were. In Jonson's *Chloridia*

> The ornament which went about the Scene was composed of Foliage or leaves, heightned with gold and enter-woven with all sorts of flowers and naked children, playing and climbing among the branches; and in the midst a great Garland of flowers in which was written, CHLORIDIA.[1]

From this time on the descriptions of these proscenia, partly owing to control by the scenic artist of the masque libretti, a control against which Jonson fought so bitterly, became more and more elaborate in their details. They form true pen-pictures of the now-vanished frames, each carefully symbolic of the theme introduced in settings and characters. "The first thing that presented itself to the eye" in Townsend's *Albion's Triumph*

> was the Ornament that went about the Scene: in the middest of which was placed a great Armes of the Kings, with Angels holding an Emperiall Crowne, from which hung a Drapery of crimson Velvet fringed with gold, tackt in severall knotts that on each side, with many folds, was wound about a Pillaster. In the freeze were festones of severall friutes in their naturall colours on which, in gratious postures, lay Children sleeping. At each end was a double sheild, with a Gorgons head, and at the foot of the pillasters, on each side, stood two Women; the one young, in a watchet Robe looking upwards and on her head a paire of Compasses of gold, the poynts standing towards Heaven; the other more ancient and of a venerable aspect, apparreled in tawney, looking downewards, in the one hand a long ruler and in the other a great paire of iron Compasses, one poynt whereof stood on the ground and the other touched part of the ruler. Above their heads were fixt compertiments of a new composition, and in that over the first was written *Theorica* and over the second *Practica*, shewing that by these two all works of Architecture and Ingining have their perfection.[2]

The same year Townsend produced a second masque, *Tempe Restored*, and here

> In the upper part of the border serving for ornament to the SCENE was painted a faire compartment of scrowles and quadratures, in which was written TEMPE RESTAVRATVM. On each side of this lay a figure bigger then the life, the one a woman with wings on her head like MERCURIE and a pen in her hand, the other a man looking downe in a booke lying open before him and a torch lighted in his hand: that figur'd Invention, this Knowledge. Neare to these were children holding ougly Maskes before their faces in action as if they would afright them, others riding on tame beasts and some blowing such wrethen Trumps as make confused noyse. In the corners sat other Children hardning of darts in Lamps. But Invention and Knowledge seeme not to be diverted from their study by these childish bugbears. In the midst of the two sides of this border in short neeces [niches] sat two ougly figures, the one a woman with a forked tongue and snaky lockes and the underpart of a Satyre; this Hagge held in her hand a smiling vizard crown'd with Roses and was figured for Envie under the Maske of friendship. On the other side was sitting as horrid a man Satyre with a wreath of poppy on his head and a Frog sitting on the forepart thereof, and above a Batt flying; this represented curious *Ignorance*.

"The rest of the Border," adds Jones, "was fild up with severall fancies which, lest I should be too long in the description of the frame, I will goe to the picture it selfe." [3] On these "fancies" the artist played his variations in following entertainments. For Shirley's *The Triumph of Peace*

> the border of the front and sides that enclosed all the Sceane had first a ground of Arbor-worke enter-mixt with loose branches and leaves, and in this was two Niches, and in them two great figures standing in easy postures, in their naturall colors and much bigger then the life; the one attired after the Grecian manner held in one hand a Scepter and in the other a Scrowle, and a picked [peaked] antique crowne on his head; his curasse was of Gold richly enchased, his robe blue and Silver, his armes and thighs bare with buskinds enricht with ornaments of Gold, his browne locks long and curled, his Beard thicke

---

[1] Part of the design for this proscenium has been preserved: *Designs*, No. 81 (Pl. XI).   [2] *Id.*, No. 107 (Pl. XXI).
[3] A pastoral frame was wrought in 1633 for *The Shepherd's Paradise*, and happily the original design has been preserved (Fig. 12).

Fig. 11. PROSCENIUM FRAME WITH EMBLEMS OF TRAGEDY AND COMEDY
Chatsworth (*Designs*, No. 181). Copyright of his Grace the Duke of Devonshire.

Fig. 12. PROSCENIUM FRAME AND STANDING SCENE FOR "THE SHEPHERD'S
PARADISE" (1633)
Inigo Jones. Chatsworth (*Designs*, No. 163). Copyright of his Grace the Duke of Devonshire.

but not long, and his face was of a grave and ioviall aspect. This figure stood on a round pedestall fained of white Marble, enrich with severall carvings; above this in a compartment of Gold was written MINOS. The figure on the other side was in a Romane habit, holding a Table in one hand and a Pen in the other, and a white Bend or Diadem about his head; his Robe was crimson and Gold, his Mantle yellow and Silver, his Buskins watchet trim'd with Silver, his haire and Beard long and white, with a venerable aspect; standing likewise on a round Pedestall answerable to the other; and in the compartment over him was written NVMA. Above all this, in a proportionate distance, hung two

Fig. 13. PROSCENIUM FRAME FOR "THE TRIUMPH OF PEACE" (1634)
Inigo Jones. Royal Institute of British Architects, London (*Designs*, No. 180).

great Festons of fruites in colors, which served for finishing to these sides. The upper part, in manner of a large Freeze, was adorn'd with severall compartments with draperies hanging downe and the ends tied up in knots, with trophies proper to feasts and triumphs, composed of Masking Vizards and torches. In one of the lesser compartments was figured a sharp sighted eye, and in the other a Golden-yoke. In the midst was a more great and rich compartment on the sides of which sate naked Children in their naturall colors, with Silver wings, in action of sounding Golden Trumpets, and in this was figured a *Caduceus* with an Olive-branch, all which are Hierogliphicks of Peace, Justice and Law.

The design for this proscenium is extant (Fig. 13), and another drawing seems connected with it (Fig. 11). The fruit and flower *motif* in Carew's *Cœlum Britannicum* took a different form. There

The first thing that presented it self to the sight was a rich Ornament that enclosed the Scæne; in the upper part of which were great branches of Foliage growing out of leaves and huskes, with a Coronice at the top; and in the midst was placed a large compartment composed of Groteske work, wherein were Harpies with wings and Lions clawes and their hinder parts converted into leaves and branches. Over all was a broken Frontispiece, wrought with scrowles and masque heads of Children, and within this a Table adorn'd with a lesser Compartiment, with this Inscription: CÆLVM BRITANNICVM. The two sides of this Ornament were thus ordered. First, from the ground arose a square Basement and on the Plinth stood a great vaze of gold, richly enchased and beautified with Sculptures of great Releive, with frutages hanging from the upper part. At the foot of this sate two Youths naked, in their natural colours; each of these with one arme supported the Vase, on the cover of which stood two young women in Draperies, arme in arme, the one figuring the glory of Princes and the other Mansuetude.

Fig. 14. PROSCENIUM FRAME FOR AN UNIDENTIFIED
MASQUE
Inigo Jones and John Webb. Chatsworth (*Designs*, No. 380). Copyright of
his Grace the Duke of Devonshire.

Their other armes bore up an Oval in which to the King's Majesty was this Impress: A Lyon with an Imperial Crown on his head; the words, *Animum sub pectore forti*. On the other side was the like composition but the design of the Figures varied, and in the Oval on the top, being born up by Nobility and Fecundity, was this Impresse to the Queen's Majesty: A Lilly growing with branches and leaves and three lesser Lillies springing out of the Stem; the words, *Semper inclita virtus.*

The whole of this proscenium, we are informed, was "heightned with Gold," and the narrator (perhaps Inigo Jones himself) deemed it "for the Invention and various composition . . . the newest and most graceful that hath ever been done in this place." Indian trophies formed the chief *motif* of the frame for the next masque, D'Avenant's *The Temple of Love*,

An Ornament of a new Invention agreeable to the Subject. On the one side upon a basement sate a naked Indian on a whitish Elephant, his legs shortning towards the neck of the beast, his tire and bases[1] of several coloured feathers, representing the Indian Monarchy. On the other side, an Asiatique in the habit of an Indian Borderer, riding on a Camel, his Turbant and Coat differing from that of the Turks, figured for the Asian Monarchy. Over these hung shields like Compartiments. In that over the Indian was painted a Sun rising and in the other an half Moon. These had for finishing the Capital of a great pillaster which served as a ground to stick them of and bore up a large freeze or border with a Coronice. In this over the Indian lay the figure of an old man with a long white hair and beard, representing the flood *Tigris*; on his head a wreath of Canes and Seadg and leaning upon a great urne out of which run water. By him, in an extravagant posture, stood a Tyger.

At the other end of this freeze lay another naked man, representing *Meander*, the famous river of *Asia*, who likewise had a great Silver Urne, and by him lay an Unicorne.

In the midst of this border was fixed a rich Compartiment, behind which was a crimson Drapery, part of it born up by naked Children tack'd up in several Pleats, and the rest was at each end of the Freeze

[1] 'Tire' stands generally for attire or dress, or specifically for headdress. 'Bases' technically applies to a short kilt worn by men below the doublet or to a short skirt (petticoat) worn by women. Very often these bases, in the masquing suits, were formed of 'labels,' thin strips of cloth, sometimes cut in the shape of leaves.

tyed with a great knot, and from thence hung down in foulds to the bottom of the Pedeſtals. In the midſt of this Compartiment in an Oval was written: TEMPLVM AMORIS. All these Figures were in their natural colours, bigger than the life, and the Compartiments of Gold.[1]

No such detailed inscription exiſts for the "front of Architecture" which graced D'Avenant's *The Triumphs of the Prince d'Amour* ; all we know is that it had "two Pillaſters at each side, and in the middle of the Coronich a Compartiment with this inscription in an Oval: *Les Triomphes du Prince d'Amour.*" The same author's *Britannia Triumphans*, however, provides an elaborate description of the specially conſtructed 'ornament' (Fig. 15).

Fig. 15. Studies for the Proscenium in "Britannia Triumphans" (1638)
Inigo Jones. Royal Inſtitute of British Architects (*Designs*, No. 253–255).

In the underpart of this were two pedeſtalls of a solid order, whereon captives lay bound. Above sate two figures in neeches, on the right hand a woman in a watchet drapery heightned with silver, on her head a *Corona Roſtrata*, with one hand holding the rudder of a ship and in the other a little winged figure with a branch of Palme and a Girland: this woman represented Navall victory. Opposite to this in the other neech sate the figure of a man bearing a Scepter with a hand and an eye in the Palme and in the other hand a booke; on his head a Girland of *Amaranthus*; his Curace was of gold with a *Palludamentum* of blue and Antike bases of Crimson; his foot treading on the head of a Serpent. By this figure was signified Right Government. Above these were other composed ornaments cut out like cloth of silver, tied up in knots with scarfings all touch'd with gold.

These Pillaſters bore up a large Freese with a Sea triumph of naked children riding on sea horses and fishes, and young Tritons with writhen trumpets and other maritime fancies. In the midſt was placed

---

[1] *Designs*, No. 210; reproduced by W. J. Lawrence in *The Elizabethan Playhouse*, i, 105. For the proscenium used in *Florimène* (1635) see *Designs*, Nos. 243 (Pl. XXVIII), 244 (Pl. XXIX).

a great compartiment of gold, with branches of Palme comming out of the scrowles, and within that a lesser of silver with this inscription—VIRTVTIS OPVS, proper to the subject of this Masque. . . . From this came a drapery of Crimson which, tied up with great knots in the corners, hung downe in foulds on the sides of the Pillasters.

Satyr *motifs* graced *Luminalia*; here

> The ornament which serv'd as a Bordure to enclose the Scene was raised on two round Basements on which were Satyres bigger than the life, bearing baskets of fruits, and knots of young Satyres clinging

Fig. 16. PROSCENIUM FRAME AND LANDSCAPE
Inigo Jones.   Chatsworth (*Designs*, No. 400).   Copyright of his Grace
the Duke of Devonshire.

about their leggs in extravagant postures.   Above these ran cornicements, which made the ground of a second order, wherein were termes of women fained of silver and children in their naturall colours standing on arches, some wantonizing about those termes and others holding great vizards before their faces.   On the heads of the Termes were cushions which served for capitals that bore the finishing of composed frontispices of great scrowles with *frutages*, from whence hung lighted Lamps.

> In the Freeze above was other young Satyres which seem'd oppress'd with the burthen of great festons, the husks of which were tied up in knots to a double compartiment composed of scrowles, quadratures and Masque heads.   In the midst hung a drapery fained of cloth of silver, and in it was written LVMINALIA.   Under all this ranne a large valens of gold, embroidered with flowers and great Tassels.

The last masque produced at court was D'Avenant's *Salmacida Spolia*, and in this, as if to present a rich flourish to a reign that was doomed to extinction, Jones provided an even more elaborate proscenium than any that he had previously designed.

THE BANQUETING HOUSE

In the border that enclosed the Sceans and made a frontispice to all the worke, in a square Neech on the right hand stood two figures of women, one of them expressing much majesty in her aspect, apparelled in sky colour, with a crowne of gold on her head and a bridle in her hand, representing Reason; the other, embracing her, was in changeable silke with wings at her shoulders, figured for intellectuall Appetite, who while she imbraceth Reason all the actions of men are rightly governed.   Above these, in a second order, were winged children, one riding on a furious Lion which hee seemes to tame with reynes and bit, another bearing an Antique ensigne, the third hovering above with a branch of Palme in his hand, expressing the victory over the Perturbations.   In a Neech on the other side stood two figures joyning hands, one a grave old man in a robe of purple, with a heart of gold in a chayne about his necke, figured for Counsell, the other a woman in a garment of cloth of gold, in her hand a sword with a serpent winding about the blade, representing Resolution. . . .

Over these and answering to the other side was a round Altar raysed high and on it the bird of Pallas, figured for Prudence.   On eyther side were children with wings, one in act of Adoration, another holding a booke, and a third flying over their heads with a lighted Torch in his hand, representing the intellectuall light accompanied with Doctrine and Discipline. . . .

Above these ran a large Freese with a Cornicement, in the midst wherof was a double Compartiment rich and full of ornament.   On the top of this sat Fame with spreaded wings, in act, sounding a Trumpet of gold.   Joyning to the Compartiment in various postures lay two Figures in their naturall colours as big as the life, one holding an Anchor, representing Safety, the other expressing Riches, with a Cornu-copia;   and about her stood Antique vases of gold.   The rest of this Freese was composed of Children, with significant signes to expresse their several qualities: Forgetfulnesse of injuries extinguishing a flaming torch on an Armour, Commerce with eares of Corne, Felicity with a basket of Lillies, Affection to the Countrey holding a Grasshopper, Prosperous Successe with the Rudder of a Ship, Innocence with a branch of Fearne. . . .

In the midst of the aforesaid Compartiment in an Ovall Table was written: SALMACIDA SPOLIA.

Thus the stage was set.   Eagerly the audience awaited the opening of the curtain.

III

THE PROSPECTIVES

WITHIN these magnificent 'ornaments,' formed like huge and richly wrought picture-frames, appeared the scenes—vistas of landscape and of sea, visions of cloud-capped mountain and of temple glorious. This does not imply, of course, that the means of securing the effects, or even the essential principles of the typical masque staging, were discovered and set forth in the earliest entertainments given during the reign of James I. Originally, as many commentators have pointed out, the masque was a brief evening's show brought into a banqueting hall, and not set there beforehand; instead of spectators coming to the entertainment, the entertainment came to the spectators. In the representative early performance of this kind groups of courtiers, disguised in masquerade fashion, drew into the hall chariots or pageant-wagons constructed in semblance of triumphal cars or else wrought into the form of movable scenes. Castles and rocks and groves thus were wheeled into princely *salons*, and around these, rather than before them, the noble actors exhibited themselves. For their use no special portion of the room was apportioned; the words spoken or sung we may imagine uttered either in the middle of the floor or else at chance-selected locations along the walls.

Such pageant-wagons had been the delight of the sixteenth century, both in England and abroad. From every Italian city, from Paris, and from the German courts come records, in plain narrative or adorned with illustrations, of allegorical disguisings and theatrical tourneys. Some were relatively simple; others, like the famous *Mascherata della genealogia degli dei* [1] performed at Florence in 1565 to honour the marriage of Francesco de' Medici to Giovanna of Austria, cost enormous sums and demanded the attention of many artists (Fig. 17). Well into the seventeenth century the chariots maintained their popularity, and even when their place was taken by formal stage-sets they continued to appear as the accompaniments of gods and heroes.

The pageant-car forms one source of masque staging during the first years of the seventeenth century. With it may be associated the traditions which the Renaissance court inherited from the medieval ages that had gone by. Of the medieval stage one thing is typical—the disposition of various 'mansions,' or houses, each representing a distinct locality, before the eyes of the audience, so that individual scenes were not shown by a succession of theatrical pictures, but were enacted by performers who stood now in one place and now in another. Obviously, the pageant-car may be regarded as a kind of mansion on wheels, and if several were brought at one time into the banqueting hall it is clear that they might present a courtly variant of the familiar multiple stage used in the performance of mystery dramas. Here would be a rock and there a castle, with perhaps a grove in the middle, action proceeding at the first, the second, or the third as occasion demanded.

The initial break with the traditions thus set and the primal step towards genuine theatrical entertainment may be seen when the rocks and groves and castles are set up beforehand to await the entry of the audience, when the wheels are removed and there is a transformation from decorated car to established scene. If, however, this marks the first movement towards a

---

[1] This masquerade was one of the most important of its time; some of the original costume designs are illustrated in this book. Lengthy descriptions of the cars and their occupants appear in Giorgio Vasari, *Vite* (Milan, 1811), xvi, and Baccio Baldini, *Discorso sopra la mascherata degl' Iddei Gentili* (Florence, 1565).

54

Fig. 17. A Pageant-wagon at Florence (*c.* 1580)
Biblioteca Nazionale, Florence (*C. B.* 3, 53; vol. ii, 75).

thoroughly theatrical conception it must be recognized that there was bound to be a period of experimentation and of sometimes indecisive questing ere the type of staging, established in the later masques, was discovered and appreciated. No wonder need we feel when we observe that the scenic styles introduced into his apprentice productions by Inigo Jones borrowed much from the practice of Elizabethan court festivities; it was but natural that this artist-architect should require years of preparation before he succeeded in making the perambulatory entertainments assume a fixed and co-ordinate form.

Our wonder should be reserved for another thing. Truly surprising is it that this man, however indebted he might be to Italian example, could, practically unaided, have made even at the very beginning such significant strides towards the establishment at Whitehall of a theatre worthy to rival those of proud and princely Italy. A glance at two masques, produced in succeeding years, 1604 and 1605, demonstrates this immediately.

DISPERSED SETTINGS: "THE VISION OF THE TWELVE GODDESSES" AND "LORD HAY'S MASQUE"

Could we have been among the specially privileged spectators who were invited to witness *The Vision of the Twelve Goddesses* on January 8, 1604, we should have been confronted by a hall so cluttered up with dispersed scenery—relics alike of perambulatory masques and of medieval simultaneous settings—that space for the audience seemed small. "The Hale [Hall]," remarks a contemporary, "was so much lessened by the workes that were in it, so as none could be admitted but men of apparance." [1] At one end of the room we should have seen a great rock or mountain, with in "the midst from the top . . . a winding stayre of breadth for three to march." Thence Iris was to descend; there some of the musicians were placed; and there, too, the whole bevy of masked ladies, in the semblance of goddesses, made their appearance. Directly opposite to this mountain, at the upper end of the hall, stood another rock-like structure, wrought to reveal a cave. Here Somnus lay sleeping until Night rose and, coming towards him, succeeded in awakening her son. Thus aroused, he waved his white wand, and immediately a small curtain stretched over part of the left-hand side of the hall was removed. Behind it Somnus made "them seem to see there a Temple." [2]

The arrangement here is a primitive one, each locality being stationary and several distinct places being represented at the same time before the eyes of the spectators. Everything, to that audience of 1604, would have been thoroughly familiar. The mountain was a scenic device hallowed by antiquity, and the cave had been a familiar theatrical appurtenance for many generations. Both were derived, through the sixteenth-century masques, from the medieval mysteries. Rocks figured freely among the pageant-cars of the Renaissance,[3] and these were evidently secularizations of that mount which seemingly appeared in nearly all representations of earlier Biblical dramas. The cardinal importance of this scenic element in medieval plays has recently been demonstrated,[4] and that in turn seems based on still more primitive iconographic traditions. A *monte* was a stable feature of the Umbrian *lauda drammatica*—a practicable mountain with stairs of ascent and at least one cave. "A hill ten and a half feet high," it was described, "with a stairway . . . all covered with

---

[1] Dudley Carleton, quoted in Sir E. K. Chambers, *The Elizabethan Stage*, iii, 280.

[2] There is no indication that Inigo Jones had anything to do with this masque, but clearly *The Vision of the Twelve Goddesses* is interesting because it presents the essential features of the earlier court entertainments which eventually that artist was to banish in favour of other methods.

[3] Sir E. K. Chambers, *The Elizabethan Stage*, i, 132.

[4] Virginia Galante Garrone, *L'Apparato scenico del dramma sacro in Italia* (Turin, 1935).

red cloth." [1]   Similar hills are recorded in the dialogue and stage directions of a vast number of medieval sacred dramas.

Taken over into the sphere of the masque, the pageant, and the masquerade, the rock or mountain had a long and distinguished career.   Many of the scenes presented by Inigo Jones were of this form.   "Rockes?" queries Plutus as he looks around him in Chapman's *Middle Temple*. "Nothing but Rockes in these masking devices?   Is Invention so poore shee must needes ever dwell among Rocks?"   The complaint was well merited.   Of all settings, the Renaissance seemed to prefer that which displayed craggy cliffs and vast mountains.   If there was a rival that rival was the temple.   Again, perhaps, taken from the temples which figured in the mysteries, this setting acquired particular interest in an age when architecture (through the discovery of Vitruvius) was assuming new importance and when the laws of perspective were eagerly being studied.   The temple of *The Vision of the Twelve Goddesses* was merely the first of many such noble edifices theatrically conceived.

An intermediate stage between the dispersed setting of this masque of 1604 and later methods may be found in Campion's *Lord Hay's Masque* of 1607.   No change of scene was attempted here, but the partial curtain concealing the Temple of Peace in *The Vision of the Twelve Goddesses* was elaborated so that the 'scene' as a whole was revealed in two distinct portions to the audience.   So important is it to understand fully the arrangement of this setting that it becomes imperative to quote at length from the printed description.   First of all, we are told of the "chaire of State" with "scaffoldes and seates on eyther side continued to the skreene," in front of which was the "dancing place."   Eighteen feet behind the screen

> an other Stage was raised higher by a yearde then that which was prepared for dancing.   This higher Stage was all enclosed with a double vale, so artificially painted that it seemed as if darke cloudes had hung before it: within that shrowde was concealed a greene valley with greene trees round about it and in the midst of them nine golden trees of fifteene foote high, with armes and braunches very glorious to behold: From the which grove toward the State was made a broade descent to the dauncing place, iust in the midst of it.   On either hand were two ascents, like the sides of two hilles, drest with shrubbes and trees, that on the right hand leading to the bowre of *Flora*, the other to the house of *Night*; which bowre and house were plac't opposite at either end of the skreene and betweene them both was raised a hill hanging like a cliffe over the grove belowe, and on the top of it a goodly large tree was set, supposed to be the tree of *Diana :* behind the which toward the window [2] was a small descent, with an other spreading hill that climed up to the toppe of the window, with many trees on the height of it, whereby those that played on the Hoboyes at the Kings entrance into the hall were shadowed.   The bowre of *Flora* was very spacious, garnisht with all kinds of flowers and flowrie branches with lights in them; the house of *Night* ample and stately, with blacke pillors, whereon many starres of gold were fixt: within it, when it was emptie, appeared nothing but cloudes and starres and on the top of it stood three Turrets underpropt with small blacke starred pillers, the middlemost being highest and greatest, the other two of equall proportion: about it were plac'd wyer artificial Battes and Owles, continually moving.

All these were evidently concealed by the 'veil,' and when the audience was seated "the vale on the right hand was withdrawne and the ascent of the hill with the bower of *Flora* [was] discovered." Later "the whole veil" was "sodainly drawne, the grove and trees of gold and the hill with *Dianas* tree" thus being "at once discovered."

Interpretation of these descriptions is a trifle difficult.   The chair of state was clearly set near the lower end of the hall, with scaffolding for the spectators running along each side wall as far as the

---

[1] Alessandro D'Ancona, *Origini del teatro italiano*, i, 246.
[2] That is to say, the window at the farther end of the hall, behind the stage.

'screen.' This word "screen" no doubt applies only to a low partition intended to divide the acting area from the auditorium, and is not a synonym for the curtain. A rectangular raised dancing floor occupied a space in the middle of the hall opposite to the state, and from that a passageway led upward to a raised stage at the other end of the hall. Precisely here it becomes a hard task to determine exactly what was done in the carrying out of the scenery. Brotanek [1] has determined that a system of dispersed sets (but placed on one platform) was employed. According to his scheme, the two 'houses' were at the extreme edges of a long, narrow stage; in the centre was a green sward with trees, behind which came the cliff and the mountain in the rear. It may be that such a reconstruction is the correct one, but another explanation is possible. Among the designs of Inigo Jones is one [2] which, with certain modifications, might conceivably have fitted this masque.[3] Nine trees are shown here, a hill with a single tree, and beyond a distant mountain. At each side are steps leading towards the top of structures seemingly marked as frames. If we were to assume that these frames extended outward at the sides, that a curtain concealed the right-hand 'house' and another curtain the rest of the set, we should come close to the description given in the text, and in that event should find ourselves confronted by a design which, while clearly introducing elements closely to be associated with the simultaneous setting, adumbrates the later unified scenes.

Some attempt was made in this masque of Campion's to introduce trick trap-work. By operation from below, the golden trees were made "to move and dance" and then range themselves in threes. At the sound of a song

> that part of the stage whereon the first three trees stoode began to yeeld and the three formost trees gently to sincke, and this was effected by an Ingin plac't under the stage. When the trees had sunke a yarde they cleft in three parts and the Maskers appeared out of the tops of them, the trees were sodainly convayed away and the first three Maskers were raysed againe by the Ingin.

So, later, the second and third trios behaved at the touch of Night's wand—at least, so they should have behaved. Unfortunately, as Campion irritatedly complains, the director, through "simplicity, negligence or conspiracy," succeeded in destroying the effect. Apparently the device had been shown to some privileged spectators earlier in the day, and some one had forgotten to put the trees back in their places—a mishap that "somewhat hazarded" the operation of the "engine."

CONCENTRATED SETTINGS: "THE MASQUE OF BLACKNESS"

In this masque a step was taken towards new things, but still the setting clung to earlier traditions. When we turn to Jonson's essay in *Blackness* we find ourselves in another world. Certainly the scenery in *Lord Hay's Masque* had been assembled at one end of the hall and thus had broken with the earlier 'dispersed' tradition, but it was, nevertheless, essentially 'simultaneous' in its effect. When the audience assembled for *The Masque of Blackness* they saw first a great curtain on which was painted a single scene of "*Landtschap* consisting of small woods and here and there a void place fill'd with huntings," and later, after this curtain had fallen, their eyes were greeted with a sea scene. A contemporary manuscript description declares that "an artificiall sea" was "seene to shoote forth it self abroad the room"; the official libretto amplifies this statement by saying that the water "flowed to the land, raysed with waves which seemed to move and in some places the billow to breake, as imitating that orderly disorder which is common in nature." Beyond the scene

> seemed a vast sea and united with this that flowed forth, from the termination, or *horizon*, of which (being the levell of the State which was placed in the upper end of the hall) was drawne by the lines of *Prospective*, the whole worke shooting downewards from the eye; which *decorum* made it more

---

[1] Pp. 229–231; in particular see his plan at p. 230. [2] *Designs*, No. 386 (Pl. XLIX).

[3] It is not suggested here that this design was made for Campion's masque—only that a similar scenic arrangement would fit in with the description provided in the libretto.

conspicuous and caught the eye a farre off with a wandring beauty; to which was added an obscure and cloudy night-piece that made the whole set of [off].

In this masque an entirely new principle was at work, the principle of the true Renaissance theatre. Instead of being composed of several distinct elements—mountain or bower, temple or house—the sea scene presented here was one and indivisible. The time had arrived when the masque was to shake off the lingering relics of the simultaneous setting and adopt that single-locality standard which, with minor exceptions, has been that of the theatre from the seventeenth century down to our own times. *Blackness*, it is true, presented no actual change of scene once the sea-piece had been revealed, and in so far it must be regarded as a pioneering and primitive essay, but the curtain painted to represent a landscape gave a suggestion of what was to come.

In another respect Jonson's masque of 1605 shadowed forth the future. The scenes already recorded—the mountain and the temple—were to a certain extent medieval in spirit and inspiration; the sea scene was an invention of the sixteenth century. Mountains and temples were popular in the Renaissance theatre, no doubt, but the seascape, with rolling waves beating on the shore and sometimes with vessels sailing by under a fair wind, closely vied with them. Again and again, in the printed *descrizioni* of Italian *intermezzi*, in original designs and in engravings, we encounter variants of this ocean scene. By introducing it thus early in his settings for the court masques Inigo Jones was testifying to the debt he owed to transalpine example.[1]

The construction of this sea devised by Inigo Jones may readily be envisaged from the instructions given by Sabbatini.[2] Three methods in all are described by him. The first, which made use of a large piece of cloth coloured to resemble water and agitated from below, may be set aside, for from Jonson's account it seems that certain characters were viewed within the waves. According to the second method, strips of wood were cut to resemble waves, and to these pieces of blue cloth were attached; by an arrangement of small levers nailed to cross-bars the boards could then be made to rise and sink. This may have been the device employed by Inigo Jones, but more probably it was the third method of which he made use. This involved the fashioning of long cylinders, shaped in wave form and covered with "cloth coloured

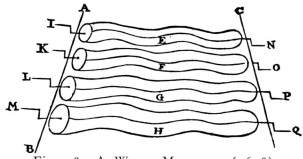

Fig. 18. A Wave Machine (1638)
Nicolà Sabbatini. Diagram in *Pratica di fabricar scene e machine*.

blue and black, with a touch of silver at the top of each board." These were provided with pivots and cranks, so that they might be turned easily. The reference to the black and silver seems to show a definite connexion between Sabbatini's description and Jonson's, although it is possible that *Blackness* introduced another device recorded by the former. This necessitated the manufacture of strips of flat boarding "painted completely black with the top touched with silver"; set between the rolling cylinders, these could be raised or lowered as desired.[3] Possibly such seas, admired though they were by contemporaries, did not always succeed in realizing the ideal. At any rate, Jonson saw fit, in his verses "To Inigo Marquess Would-bee," to ridicule the efforts which the artist made:

> Thy Canvas-Giant at some channell a'mes,
> Or Dowgate torrent falling into Thames.[4]

[1] Enid Welsford, p. 175, argues that in *Blackness* Jones took suggestions from the pageant tournament given at Florence in 1579 in honour of the marriage of Francesco de' Medici to Bianca Capello.

[2] ii, 27, 28, 29. Furttenbach also discusses this subject in *Mannhafter Kunstspiegel*, p. 135.

[3] ii, 30. [4] *Poems*, ed. B. H. Newdigate, p. 298.

The waves must have extended from near the front of the stage backward to the rear shutter (the frame painted to represent a distant ocean). Above was the cloudy night-piece, and this, since Night herself descended from it, can have been constructed only according to the method which Sabbatini describes as the "divided heavens."[1] "When it is desired," remarks that author,

> to make the machines rise into the heavens or descend to the stage, it is necessary to divide the heavens into sections. This will arouse delight and admiration among the spectators, who fail to see how these machines descend to the stage and then disappear into the sky again.

Each section consisted of a curved frame covered with cloth; several of these were then nailed to the roof of the hall so that the spaces between them were sufficiently masked from the audience yet were adequately wide to allow of the lowering from above of single figures or of aerial chariots (Fig. 19).[2]

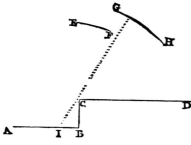

Fig. 19. Cross-section of the Divided Heavens (1638)

AB is the level of the hall floor, and CD that of the stage.
Nicolà Sabbatini. Diagram in *Pratica di fabricar scene e machine*.

Blackness, as we have seen, presented several examples of moving 'scenes' and thus introduces us to one of the most characteristic Renaissance devices—that which was technically known as the 'machine.' This word is used first apparently in *Oberon*, no doubt derived directly from the Italian *macchina*; earlier than that, in *Blackness*, *Hymenæi*, and *Lord Hay's Masque*, its place was taken by the more homely 'engine.' In the first it applied to a sea scene, in the second to a cloud effect, and in the third ("an Ingin plac't under the stage") to the transferring of trees from one part of the stage to another. The examples indicate the wide significance of the term and the variety of uses to which the machine itself was put in those times. Scenes and machines were the two basic elements in the presentation of a theatrical performance during the early seventeenth century. Here in Jonson's masque we are at the beginning of Renaissance stage practice in England.

Changing Scenes: Italian Intermezzi

Blackness was modern, as *The Vision of the Twelve Goddesses* was ancient, but one thing it lacked. A Renaissance sea scene it had, and a "divided Heaven"; its setting was concentrated on a single platform, and it made use of primitive mechanical effects. In all these things it belonged in spirit to the movement which had inspired Italian architects to make glorious the courts of those princes they served. At the same time this production must be regarded as a trial essay, wanting that particular feature which had already become the most representative element in the theatrical performances of Italy. Scene and machine appeared in this masque, but of scene-change there was none, and scene-change had become an admired ideal of the Renaissance theatre.

That that should have been so may at first seem strange, for this was the age when the unities of place and time were becoming firmly established, and when false ideals of scenic illusion kept men's minds dominated and overawed. The age was, however, one also of splendour and excitement. The rich kaleidoscopic colours of life were making their appeal as they had never done before, and with all the flaunting of gorgeous raiment, the proud tourneys of flashing silver and glittering gold, the magnificent triumphal processions, audiences craved for and demanded a bold movement on the stage. So far as the regular theatre was concerned, the English playhouse found a solution in a drama of swift rhythm, of stirring alarms and of spectacular groupings, when players appeared in

---

[1] ii, 37.

[2] Furttenbach in his *Architectura civilis*, p. 28, calls these sections *cerchie*. Possibly the reference to "a hoope and blewe Lynnen cloth" in a Revels account of 1579 indicates their early use at court (A. Feuillerat, *Documents relating to the Office of the Revels in the Time of Queen Elizabeth* (Louvain, 1908), p. 308).

resplendent costumes against backgrounds which, because of their simplicity, could be imaginatively altered at a moment's notice, and which, because they made no direct visual appeal, did not offend any save those who, like Philip Sidney, were strictest classicists. For Italy, however, that solution could not serve; pictorial scenes had been invented and were applied to the production of tragedy and of comedy, while critical theory maintained a tireless vigil on dramatic representations. The dramatists and directors there found themselves compelled to restrain their plays within the scope of a single setting—the typical tragic, comic, and pastoral scenes of Serlio—and within the narrow periods prescribed by the unity of time.

Yet audiences demanded more, and since it is always the public's will which rules in the theatre, a way of escape had to be discovered. To find this means of escape, to present the vividly colourful and the excitingly mobile, one course alone lay open, the provision of scenic movement in the *intermezzi*.[1]

Essentially symbolic of the whole theory and practice of the Italian stage during this period is the production of Antonio Landi's comedy *Il Commodo* at Florence in 1539.[2] Before the play began there appeared the figure of Aurora, representing the dawn; then the audience saw

> little by little the sun rising in the stage heavens. This sun, moving softly, demonstrated act by act the hour of the fictional day, until about the close of the fifth act it eventually disappeared, and the figure of Night descended.

It is obvious that here an attempt was being made to reach accord between the newly invented perspective settings and critical theories concerning the unities. Unity of place is preserved by the scene, while the sun's movement across the sky proved the careful retention of the unity of time. To watch such a simple play, however, the audience was not prepared, and accordingly Giovan Battista Strozzi was called in to invent a series of *intermezzi* for the intervals between the acts. The first was of shepherds, the second of nymphs and Tritons, the third of Silenus, the fourth of Amazons. Hardly any single play could have demonstrated more clearly the triple forces at work in the Italian theatre of the Renaissance.

The explanation of the position occupied by these *intermezzi* demands a glance at the formal division of tragedies and comedies during these years. An observation of classic plays had shown that a five-act division was desirable, if not positively necessary. Usually in the critical writings of the time authors were content to quote Horace and impose the rule; but among them were some who, like Leone di Somi,[3] inquired more curiously. For di Somi the justification of a fivefold division was to be found in the facts that drama should form a mirror of life, and that man, the perfect creation of nature, has five fingers, five toes, five extremities, and five senses.[4] For various reasons, fantastic and practical, five became the established number of acts in any seriously considered tragedy or comedy, intervals being thus provided during the performance of any play.

It was on these intervals that the scenic artists avidly seized. Prevented within the play from presenting anything more than a single and formal set, tragic or comic or pastoral in accordance with the drama's style, they sought and found an opportunity in the entertainments presented during the periods of intermission. Naturally there was opposition, but in spite of that opposition the *intermezzi* had by 1572 assumed an overwhelming importance in the Italian theatre: that year Piccolomini was forced to complain that "nowadays more attention is paid to these *intermezzi* than to the

---

[1] A summary discussion of the *intermezzi* and their significance appears in John W. Cunliffe's introduction to his *Early English Classical Tragedies* (Oxford, 1912).

[2] *Apparato et feste nelle noze dello illustrissimo Signor Duca di Firenze, & della Duchessa sua Consorte* (Florence, 1539).

[3] *The Development of the Theatre* (second edition), pp. 240–244.

[4] Leone di Somi's cogitations on the mystery of the number five find an echo in the familiar musings of Sir Thomas Browne in *The Garden of Cyrus* (1658). A note on the subject as it relates to the drama's five acts appears in the *Annotationi di M. Alessandro Piccolomini, nel libro della Poetica d' Aristotele* (Venice, 1575), p. 182. The dedication to this volume is dated 1572.

plays themselves." [1]   The attack upon the *intermezzi* came from two sources: the alarmed play-wrights objected to the show and spectacle because, they deemed, these took from real interest in the dramas themselves; others, more severely critical, argued grimly that, since all tragedies should have choruses incorporated in the action, the intermission entertainments were wholly out of place, even although most of the latter were prepared, with Angelo Ingegnieri, to admit that "in pastorals and comedies, while not strictly proper, they provided a rich embellishment." [2]

One solution of these problems there was—the creation of *intermezzi* which should in some way harmonize with the theme of the play being presented on the same occasion.   Antonio Ongaro thus emphasized in the introduction to his *L'Alceo* (Ferrara, 1614) [3] that his intermission entertain-ments were strictly related to his main subject, and hence could be regarded as the equivalents of ancient classical choruses, while Leone di Somi devoted fair space to a discussion of the appropriate *intermezzi* for various types of play.   In general, it is difficult to trace the relationship between such scenic performances and the drama during the late sixteenth and early seventeenth centuries, but it is at least interesting to note that the effort to combine these two elements both stylistically and in theme was not unknown at this time.

To indulge in any lengthy account of the various shows of this nature were needless, but one example may perhaps be chosen to indicate what, by the end of the sixteenth century, these things had become in the hands of the many artists who were here applying their genius.   Choice may be made of the magnificent spectacle presented by Bernardo Buontalenti at Florence in 1589, of which many accounts remain to us. [4]   The play was a comedy—*La Pellegrina*, by Girolamo Bargagli—but that need not concern us.   Indeed, it is to be observed that the same *intermezzi*, composed by Giovanni de' Bardi, after being shown with *La Pellegrina* on May 2, were repeated on May 6 for another comedy, *La Zingana*, and again on May 16 for still a third comedy, *La Pazzia*, the second and the third being acted by the famous troupe of the Gelosi.   For *La Pellegrina* itself a view of the "City of Rome" appeared, but that, splendid though it may have been, was as nothing to the settings prepared for the intermission entertainments.   First came a musical interlude in which an allegorical figure seated on a slowly descending cloud against a starry background "sang a most exquisite song."   Then came a wondrous scene of cloud and sky, the clouds passing through the air and disappearing behind a magnificent temple.   In this *intermedio* appeared no less than forty-four musicians.   When the time for the second *intermedio* arrived "the setting changed again and showed a prospect all of mountains, rocks and fountains."   Amid these slowly rose a mountain representing Parnassus on which were seated eighteen nymphs chanting a lyric.   Suddenly the set divided and two dark caverns were revealed, and from these issued twelve musicians.   In the third *intermedio* was another cavern in a dark wood whence came thirty-six musicians and four ballet dancers: this was "a very fine musical ballet, a lovely and magnificent *intermedio*."   During its course appeared a fearsome Dragon, which was finally put to death by Apollo, who descended from the skies.   Soon the time came for the fourth *intermedio*.   Once more the prospect changed, and there "passed through the air" a deity "in a golden chariot" drawn by two dragons.   In a cloud were seen diverse spirits, and below a Hell, with Lucifer, "a terrible monster," and other "infernal furies" working at Vulcan's smithy and singing "lovely, but dismal, madrigals."   The fifth *inter-*

---

[1] *Op. cit.*, p. 180.

[2] *Della Poesia rappresentativa e del modo di rappresentare le favole sceniche* (Ferrara, 1598; reprinted in *Delle Opere del Cavalier Battista Guarini* (Verona, 1738), iii, 494, 496).

[3] P. 41.

[4] F. Baldinucci, *Notizie de' professori del disegno* (*Opere* (Florence, 1774), viii, 41–70); Bastiano de' Rossi, *Descrizione dell' apparato, e degl' intermedi* (Florence, 1589); *Li sontuosissimi Apparecchi . . . fatti nelle nozze della gran Duchessa d' Fiorenza* (Venice, 1589); Giuseppe Pavoni, *Diario . . . delle feste celebrate nelle solennissime nozze delli Serenissimi Sposi* (Bologna, 1589).   Many of Bernardo Buontalenti's designs are yet extant: see A. Warburg, *I Costumi teatrali per gli intermezzi del 1589 : i disegni di Bernardo Buontalenti e il libro di conti di Emilio de' Cavalieri* (*Atti dell' Accademia del R. Istituto Musicale di Firenze*, xxxiii (1896), 103–145).

medio presented a most realistic sea with vessels riding the waves.   Amid these waves was shown a shell bearing Amphitrite accompanied by dolphins and Tritons.   As these sang their songs a ship with twenty men aboard came on stage: it "sailed across and tacked with such skill as seemed incredible to the onlookers."   The watchman in the crow's-nest sang a madrigal while a dolphin danced below—this, according to contemporaries, was a stupendous show.   Finally came the sixth and last entertainment, with an enormous "Paradise," full of clouds, Jove in the middle surrounded by his fellow-deities.   Fifty musicians were concealed in these clouds, and forty others came on the stage below.   "The grandeur of the spectacle," declared one eyewitness, "cannot be told; he who did not actually see it must fail to credit its wonders."

Of such sort were the shows that had become popular in Italy by the end of the sixteenth century —extravagant allegorical interludes introducing the gods and goddesses in settings which ever became more and more elaborate.   Of such sort, too, were those which Inigo Jones was striving to establish at Whitehall.   In *Blackness* he had succeeded in achieving part of his object; at least, he had created one independent scene equivalent to the seascape which formed the fifth of the Florentine *intermezzi* in 1589.   What now was required was the finding of means whereby there might be achieved the scenic change so characteristic of these Italian spectacles.

Periaktoi: "The Masque of Hymen"

Jonson's masque was presented at Whitehall in 1605; the same year, eight months later, Inigo Jones was experimenting at Oxford, there introducing methods which later he was to use at court. From a study of Vitruvius, and no doubt from practical experience of the Italian stage, he had become aware of those triangular frames which the Greeks called περίακτοι.   When exactly such *periaktoi* were first employed in the modern theatre is uncertain, but we know that they were in use during the sixteenth century; both Sabbatini[1] and Furttenbach[2] record their employment towards the middle of the century that followed—indeed, the former confesses that he regards them as providing the best method known to him of effecting a change of scene.   The procedure was relatively simple.   Frames were constructed of "light wood having the bases and tops in the form of equilateral triangles."   These were then set upon pivots which, brought below stage, could be turned by means either of cords or handles.   According to Furttenbach's arrangement, two of these *periaktoi* were set edge to edge (Fig. 20), but evidently Sabbatini thought of them as taking the place of ordinary wings placed at each side of the stage in front of the back-shutter.

At Oxford the disposition of the *periaktoi* seems to have been different from the plan suggested by either.   That they were employed then is distinctly stated by Isaac Wake in his *Rex Platonicus* (1607)[3]—"peripetasmata" he calls them, and informs us that, "to the amazement of all," by their means the scenes were changed not only for various plays but within the bounds of a single drama. Wake's account is expanded by Philip Stringer;[4] from his remarks it appears that a "false wall fair painted and adorned with stately pillars" was erected at the upper end of the hall—"which pillars," says Stringer, "would turn about, by reason whereof, with the help of other painted clothes, their stage did vary three times in the acting of one Tragedy."   The assumption has been that *periaktoi* of the usual kind were employed, but one wonders whether the reference to the turning pillars does not indicate a slightly different device.   In the Huntington Library copy of *Candy Restored*, a play presented in 1641, a stage plan shows the use of revolving frames which, instead of being triangular, are flat (Figs. 110, 111).[5]   From Stringer's description it would seem that Jones arranged three or

---

[1] ii, 7.
[2] *Mannhafter Kunstspiegel*, pp. 257–259; *Architectura civilis*, p. 28 (where they are called *telari*).
[3] *Cf.* Sir E. K. Chambers, *The Elizabethan Stage*, i, 233.
[4] J. Nichols, *The Progresses of James the First* (1828), i, 538.   [5] *Infra*, pp. 151–153.

four frames of this kind in a row behind his actors, the pillars forming the central pivots; turning, they would carry the rest of the frames with them. Three changes of scene could easily have been achieved by this method, since during the performance of an act it would have been a simple procedure to place a differently painted 'cloth' over one already used. If this interpretation be the correct one —and none other seems to fit Stringer's report—then we have here the first known reference to the use of revolving flat frames. A few months after this experiment at Oxford Inigo Jones prepared the scenery for Jonson's *Hymenæi*, produced in honour of the wedding of the Earl of Essex and Frances Howard, daughter of the Earl of Suffolk. Here, we are told, the curtain was drawn to reveal an altar and "a *Microcosme* or *Globe*, figuring Man," set against a background of clouds. The "ΜΙΚΡΟ-ΚΟΣΜΟΣ or *Globe*" was "fill'd with *Countreys*, and those gilded; where the *Sea* was exprest, heightened with silver waves. This stood, or rather hung (for no *Axell* was seene to support it) and turning softly, discovered the first *Masque* . . . which was of the *men*, sitting in faire *composition*, within a *mine* of severall metalls." Above sat the figure of Reason "as in the braine, or highest part of *Man*." A contemporary informs us that Ben Jonson himself manipulated the winch for turning this machinery.

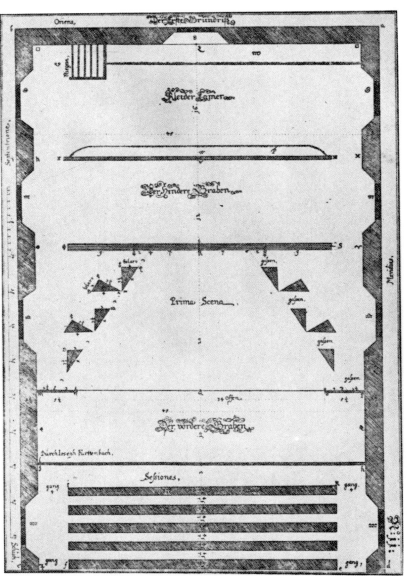

Fig. 20. GROUND-PLAN OF A STAGE SET WITH PERIAKTOI
(1663)
Joseph Furttenbach. Plan in *Mannhafter Kunstspiegel*.

Obviously use was being made here of "peripetasmata" similar to those employed at Oxford. The scene may readily be reconstructed—the altar towards the front of the stage, and behind the vast globe painted to represent the countries of the world, the sea blue with wavy silver lines, and the continents marked out in gold. Although no axle was visible, it seems likely that the same device as before was utilized, and Ben Jonson, we may believe, was stationed below-stage. The first side of the globe displayed to the audience was convex; turning, it showed a concave, painted to resemble a mine, with the masquers in their appointed seats. Since eight men were accommodated in it, together with the figure of Reason above, we may imagine that the "microcosmus" must have been at least ten or twelve feet in diameter. Whether the device was original to Jones, or whether he borrowed it from some Italian source, we cannot tell; it is interesting, however, to observe that in 1637 *Le Nozze degli dei*, a musical production by Giovanni Carlo Coppola, showed two globes hanging in the air, the first scene displaying "the world as if in a chaos" (Fig. 21).

Fig. 21. THE GLOBE OF THE WORLD IN "LE NOZZE DEGLI DEI" (FLORENCE, 1637)

Alfonso Parigi. Etching by Stefano della Bella.

The microcosmus occupied most attention in *Hymenæi*, but considerable effort, too, seems to have been devoted to the management of the clouds. Apparently at each side stood great statues of Atlas and Hercules; these, "in varied postures, bearing up the Clouds," served almost as the pillars of a proscenium arch. In all probability one section of the sky was fixed permanently to these figures so as to complete a frame for the scene beyond. The other clouds, however, were not stationary. At one point they opened, "and, the ayre clearing, in the top thereof was discovered IVNO," while "round about her sate the spirites of the ayre in severall colours making musique," and, "above her, the *region of fire* with a continuall motion was seene to whirle circularly, and IVPITER, standing in the toppe." The deities then descended "in two great cloudes that put foorth themselves severally and with one measure of time"; these "were seene to stoupe and fall gently downe upon the earth." Later still the whole scene became "cover'd with cloudes, as [in] a *night*."

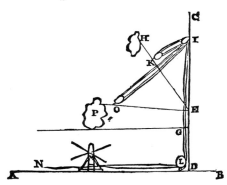

Fig. 22. A Cloud Machine
(1638)

Nicolà Sabbatini. Diagram in *Pratica di fabricar scene e machine*. The cloud is lowered from H to P and controlled at the capstan (M) below stage.

Obviously here Jones was applying certain principles which had been established in Italy and which were to be set down in description by Sabbatini. The reference to the 'stooping' of the two clouds gives us a clue to at least one device. In the Italian technician's work [1] we are told "how to lower a cloud, with persons in it, from the rear of the sky forward to the centre of the stage." His machine, it is true, was designed to bring the cloud from the top of the back-shutter down to the middle of the acting area, whereas it is apparent from the description of the masque that Inigo Jones's two clouds moved parallel to the stage front from the extreme upper corners of the 'heavens'; but the procedure, almost certainly, was the same in each instance. To procure the desired result one of two methods might be employed. Where there was sufficient back-stage space a strong beam, 25 feet long, was constructed to serve as a lever, the fulcrum being out of the spectators' range of vision. On the front end was placed the platform containing the character who had to descend, the beam being concealed by a frame painted to resemble clouds; at the other end a rope, carried to a pulley in the roof, thence to a pulley on the stage floor immediately below, and from there to a capstan, controlled the raising and lowering of the machine. Where the back-stage space did not permit the introduction of such a large machine a second device could be employed (Fig. 22). Here a shorter beam was pivoted to an upright, and a set of ropes and pulleys operated from a capstan enabled the director to bring the cloud platform down from the heavens or restore it to its original position. Presumably in *Hymenæi* two such machines, worked from the sides instead of from the back, produced the effects described in Jonson's descriptions.

Not much opportunity was provided for scenic effects in the same author's *Entertainment at Theobalds* of 1607, although some hints were given there of later devices. According to the description, "a traverse of white" concealed the stage; this was drawn to reveal "a gloomie obscure place, hung all with black silkes," no doubt simply a curtained interior occupying the front part of the stage area. These black curtains in turn vanished and discovered the scene proper, "a glorious place, figuring the *Lararium* or seat of the Household-Gods, where both the *Lares* and *Penates* were painted in copper colour; erected with Columnes and Architrabe, Freeze and Coronice." Beyond could be seen, "as farder off, in *Landtschap* . . . clouds riding." Unquestionably we have here a definite change of scene, although the first, the "obscure place," probably consisted of little more than an ordinary set of black curtains corresponding to the landscape curtain of *Blackness*. In this *Entertainment* further use was made of descents and ascents. At one side hung suspended "a boy figuring Good *Event*" with "nothing seene to sustaine him by all the time the Shew lasted"; at the

[1] ii, 45. The first of Sabbatini's methods is described, with minor variations, by Furttenbach in *Mannhafter Kunstspiegel*, p. 126 (Fig. 28).

THE PROSPECTIVES

other side "Mercurie descended in a flying posture," no doubt suspended on a rope passing through a pulley set in the roof.

Much cloud-work appeared in Marston's *Huntingdon Masque*. Here also the stage was concealed by a traverse, which "slyded away" to reveal the scene. "Presently a cloud was seen to move up and downe almost to the topp of the great chamber," while later "Ariadne rose from the bottom of the roome, mounted upon a cloud, which waved up untill it came nere Cynthia." It seems probable that in this instance also the first scene was prepared by the simple use of a curtain, since the stage directions call for the winding of cornets and the drawing of another traverse which showed "the syde of a steepely assending wood, on the top of which, in a fayre oak, sat a golden eagle, under whose wings satt in eight severall thrones the eight Masquers." The description seems to show the same principle at work which had already served at Theobalds and which was adumbrated in *Blackness*.

"The Masque of Beauty" and "The Masque of Queens"

After this came the next great masque at Whitehall, Jonson's *Beauty*, in which, according to the Venetian ambassador, "the apparatus and the cunning of the stage machinery was a miracle."[1] Who precisely designed the settings we do not know, but certainly their execution was carried out by William Portington, the King's master-carpenter.[2] Old principles were here pursued. The curtain was painted to resemble a night scene, and, this drawn, the main set appeared, "a *Island* floating on a calme water," with, in the centre, a great "throne of beauty . . . divided into eight *squares* and distinguish'd by so many *Ionick* pilasters." Evidently the island was built upon a wagon which moved forward during the course of the masque, while the "throne" was constructed on the principle of the *periaktoi*, supported on a central pillar,[3] for, "as the whole *Iland* mov'd forward on the water," it "had a circular motion of it owne, imitating that which we call *Motum mundi*, from the *East* to the *West*, or the right to the left side."[4] It seems from the description that the base of the throne was concealed by a circular series of steps which, as the main edifice turned, "had a motion contrary." Thus, with "these three varied Motions"—calculated to set the eyes of the audience rolling—"at once the whole *Scene* shot it selfe to the land." No change of scene was attempted in this masque; only the moon, personified, in a silver chariot, was seen "to ride in the clouds above." Presumably nothing more was done than cause this chariot machine to run along a beam concealed in the painted cloud-work.

The turning machine, based on the Greek *periaktoi*, made still another appearance in *Queens*, which the French ambassador found "very sumptuous and, if I may say so, rather ornate than artistic." In this for the first time an effort was made to effect a genuine scene-change. At first came "an ugly *Hell*," evidently discovered by the drawing of a curtain to the accompaniment of "a strange murmur with a kind of hollow and infernall musique." After some action "lowde musique" sounded, "with which . . . the *hell* . . . quite vanished, and the whole face of the *Scene* altred, scarce suffring the memory of such a thing." In its place was seen "a glorious and magnificent building, figuring the *house of fame*." This is described as having "for the lower columnes . . . *Statues* of the most excellent *Poets*" and "for the upper . . . those great *Heroes* which these *Poets* had celebrated." "Betweene the pillars, underneath, were figur'd *Land-battailes*, *Sea-fights*, *Triumphs*, *Loves*, *Sacrifices*, and all magnificent subiects of honour." Above was a throne for the

---

[1] *Calendar of State Papers* (*Venetian, 1607–10*), xi, 86.
[2] Sir E. K. Chambers, *The Elizabethan Stage*, i, 180.
[3] See the Office of Works account in P. Reyher, p. 358.
[4] It is to be noted that the moving island, a device also used in *Neptune's Triumph*, was another Italian 'machine.' It occurs in *Le Nozze degli dei*: there the nymphs *vengono sopra un' Isoletta mobile*.

67

masquers, and it, "being *Machina versatilis*, sodainly chang'd" in the course of the performance, "and in the place of it appear'd *Fama bona*." [1]

The precise arrangements used in this masque require some detailed consideration. It is to be noted that the original designs by Inigo Jones for the House of Fame are extant. The first of these [2] shows a building with a large central doorway, with columns formed like statues and with spaces for the allegorical pictures which Jonson mentions. The second storey has a large trifoliated arch in which are seated the eight masquers in pyramidal form. Quite clearly, these characters must have been placed on one side of a circular platform which, turning, revealed on the other side

Fig. 23. VULCAN'S CAVE IN "L'EDUCATIONE D'ACHILLE" (TURIN, 1650)
Biblioteca Nazionale, Turin.

the figure of Fame. With this design may be taken another showing the main entrance to the House of Fame and two pairs of supporting statues. [3]

The reference to the "machina versatilis" obviously has to be limited to the means by which the vision of the masquers is changed to that of Fame, but it is still possible that, although its strict application be to the upper platform, upon which the masquers were seated, by this device also the poetical Hell was changed into a noble palace. Hell scenes were usually of a cavernous kind, and one can readily imagine a frame, set upon a revolving platform, one side of which appeared as the building figured in Jones's sketch and the other displayed a concaved rock, perhaps somewhat similar to Vulcan's cavern in a later Turin ballet (Fig. 23). A cloth painted to resemble rock-work might readily have concealed the masquers seated above and the corresponding figure of Fame.

In *Queens* the Italianate elements become more deeply pronounced. Hell scenes had, of course, been regular accompaniments of medieval productions, but the "poetical Hell" of the Renaissance

---

[1] P. Reyher, p. 366, quotes from an Audit Office account which refers to the "fitting and setting up of diverse running scaffoldes, fframing and setting up a great Stage for a maske all the height of the Banquettinghouse w[i]th a floore in the middle of the same, being made w[i]th sondry devices with great gates and turning doores belowe and a globe and sondry seates above . . . to be turned rounde aboute."

[2] *Designs*, No. 14 (Pl. IV). [3] *Id.*, No. 15.

breathed the spirit of a new age.   Repeatedly we encounter localities of this sort in the *intermezzi*, and Jones was to make several essays of a like kind in later years.   The House of Fame, too, suggests the influence of Italian architectural ideas, and it is possible that a considerable hint was given to the contrivers of this masque by one particular production, *Il Giudizio di Paride*, composed by M. A. Buonarotti and designed by Giulio Parigi at Florence in October 1608, about six months before *Queens* was presented at Whitehall.[1]   This Florentine show was destined to stand Jones in good stead; from it he later borrowed many ideas.

At best, the turning scene made use of in *Queens* was a poor thing, limited in its effects and no doubt somewhat cumbersome in the then primitively mechanized back-stage area at Whitehall. Soon Jones was to experiment with other methods.   *Queens* was produced on February 2, 1609; already in the preceding February the artist-architect seems to have tried out other means of securing his effects.   The *Hue and Cry after Cupid*—"a singular brave masque," according to Sir Henry Saville [2]—was penned by Jonson to celebrate the marriage of Viscount Haddington, and on it much money seems to have been expended.   For this show the artist designed a kind of proscenium arch, consisting of "two *pilasters*, chardg'd with spoiles and *trophees* of *love* and his *mother*."   Behind this came the scene, "a high, steepe, red cliffe, advancing it selfe into the cloudes."   "Beyond the cliffe," writes Jonson, "was seene nothing but cloudes, thick and obscure."   On a sudden, however, a bright sky broke forth, and the audience saw the chariot of Venus drawn by two swans, together with a vision of the Three Graces.   This chariot came to rest on the cliff, and from it Venus descended "by certayne abrupt and winding passages" to meet with Vulcan.   The latter suddenly exclaimed, "Cleave, solid Rock!"

> at which, with a lowd and full musique, the Cliffe parted in the midst and discovered an illustrious Concave, fill'd with an ample and glistering light, in which an artificiall *Sphere* was made of silver, eighteene foot in the *Diameter*, that turned perpetually.

It is, perhaps, somewhat difficult to interpret this scenic change exactly.   The reference to a "concave" might suggest that the turning machine was employed here as in *Queens*, but the word "cleave" seems to demonstrate that the rock was composed of flats, part of which moved away in order to reveal the scene within.   If so, then in this entertainment Inigo Jones was trying out for the first time Vitruvius's alternate device, the *scena ductilis*.   According to such an interpretation, we may imagine the regular 'divided heavens,' with their painted skies and behind a back-shutter filled with clouds.   Centre stage stand the rock wings, ready to be removed at Vulcan's cue.

The arrangement thus postulated reminds us of a scenic device which, as the designs made by Mahelot and his companions for the Hôtel de Bourgogne demonstrate, came to be characteristic of the Parisian theatre.[3]   Here a front scene was shown by means of a simple flat which removed to reveal a larger set beyond; technically the device was known in France as the *ferme*.   Whether it had already been established at the time when Jonson put forward his *Hue and Cry after Cupid* is hard to determine, but clearly there is a close connexion between this front flat and the rocks which divided in that masque and in *Oberon*.[4]

"TETHYS' FESTIVAL"

If the *scena ductilis* was utilized in *Hue and Cry after Cupid*, we may regard this production as marking the commencement of a fresh period in masque invention.   From its style we proceed

---

[1] E. Welsford, p. 183.

[2] Sir E. K. Chambers, *The Elizabethan Stage*, iii, 381–382.

[3] H. C. Lancaster, *Mémoire de Mahelot* (Paris, 1920), pp. 119, 142.   My attention was drawn to this by a dissertation of George Kernodle on perspective methods in Renaissance staging (Yale University).   [4] See *infra*, p. 73.

straight forward to the *Tethys' Festival* of Daniel and to Jonson's *Oberon*. In the former there was an ornate proscenium arch, with a curtain painted to resemble clouds, which, being removed, revealed the first scene of

> a Port or Haven, with Bulworkes at the entrance and the figure of a Castle commaunding a fortified towne. Within this Port were many Ships, small and great, seeming to lie at Anchor, some neerer and some further off, according to perspective. Beyond all appeared the Horison or termination of the Sea, which seemed to move with a gentle gale, and many Sayles, lying some to come into the Port and others passing out.

From this description it seems almost certain that Jones was using here a set of four *periaktoi* in association, the turning machine being now employed not to make a central scene revolve, but to present opportunity for a complete change of setting. One may legitimately imagine at least two such prisms on each side, painted to resemble fortifications, and a distant view on the shutter of a sea with ships at anchor or sailing forth under full-spread masts. Above would come the familiar sections of the 'divided heavens.'

At a given signal the sea suddenly passed from the eyes of the spectators; "the Port vanished, and *Tethys* with her Nymphes appeared in their severall Cavernes, gloriously adorned." Five niches were provided,

> whereof that in the middest had some slender pillowes of whole round and were made of moderne Architecture in regard of roome. These were of burnisht gold and bare up the returnes of an Architrave, Freeze, and Cornish of the same worke; on which upon eyther side was a Plinth directly over the pillers, and on them were placed, for finishings, two Dolphins of silver, with their tailes wreathed together, which supported ovall vases of gold.
>
> Betweene the two pillers, on eyther side, were great ornaments of relievo; the Basement were two huge Whales of silver. . . . The seate or Throne it selfe was raised sixe steps, and all covered with such an artificiall stuffe as seemed richer by candle then any cloth of gold. The rests for her armes were two Cherubines of gold. Over her head was a great skallop of silver, from which hung the foldes of this rich drapery.
>
> Above the Skallop, and round about the sides, was a resplendent freeze of iewell glasses or lights. . . .
>
> The part which returned from the two Plinthes that bare up the Dolphines was circular and made a hollownesse over Tethys head, and on this circle were 4 great Chartuses [cartouches] of gold, which bore up a round bowle of silver in manner of a fountaine, with mask-heads of gold, out of which ran an artificiall water. On the middest of this was a triangular basement, formed of scrowles and leaves, and then a rich Vayle adorned with flutings and inchased worke, with a freeze of fishes and a battaile of Tritons, out of whose mouthes sprang water into the Bowle underneath. On the top of this was a round globe of gold full of holes, out of which issued aboundance of water, some falling into the receipt below, some into the Ovall vase, borne up by the Dolphines, and indeed there was no place in this great Aquatick throne that was not filled with the sprinckling of these two naturall seeming waters. The Neeces [niches] wherein the Ladies sate were foure, with Pillasters of gold, mingled with rustick stones, shewing like a minerall, to make it more rocke and Cavern-like, varying from that of *Tethys* throne. Equall with the heads of the Pillars was an Architrave of the same work; above was a circular frontispice, which rose equall with the Bowle of the fountaine fore-discribed. On the rustick frontispice lay two great figures in Rileve, which seemed to beare up a Garland of Sea-weeds; to which, from two antick Candlestickes which stood over the Pillasters, were hanging Labells of gold; and these were the finishings of the top of the two Neeces next to that of *Tethys*.
>
> In the space betweene the frontispice and the Architrave stood a great Concave shell, wherein was the head of a Sea-god, and on either side the shell to fill up the roome, two great mask-heads in perfile. The other two Neeces, which were outermost, were likewise borne up with Pillasters of gold,

and, for variation, had square frontispices, and against the streight Architrave of the other was an Arch. All these were mingled with rustick, as before.

In the middle, betweene the frontispice and the Arch, was a Bowle or fountaine made of foure great skallops, borne up by a great maske head, which had likewise foure aspects; and lying upon this Arch (to fill up the Concaves) were two figures turned halfe into fishes; these with their heads held up the sides of this Bowle; above this were three great Cherubines heads spouting water into the Bowle. On the middest of the square frontispice stood a great vase adorned.

The rest of the ornaments consisted of maske-heads, spouting water, swannes, festons of maritime weedes, great shels and such like; and all this whole Scene was filled with the splendor of gold and silver; onely some beautifull colours behinde to distinguish them and to set off the rest.

The whole worke came into the forme of a halfe round.

That the change from one scene to the other was produced by means of *periaktoi* seems certain from the references to the concave niches. If the bulwarks and fortifications were painted on one flat 'face' of each prism, then on the revolving of these there could easily have been shown a series of four cavern-like enclosures; the prisms would thus have only two sides instead of three. So far as Tethys' bower was concerned, we may believe that it was revealed by the drawing back of the shutter representing the seascape. In the space beyond there might easily have been set the platform containing her throne. That such a method was employed seems suggested also by the fact that, towards the end of the masque, "lowde Musicque soundes" and there appears "a most pleasant and artificiall Grove." This third scene might readily have been prepared by affixing variantly painted strips of canvas to the up-stage sides of the *periaktoi* during the performance of the maritime episodes. One thing, however, is new—the arrangement of the parts of the setting in a "halfe round." That phrase no doubt alludes to the placing of the *periaktoi* at each side of the stage, immediately in front of the back-shutter, instead of the large central 'scene' presented in the House of Fame. It is to be suspected also that one particular device employed by Sabbatini was made to serve in this masque.[1] "The second method of opening the shutter," as he describes it, involves making this shutter in four parts, so that the two inner sections are hinged to the two outer. "The reverse sides," we are told, "are painted in conformity with the faces of the *periaktoi*," and consequently when they are opened inward form part of a new setting. To open them in this way cords drawn to the sides are controlled by men concealed from sight by the upper pieces of scenery. Daniel's description seems to imply that the throne of Tethys was directly joined to the niches at the sides, and this of Sabbatini's is likely to have been the method employed.

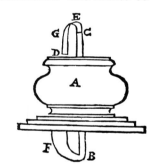

Fig. 24. A Foun-
tain Machine

Nicolà Sabbatini. Diagram
in *Pratica di fabricar scene
e machine.*

Sabbatini helps us also to interpret the references to the water flowing into the bowls.[2] The device employed here was fairly simple. In the middle of the basin a tube was fixed, sufficiently wide to allow the passage of a folded piece of cloth. To this cloth was attached a series of short rods about 6 inches long, and the whole was painted blue in semblance of water. One end of the strip of cloth was passed downward through the tube, carried below-stage out of sight of the audience, and sewn to the other end. The flowing of the water was then simulated by one man pushing the rods upward while another, controlling the operation from above, contrived to make the cloth spread out. The same procedure in a reverse direction could make it seem as if a constant stream was passing into a container from a spring or a fountain-head (Fig. 24).[3]

---

[1] ii, 14.   [2] ii, 36.
[3] The water-flowing device had already been used in *Beauty*. It reappeared in *Inner Temple, Flowers*, and *Tempe Restored.*

STUART MASQUES AND THE RENAISSANCE STAGE

"THE MASQUE OF OBERON" AND "THE LORDS' MASQUE"

"A very stately maske," Ben Jonson's *Oberon*, followed *Tethys' Festival*, and fortunately, although the author's description is brief and inconclusive, some clear knowledge of the methods employed may be gained from several original designs prepared by Inigo Jones. One of these[1] is marked by the artist "2 sceane K: Oberons Pallace," thus definitely determining its provenance, while another (Fig. 1)[2] clearly represents an original sketch for the same design. The first scene, as described by Jonson, was "all obscure and nothing perceiv'd but a darke Rocke, with trees beyond it, and all wildnesse that could be presented." The second, revealed when this "whole Scene opened," showed "the *Frontispice* of a bright and glorious *Palace*, whose gates and walls were transparent."

From the description itself one might have imagined that the first scene was merely a painted curtain, but Jones's design shows clearly that this was not so. Here the palace stands revealed in the midst of rocks and mountains, its 'discovery' evidently having been effected by drawing away some flats painted to represent rocks. These rocks themselves are clearly shown in another design,[3] which, although it presents some variations, is so closely akin to the other that we must assume its connexion with this masque. A set of notes appended to Fig. 1 provides some indication of the size of the set. The "heyght of the middell space" was 9 feet and its breadth 5 feet; the terms were 4 feet 1 inch high and the second pillars 7 feet; while "the heyght of ye Tour [tower] to ye batelmentes" was 11 feet.

This palace in turn 'opened' to discover "the nation of *Faies*," probably by the drawing back of other shutters. Concerning the drawing of these shutters a word may be said. Certainly there is shown here a consciousness of the *scena ductilis*, whereby flat frames might be removed in order to display a new setting, but we should err if we assumed that Inigo Jones, thus early in his career, had divined the principles of that method of scene-shifting which was to be the standard of the later seventeenth and eighteenth centuries. At this time he did not go farther than see the possibilities of drawing back a frame or shutter in order to discover something beyond; there seems to have been no appreciation on his part of the way in which one shutter-frame might be substituted for another. To all intents, the scene of rocks with which *Oberon* began was a 'back' scene; it was at least represented in the flat, and so corresponded to the rear perspective with which the wing type of setting normally terminated. Many years had to elapse before the use of flat frames in grooves, combining wings and rear shutters, was put into practice.

Regarding Jonson's next masque, *Love freed from Ignorance*, not much information has come down to us, for the author's stage directions are meagre in the extreme. Not a single clue is there to determine the nature of the setting, but no doubt Percy Simpson and C. F. Bell are right in suggesting that we have a representation of the prison from which the Daughters of Morn were released.[4] *Love Restored* is equally scanty in its information, but luckily the next important masque, *Lords*, was prepared by a writer, Campion, less churlish in his stage descriptions than Jonson. The scene for this, we are informed,

> was divided into two parts from the roofe to the floore, the lower part being first discovered [when] there appeared a Wood in *prospective*, the innermost part being of releave or whole round, the rest painted. On the left hand from the seate was a Cave, and on the right a thicket.

After some action

> the upper part of the Scene was discovered by the sodaine fall of a curtaine; then in clowdes of severall colours (the upper part of them being fierie and the middle heightned with silver) appeared eight

---

[1] *Designs*, No. 42; reproduced in *The Works of Ben Jonson*, ii, 286–287.   [2] *Id.*, No. 43.
[3] *Id.*, No. 40; reproduced in *The Works of Ben Jonson*, ii, 284–285.
[4] *Id.*, No. 17; reproduced in E. Welsford, p. 256.

Starres of extraordinarie bignesse. [These] mooved in an exceeding ſtrange and delightfull manner, and I suppose fewe have ever seene more neate artifice then Maſter *Innigoe Jones* shewed in contriving their Motion.

Later "the Starres suddainely vanished as if they had been drowned amongſt the Cloudes," and these clouds in their turn gave way to "an Element of artificiall fires, with severall circles of lights

Fig. 25. A Cloud Palace in "La Contesa" (Ferrara, 1632)
Francesco Guitti. Etching by Battiſta Torre.

in continuall motion, representing the house of Prometheus." A "bright and transparant cloud" now descended from one side of the ſtage, as it came down breaking

in twain, and one part of it (as with a winde) was blown overthwart the Scœne. While this cloud was vanishing, the wood, being the under-part of the Scœne, was insensibly changed and in place thereof appeared foure Noble women-ſtatues of silver, ſtanding in severall nices [niches], accompanied with ornaments of Architecture, which filled all the end of the house and seemed to be all of gold-smithes work. The firſt order consiſted of Pillaſters all of gold, set with Rubies, Saphyrs, Emeralds, Opals and such like. The Capitels were composed and of a new invention. Over this was a baſtard order with Cartouses reversed, comming from the Capitels of every Pillaſter, which made the upper part rich and full of ornament. Over every ſtatue was placed a hiſtory in gold, which seemed to be of base releave. The conceits which were figured in them were these. In the firſt was *Prometheus*, embossing in clay the figure of a woman, in the second he was represented ſtealing fire from the chariot-wheele of the Sunne; in the third he is expreſt putting life with this fire into his figure of clay; and in the fourth square *Iupiter*, enraged, turns these new made women into ſtatues. Above all, for finishing, ran a Cornish, which returned over every Pillaſter, seeming all of gold and richly carved.

73

During the course of the ensuing action these four statues were "transformed into women." Not content with this, Jones contrived to change "the whole scoene" once more; it became "a prospective with Porticoes on each side, which seemed to go in a great way; in the middle was erected an Obeliske, all of silver, and in it lights of severall colours." This obelisk "was of that height that the toppe thereof touched the highest cloudes, and yet *Sybilla* did draw it forth with a threed of gold."

Fig. 26. A Cloud Scene

Inigo Jones. Chatsworth (*Designs*, No. 382). Copyright of his Grace the Duke of Devonshire.

Obviously in reading this description we find ourselves in the presence of something much more elaborate than any masque had previously offered. To interpret the description aright is, however, a by no means easy task. One may imagine, perhaps, with some assurance two curtains, probably painted, the first stretched over the lower half of the stage and the second concealing the heavens. The scene at the start is a landscape with cave and thicket, each of these no doubt being depicted by means of wings, perhaps of the *periaktoi* kind, and a perspective forest painted on a shutter. The upper curtain now falls to display a large cloud which is drawn back to reveal the house of Prometheus. A cloud-machine then descends and,

rising, discovers a changed scene below, with four niches in which stand lifesize statues. Once the statues have altered to real women a transformation occurs, and a familiar Renaissance street scene takes its place. The fact that there are three distinct settings, taken in association with the further fact that niches again are used, leads one to believe that the system of *periaktoi* was still in service. If one 'face' of each prism was painted to represent trees or caves it would have been an easy task to turn these round to display a series of alcoves, while a third turning of the wings could have revealed the various "Porticoes." The cloud machines were, in all probability, the same as those already employed in earlier masques. Perhaps, however, the device already described, whereby the cloud swung forward in its descent, was in this instance supplanted by one more fitted to deal with the not inconsiderable weight of the masquers who were lowered from the house of Prometheus. Of such devices two are recorded by Sabbatini.[1] The first demanded the placing of two stout beams so as to form a swallow-tail groove stretching from the heavens to the floor of the hall. Into this is set a stout piece of wood about 6 feet long, with

[1] ii, 43, 44.

a strong arm attached to its upper end and supported by a brace to the lower end. By means of a rope taken through a pulley in the roof this entire framework (triangular in shape) can be raised or lowered. The cloud platform is now attached to the outer end of the horizontal arm, the machine itself being concealed partly by the frame painted to resemble clouds, partly by the setting of the supporting beams behind the back-shutter with strips of cloth designed to conceal the gap through which the arm must necessarily pass. Sabbatini's second machine does not differ materially from this first one. The vertical beams are in this instance so placed as to make a guide groove; in this

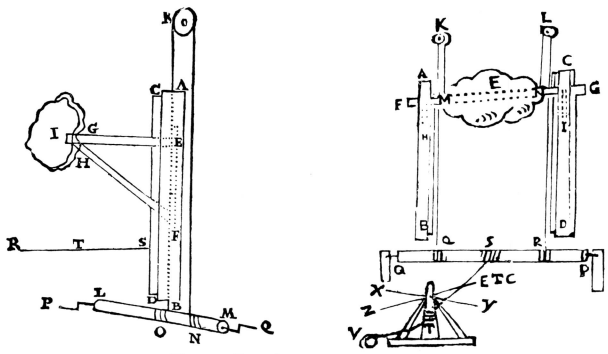

Fig. 27. Two Cloud Machines (1638)

Nicolà Sabbatini. Diagrams in *Pratica di fabricar scene e machine*. The second shows two upright grooves (AB and CD), with a machine supported between them; the first gives only one upright (AB), with the machine set at right angles to the main bar.

runs a horizontal bar, to the front of which is attached the platform for the characters and the surrounding cloud-frame (Fig. 27).

The obelisk which was drawn up "by a threed of gold" must have been made in sections. Sabbatini[1] describes a method of making a mountain rise from below stage, but this method involves a deep space underneath the acting area. In all probability Jones simply constructed his obelisk out of a long strip of cloth attached to a series of small frames; by attaching a golden cord to the upper frame the whole could easily be drawn upward towards the heavens. More precise information is provided by Sabbatini concerning the means of changing the statues into living persons.[2] The procedure here was to cut out a piece of cloth in the shape desired; this, when painted, had its top attached to the end of a smooth rod about 6 feet long which passed through a hole bored in the stage-floor. Behind the painted flat stood the actor who was later to appear, and when the moment of transformation arrived it was a simple matter to have the rod drawn down below stage, leaving the painted cloth crumpled up and almost out of sight on the ground.

[1] ii, 24.   [2] ii, 24, 25.

"THE MIDDLE TEMPLE MASQUE"

The same year, 1613, saw the production of another sumptuous performance, Chapman's *Middle Temple*. The first scene for this show consisted of

an Artificiall Rock, whose top was neere as high as the hall it selfe. This Rock was in the undermost part craggy and full of hollow places, in whose concaves were contriv'd two winding paire of staires by whose greeces the Persons above might make their descents and all the way be seene. All this

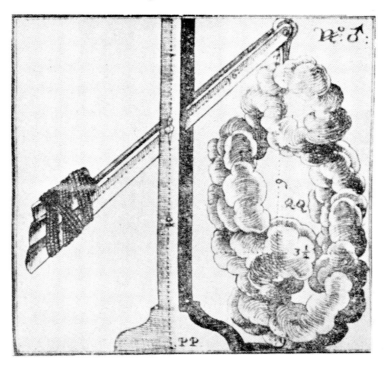

Fig. 28. A Cloud Machine (1663)
Joseph Furttenbach. Engraving in *Mannhafter Kunstspiegel*.

Rocke grew by degrees up into a gold-colour, and was run quite through with veines of golde. On the one side whereof, eminently raised on a faire hill, was erected a silver Temple of an octangle figure, whose Pillars were of a compos'd order and bore up an Architrave, Freese and Cornish, over which stood a continued Plinthe, whereon were advanc't Statues of silver. Above this was placed a bastarde Order of Architecture, wherein were kerv'd Compartements, in one of which was written in great golde Capitalls, HONORIS FANVM. Above all was a *Coupolo* [cupola] or Type, which seem'd to be scal'd with silver Plates.

For finishing of all upon a Pedestall was fixt a round stone of silver, from which grew a paire of golden wings, both faign'd to bee Fortunes. . . . About this Temple hung Festons, wreath'd with silver from one Pillars head to another. Besides, the Freese was enricht with kervings, all shewing Greatnes and Magnificience.

On the other side of the Rocke grewe a Grove, in whose utmost part appear'd a vast, wither'd and hollow Tree, being the bare receptacle of the Baboonerie.

During the performance "the middle part of the Rocke began to move, and being come some five paces up towards the King, it split in peeces with a great crack," while "the peeces of the Rocke vanish't." Later on the upper part of the rock was sodainly turn'd to a Cloude, discovering a rich and refulgent Mine of golde. . . . Over this golden Mine in an Evening sky the ruddy Sunne was seen ready to set and behind the tops of certain white Cliffes by degrees descended, casting up a banke of clouds, in which awhile hee was hidden.

The stage descriptions here indicate that the scenic changes were conducted much in the same manner as had attended the manipulation of preceding masques. The central rock, we must believe, was built on a wagon such as bore up the island in *Queens*, and its formation must have been similar to that used in *Oberon*. Presumably portions moved to the sides in order to reveal flats painted to resemble clouds, these in their turn moving away to show the "Mine" and the sunset beyond. Sabbatini does not specifically describe any method for simulating a sunset, but obviously his instructions explaining "how to make part of the heavens grow slowly clouded"[1] might readily have been adapted to this purpose. To carry this into effect a frame was made to correspond to each opening in the 'divided heavens'; to this frame at the back were attached several supports made of strong, thin wood. By drawing the frame along so that it covered the original strip of sky different-coloured clouds could easily be made to appear (Fig. 29).

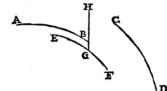

Fig. 29. A Device for changing Clouds (1638)

Nicolà Sabbatini. Diagram in *Pratica di fabricar scene e machine*. The cloud frame EF is drawn over AB by means of the handle, HG.

"The Masque of the Inner Temple"

The same year Beaumont was responsible for the masque presented by the Inner Temple and Gray's Inn. Here also "the Fabricke was a Mountaine with two descents," covered by a pair of curtains; evidently a combination was being made of the horizontally divided stage of *Lords* and the practicable rock set of Chapman's masque. "The first Travers was drawne," we are informed,

> and the lower descent of the Mountaine discovered, which was the Pendant of a hill to life, with divers boscages and Grovets upon the steepe or hanging grounds thereof; and at the foote of the Hill foure delicate Fountaines, running with water and bordered with sedges and water flowers.

In this part of the masque five Hyades descended "softly in a cloud from the firmament to the middle part of the hill." Then came what is styled "the Main Masque." The second traverse was drawn,

> and the higher ascent of the Mountaine is discovered, wherein, upon a levell, after a great rise of the Hill, were placed two Pavilions, open in the front of them. The Pavilions were to sight as of cloth of gold, and they were trimmed on the inside with rich Armour and Militarie furniture, hanged up as upon the walles; and behind the Tents there were represented in prospective the tops of divers other Tents, as if it had been a Campe. . . . In the midst betweene both the Tents upon the very top of the hill, being a higher levell then that of the Tents, was placed *Jupiters* Altar, gilt, with three great Tapers upon golden Candlesticks burning upon it.

The stage of two levels does not present much difficulty, but the reference to the descent of the cloud machine suggests a minor problem. A firmament, or "heavens," was attached to the roof, and from this the machine came down, apparently in front of the second traverse. That being so, one must, it seems, assume that the second, or rather upper, scene of pavilions was set back, concealed by a curtain painted to resemble the sky. When the cloud machine was lowered from an opening in the heavens it came to rest upon the forward edge of the upper scene (the top of the lower hill), and when the curtain was removed the pavilions were rendered visible, set back at least

[1] ii, 38.

some few feet from this position. It is clear that no vital experimentation was indulged in for this performance.

Fig. 30. A Cloud Scene in "Il Gridellino" (Turin, 1653)
Biblioteca Nazionale, Turin.

"Somerset's Masque"

The next masque, also given in the year 1613, was Campion's entertainment in honour of the Earl of Somerset, but in this Inigo Jones had no share,[1] the scenic devices being the work of an Italian, Constantino de' Servi—and, it appears, not nearly so successful in execution as those put forward by the English artist. De' Servi,

> being too much of him selfe and no way to be drawne to impart his intentions, fayled so farre in the assurance he gave that the mayne invention, even at the last cast, was of force drawne into a farre narrower compasse then was from the beginning intended.

For the stage he contrived "an Arch Tryumphall, passing beautifull, which enclosed the whole Workes," and a curtain was drawn to reveal the scene.

> On the upper part there was formed a Skye of Clowdes very arteficially shadowed. On either side of the Sceane belowe was set a high Promontory, and on either side of them stood three large pillars of golde. The one Promontory was bounded with a Rocke standing in the Sea; the other with a Wood. In the midst betwene them apeared a Sea in perspective with ships, some cunningly painted, some arteficially sayling. On the front of the Sceane, on either side, was a beautifull garden, with six seates a peece [and beyond] the mayne Land, and in the middest a paire of stayres made exceeding curiously in the form of a Schalop shell.

[1] During the latter part of 1613 and throughout 1614 he was travelling abroad.

78

THE PROSPECTIVES

Towards the end of the masque "out of the ayre a cloude descends" bearing six knights, while on the two promontories the golden pillars are transformed into six other knights. This done,

> the whole Sceane is changed: for whereas before all seemed to be done at the sea and sea-coast, now the Promontories are sodainely remooved and London with the Thames is very arteficially presented in their place.

During this scene four practicable barges arrive and depart.

The transformation of the pillars into men is a device we have already encountered, but the moving of the vessels is new. Sabbatini aids us in his description of "how to make ships and galleys or other vessels seem to move along the sea." [1] The method was to cut out a shape from flat board and paint this so that it might seem in the round. After having been attached to a base the vessel was set in a swallow-tail groove running across the stage (Fig. 31). Inigo Jones used this device later and earned Jonson's disapproval:

> And stradling shewes the boyes browne-paper fleet
> Yearely set out there, to sayle downe the street.[2]

One might suspect, too, that possibly a different method of scene-shifting was employed in this performance. It may be, of course, that *periaktoi* were made to serve in the transformation of the seascape to the view of London, but the description of the former seems so closely associated with representations of similar sets worked out by another method that we might presume all to have been constructed in the same manner. During the century from 1550 to 1650 the commonest of all scenic devices was the angled wing. Such wings had been recorded by Serlio and still provided the basis of Sabbatini's stagecraft. Briefly they may be defined as wings made of two frames—one rectangular placed parallel to the stage-front, and the other with lower and upper edges cut to fit the raked floor and to accord with the perspective lines. The second frame was attached to the first in such a position that, when set on the stage, it lay along a line drawn to the vanishing-point. With a series of two or three such wings (or 'houses'—*case*, as they were called in Italy), together with back-shutters, per-

Fig. 31. A Device for showing Ships in Movement (1638)

Nicolà Sabbatini. Diagram in *Pratica di fabricar scene e machine*. The waves are shown at DE and FG; BC is the groove in which the ship moves.

spective settings could readily be prepared, although it must be recognized that the violent perspective used in the Renaissance theatres demanded that the rearmost flats should be exceedingly small. Referring to the dwarf Jeffery Hudson, Jonson ridiculed these scenes as the "Lane where Tom Thumb, Jeffrey meets."

There are, of course, many illustrations of these 'Serlian' wings to be found in Italian sources; here may be taken a hitherto unreproduced plan of English provenance—a ground-plan, elevation, and section prepared by John Webb for the production of *Florimène* in 1635 (Fig. 32). This shows, first, a "Profyle of ye stage for ye proportioning ye shortning sydes of sceanes with Triangular frames when there is but one standing sceane, comparted by the sceane of ye Pastorall of Florimene in ye hall at Whitehall 1635," and, second, a "Ground platt for ye standing sceane with Triangular frames." It is the latter of the two plans which is of particular interest. To the left are the four

---

[1] ii, 31. See also Furttenbach, *Mannhafter Kunstspiegel*, p. 136.
[2] *Poems*, ed. B. H. Newdigate, p. 296.

'Serlian' wings, and to the right these are displayed as they would appear when set upon the stage. The diagonal line on which the 'perspective' faces were intended to stand is clearly indicated.

Fig. 32. GROUND-PLAN AND ELEVATION FOR "FLORIMÈNE" (1635)
John Webb.   British Museum, MS. Lansdowne, 1171, ff. 13b and 14.

The principal disadvantage of the angled wing was the difficulty of devising a change of setting. One method described by Sabbatini need hardly be seriously considered, so cumbersome and impracticable would it be likely to prove. Briefly, this consisted of having a curved rod or rail at the top of each 'house' and a roll of canvas, painted for the second scene, attached to a pole at the outer end of the front face. When the time arrived men deputed for the purpose brought this pole round over the front of the house and so covered the frame with the second canvas. At best, such a method of scene-change must have been of a makeshift sort, and we cannot believe that much use was made of the device. Sabbatini's other plan was to have additional frames set behind the various houses; these, guided by grooves, could be run up-stage so that the one behind the first house covered the second house, that behind the second house covered the third, and so on. One may believe that this method, thoroughly practical, was the one regularly in use during the period. At the same time, of course, it was a simple matter to draw back the two shutters at the rear of the stage in order to reveal others immediately behind.[1]

"THE MASQUE OF FLOWERS," "MERCURY VINDICATED," AND "BROWNE'S MASQUE"

If, indeed, this system of angled wings was made use of in *Somerset's Masque*, apparently it was not copied, at least for the purpose of showing a change of scene, in the next masque of which we have definite record, *Flowers*. Here there was shown a traverse "painted in *Perspective*, like the wall of a Cittie, with battlements, over which were seene the Tops of houses." It seems probable that the traverse was not a curtain, but some kind of shutter, since it had in the middle "a great gate, and on either side a Temple . . . in either of which opened a little gate"—all these gates being practicable.   To the sound of loud music this traverse was removed, and there appeared a formal

[1] ii, 5, 6.

garden, with a fountain and great silver statues. The precise appearance of this lovely place, fragrant with blossom and glittering with myriads of lights, is elaborately described for us, but, unfortunately, lacking any pictorial evidence, we must find it impossible to determine precisely how

it was composed. All that may be said is that probably the garden was shown by means of perspectively painted wings with a central 'mount' recalling the rocks which had already figured in a number of earlier masques. No attempt was made to change the setting once it had been revealed by the drawing of the traverse.

One might suppose that Ben Jonson's next masque, *Mercury Vindicated*, was equally simple. The first scene was "a laboratory or Alchymists workehouse"—almost certainly shown by means of front flats, the traverse of *Flowers*. This removed, there appeared a "glorious bowre." Although there is no description of the sets, one may believe that the procedure adopted in these two productions was identical. The same year, 1615, saw the performance of William Browne's *Inner Temple Masque*, sometimes called *Ulysses and Circe*. In this "on one side the hall towardes the lower end was discovered a cliffe of the sea," with "a sea . . . done in perspective on one side the cliffe." The reference here to "one side the hall" seems to indicate that the stage was divided vertically, and that this sea with the grove occupied only half of the available acting area. That

Fig. 33. A Gateway
Inigo Jones. Chatsworth (*Designs*, No. 403). Copyright of his Grace the Duke of Devonshire.

such a supposition is correct finds justification when we discover that, during the performance, "a travers was drawne at ye lower end of the hall," revealing

> an artificiall wood so nere imitatinge nature yt I thinke had there been a grove like yt in ye open plaine birds would have been faster drawne to that then to Zeuxis grapes. Ye trees stood at the climbeinge of an hill & lefte at their feete a little plaine wch they circled like a crescente.

Apparently on this hill were gates, for these, at a touch of Circe's wand,

> flew open, makinge as it were a large glade through the wood & alonge ye glade a faire walke, two seeminge bricke walles on eyther side, over wch the trees wantonly hung; a great light (as ye Suns suddaine

unmaskinge) being seene upon this discovery. At yᵉ further end was describe an arbor, very curiously done, haveinge one entrance under an architreave borne up by two pillers wᵗʰ their chapters & bases guilte, yᵉ top of yᵉ entrance beautifide with postures of Satyres, Wood-Nymphes & othr anticke worke, as also yᵉ sides & corners; the coveringe archwise interwove wᵗʰ boughes, yᵉ backe of it girt round wᵗʰ a vine & artificially done up in knottes towrds yᵉ toppe. Beyond it was a wood-scene in perspective.

"THE VISION OF DELIGHT," "LOVERS MADE MEN," AND "PLEASURE RECONCILED TO VIRTUE"

Browne's masque clearly introduced nothing new. The divided stage was already old-fashioned in 1615, and the gates opening to reveal a vista are strongly reminiscent of the cleaving of the rocks in *Oberon*. "The scene chang'd" in Jonson's *The Golden Age Restored*, but by this time the crabbed old author was being very parsimonious in his notices of scenic display, and we have no means now of knowing what either of the two sets represented. A little more information is provided in the text of *The Vision of Delight*. The scene here was "a Street in perspective of faire building," almost certainly a Serlian setting made up of angled wings. Later this scene "changed to Cloud" and thence "to the Bower of *Zephyrus*," the bower itself opening to discover the masquers. One may reasonably suppose that cloud frames were substituted to effect the first change and that these in turn had their places taken by frames representing parts of the bower. The opening of the bower was no doubt realized by drawing back the two rear shutters. The only other possible interpretation of the stage descriptions is that the second scene of clouds was a kind of front set, possibly created by means of descending machines, these front clouds concealing the alteration of the rear part of the set from street to bower. Here, too, direct influence of Italian shows has been sought;[1] suggestions are thought to have been taken from the entertainments presented at Florence for the marriage of Francesco de' Medici to Bianca Capello and from others celebrating the marriage of Cosmo de' Medici to Maria Maddalena of Austria in 1608.[2]

FIG. 34. A GARDEN WITH A PAVILION

Inigo Jones. Chatsworth (*Designs*, No. 406). Copyright of his Grace the Duke of Devonshire.

Lovers made Men, otherwise known as *The Masque of Lethe*, is the next English court production of which we have any certain knowledge; its settings, apparently, were prepared by Nicholas Lanier. Before the stage appeared an "Arch-Triumphall," through which was seen Charon's barque setting off from the shore. On land was "a grove of myrtles . . . presented in perspective and growing thicker to the outer side of the Scene." This was a static set, no alteration being

[1] E. Welsford, pp. 199–202.

[2] *Descrittione delle feste fatte nelle nozze de' serenissimi principi di Toscana, D. Cosimo de' Medici, e Maria Maddalena, Arciduchessa d'Austria* (Florence, 1608).

attempted.   Slightly more elaborate was the production of *Pleasure reconciled to Virtue*, the appearance of which may be reconstructed both from Jonson's libretto and from the account of it given by Busino.[1]   First of all, the audience saw a large curtain, "painted to represent a tent of gold cloth with a broad fringe; the background was of blue calicoe powdered all over with gold stars."   This dropped and revealed the main scene, which, in Jonson's words, "was the Mountaine *Atlas*, who had his top ending in the figure of an old man, his head and beard all hoary and frost, as if his shoulders were covered with snow; the rest Wood and Rocke [and] a *Grove* of *Ivie* at his feet."

Fig. 35. A Forest with a Palace

Inigo Jones.   Chatsworth (*Designs*, No. 398).   Inscribed: "first sceane a pallas in trees pinted a shutter."
Copyright of his Grace the Duke of Devonshire.

Busino informs us that his "enormous head was alone visible up aloft under the very roof of the theatre and it rolled its eyes and moved itself very cleverly."   In the midst of the performance the grove vanished and the musicians were discovered sitting at the foot of the mountain, which itself later opened and closed again.   According to Busino, the means employed for this effect was "two doors which were made to turn"—words which seem to suggest the employment of flat *periaktoi* similar to those later employed in *Candy Restored*.[2]   What precisely was displayed when the mountain thus opened we cannot tell, but Busino says that "from behind the hills of a distant landscape the day was seen to dawn, some gilt columns being placed along either side of the scene so as to aid the perspective and render the distance greater."   One may suspect that nothing very

[1] M. Sullivan, xv, 108–114; *Calendar of State Papers* (*Venetian*, 1617–19), xv, 110–112; E. Welsford, pp. 206–207.
[2] *Infra*, pp. 151–153.

new was attempted here; in any case, the central mountain was by now an old device. "Mr Inigo Jones," commented a contemporary, "hath loſt in his reputacon."

For a full decade, unfortunately, it is almoſt impossible to discover evidence relating to his scenic efforts. He may during those years have made efforts to reſtore his faded preſtige, but the libretti of the masques then produced are sparing of directions. All that is known for certain regarding the visual appearance of *News from the New World* is that ſpectators were regaled with a view of "the Region of the Moon." Not even so much is known of *Gipsies*. *Augurs* provides a good inſtance of the tantalizing taciturnity of the masque writers at this period. The text indicates that the scene for the firſt antimasque[1] was "the Court Buttry-Hatch," and towards the close of the production, we are told, "the heaven opened and *Jove* with the Senate of the Gods were discovered." Two other ſtage directions show that "the Earth" was made to rise and that at the end "the whole Scaene shut." In the dialogue, certainly, Apollo is called upon to point and say:

> Yond, yond afarre
> They closed in their Temple are;

but, lacking any precise indication of a temple scene in the text, we might well have been excused for believing that this building exiſted only in imagination. Yet this belief would have been erroneous. Among the designs of Inigo Jones is one sketch definitely marked "The Colledge of Augures" (Fig. 36).

"Time Vindicated," "Neptune's Triumph," and "Love's Triumph"

Three changes of scene were essayed in *Time Vindicated*. This we know from the remarks of Sir John Aſtley, who recorded a view of Whitehall, a cloud scene, and a foreſt, but again the text has omitted indication of all the effects. The firſt scene is not noted, and only a brief note preserves the information that towards the end of the masque "the whole Scene" was "chang'd into a Wood." For the second set there was "Loud MUSIQUE, to which the whole Scene opens, where *Saturne* sitting with *Venus* is discover'd above." Slightly fuller are the directions for *Neptune's Triumph*, a masque planned for production in January 1624, but for various reasons laid aside. Its scenery was utilized for a revision, presented the following year as *The Fortunate Isles*. Whether there was a proscenium arch is doubtful; more probably two side-wings, representing "Pillars, dedicated to *Neptune*," were used as a half-proscenium. These are well shown in Inigo Jones's extant design,[2] which presents also a view of the palace of Oceanus, obviously made from a set of Serlian angled wings. Since this formed the second scene, and since Jonson specifically declares that when the masque began "all that [was] discovered of a *Scene*" was the pillars, we muſt believe that a curtain was operated behind the front wings. That removed, there was shown the island of Delos (evidently a practicable set on wheels, for later it moved forward), and a vaſt heaven opened while "*Apollo*, with *Mercury*, some *Muses* and the Goddesse *Harmony* make the musique." After the maritime palace had been revealed the audience saw a sea prospect with a fleet in full sail. To interpret these descriptions is difficult. One suſpects that the island of Delos muſt have been represented by a low border which could eventually be run to the side, and that both the second and the third scenes were carried out by means of those angled wings which were used for the intereſting woodland set used in the French paſtoral of 1626.[3]

Difficulties—arising from paucity of direction—pursue us when we turn to *Love's Triumph*. Not the slighteſt hint of description is there of the firſt set; all we know is that it opened to discover a temple by a shore, with "a hollow rocke, filling part of the Sea-prospect." Herein was

---

[1] The term 'antimasque' has been fully discussed by E. Welsford. Briefly it may be defined as that portion of the masque intended, by the introduction of grotesque characters, to set off and make more beautiful the appearance of the chief masquers.

[2] *Designs*, No. 65 (Pl. IX). [3] *Id.*, No. 67 (Pl. X).

presented a maritime triumph; "which ended, the scene changeth to a Garden, and, the heavens opening, there appeare foure new persons in forme of a *Constellation*." Through this constellation passed Venus, seated on a cloud; the cloud descended to earth and, vanishing, left a throne. After a time this throne too disappeared—"in place of which there shooteth up a Palme-tree with

Fig. 36. The College of Augurs in "The Masque of Augurs" (1622)
Inigo Jones. Chatsworth (*Designs*, No. 63). Inscribed: "The Colledge of Augures."
Copyright of his Grace the Duke of Devonshire.

an imperiall Crowne on the top, from the roote whereof Lillies and Roses twining together and imbracing the stemme flourishing through the crowne." The cloud-work is familiar; presumably a machine lowered Venus, who, stepping backward from the platform, found a station upon a throne placed immediately behind. One imagines that the vanishing of the throne was managed by simply drawing up a canvas which was cut and painted to resemble the palm-tree.

"Chloridia"

If, however, exact information is scanty for this mid-period of masque development the later thirties of the century present a rich array of material, both descriptive and pictorial. Most of the designs of Inigo Jones belong to these years, and many of the masques, being penned by authors less intent on their literary pre-eminence than Jonson, give more elaborate notations upon the effects secured or intended. For *Chloridia* Jonson and Jones were still in collaboration. The latter's design for the proscenium is still extant. "The curtain," we are informed by the writer,

> being drawne up, the *Scene* is discover'd, consisting of pleasant hills, planted with young trees, and all the lower bankes adorned with flowers. And from some hollow parts of those Hills, Fountaines come gliding downe; which, in the farre-off Landshape, seem'd all to be converted to a river. Over all a serene skie, with transparant cloudes, giving a great lustre to the whole worke, which did imitate the pleasant *Spring*.

Two designs by Jones reveal the precise appearance of this set.[1] At one side of the stage "a bright Cloud begins to breake forth" and reveals Zephyrus, while at the other side "in a purplish Cloud" appears Spring herself. This part of the action over, "a part of the under-ground" opens, and out comes "a Dwarfe-Post from Hell." A tempest rises, and presumably dark clouds take the place of the "bright" ones, when suddenly there is calm,

Fig. 37. A FOREST SCENE
Inigo Jones. Chatsworth (*Designs*, No. 395). Copyright of his Grace
the Duke of Devonshire.

> and the *Scene* is changed into a delicious place, figuring the bowre of *Chloris*, wherein an arbour fayn'd of Goldsmiths worke, the ornament of which was borne up with *Termes* of *Satyres*, beautifi'd with *Festones*, Garlands and all sorts of fragrant flowers. Beyond all this, in the skie a farre off appear'd a *Raine-bow*.

Once more

> the farther *Prospect* of the *Scene* changeth into ayre, with a low *Landshape* in part covered with clouds; and in that instant, the Heaven opening, *Juno* and *Iris* are seene; and above them many *aery spirits*, sitting in the cloudes. . . . Here out of the Earth ariseth a Hill and on the top of it a globe, on which *Fame* is seene standing with her Trumpet in her hand; and on the hill are seated four Persons.

After some speech Fame takes wing and "begins to mount" while "the hill sinkes and the Heaven closeth."[2]

[1] *Designs*, Nos. 82, 83 (Pl. XII); *The Works of Ben Jonson*, i, 334–335.
[2] E. Welsford, p. 218, notes that the ascent of Fame was borrowed from *Il Giudizio di Paride*. It is well known that Jonson thought little of the manner in which the ascent was manipulated:

> "The ascent of Ladie Fame, which none could spie,
> Not they that sided her, Dame Poetry,
> Dame History, Dame Architecture too
> And Goody Sculpture, brought, with much adoo,
> To hold her up."   (*Poems*, ed. B. H. Newdigate, p. 296.)

THE PROSPECTIVES

There can be no doubt but that these were most ambitious effects. The changes almost certainly were made by means of the Serlian angled wings, already thoroughly familiar, and old devices for heavenly apparitions were being made use of; but the descriptions make it certain that the entire masque was richer in scenic changes than any other, previously produced, of which we have record. The tempest may have been shown by means of the extra frames already described,[1] although Sabbatini noted another method, whereby pieces of canvas painted to resemble clouds were rolled up at the upper ends of the sectional heavens; one end of the canvas was attached to the frame, and to the other end were sewn cords which, passing through pulleys, could draw the fresh cloth down

Fig. 38. Setting for "La Fenice rinovata" (Fossano, 1644)
Biblioteca Nazionale, Turin.

over the old. If the "bright" clouds were shown by means of lights placed immediately behind the frames these pieces of cloth would obviously serve to darken the stage.[2] The same procedure, declared Sabbatini, might be employed to make a rainbow appear in the sky.[3] Already there have been instances of mountains or other objects rising from below stage, but these seem to have been merely flat pieces of scenery: the mountain in *Chloridia*, since figures were seated on it, was three-dimensional. Four chapters in Sabbatini's book are devoted to the discussion of methods whereby "men might be brought through a stage-trap quickly," [4] and one of these was probably used here. A lever, of length proportionate to the weight of the object to be raised, was set in position with its fulcrum a short distance from the trap. On one end was set the object, which ascended when the other end was lowered. It seems likely, since there was not great depth below the acting area, that the mountain must in some way have been masked, possibly by a low border, before the time came for its raising.

[1] *Supra*, p. 77.   [2] ii, 40.   [3] ii, 41.   [4] ii, 18–21.

"Albion's Triumph"

The ambitious staging of *Chloridia* was followed by equally ambitious sets in *Albion's Triumph*, written by Aurelian Townsend. The 'ornament,' or proscenium frame, was a rich and elaborate one,[1] with a curtain which was drawn up to reveal the first scene :

a *Romane Atrium*, with high Collombs of white Marble and ornaments of Architecture of a composed maner of great proiecture, enrich with carving, and betweene every retorne of these Collombs stood

Fig. 39. A Roman Atrium in "Albion's Triumph" (1632)
Inigo Jones. Chatsworth (*Designs*, No. 108). Copyright of his Grace the Duke of Devonshire.

Statues of gold on round pedestalls, and beyond these were other peeces of Architecture of a Pallace royall.

Over all was a serene skie, out of which a cloude began to breake foorth, and as it discended a person was discovered sitting in it.

The original design for this scene has been preserved (Fig. 39); clearly it was based on Giulio Parigi's set in *Il Giudizio di Paride*.[2] The Roman atrium then vanished, and in its stead there appeared "the Forum of the City of *Albipolis* and *Albanactus* triumphing, attended like a Roman Emperor . . . seene a farre off to pass in pomp." This episode over, "The Scene is turned into

[1] *Supra*, p. 47.

[2] E. Welsford, p. 223, suggests that the last scene may have been inspired by the second *intermedio* in this production. The 'forum' set is reproduced in *Designs*, p. 62.

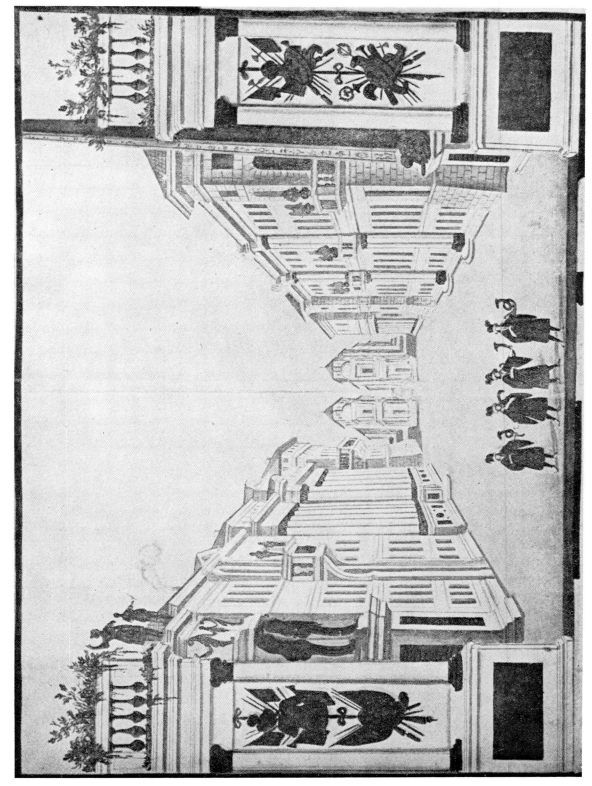

Fig. 40. Setting for "L'Unione perla peregrina" (Turin, 1660)

Biblioteca Nazionale, Turin.

an Amphitheater, with people sitting in it." Again "The Scene is changed into a pleasant Grove of straight Trees which, rising by degrees to a high place, openeth it selfe to discover the aspect of a stately Temple: all which was sacred to Iove." In the grove appeared Albanactus and his counsellors, with "sacrificers" and priests, who in their turn leave the stage, which suddenly changes to reveal "a Landscipt, in which was a prospect of the Kings Pallace of *White-hall* and part of the Citie of *London* seene a farre off." Cloud effects had accompanied the entire presentation of

Fig. 41. A Triumphal Procession in "Albion's Triumph" (1632)
Inigo Jones. Chatsworth (*Designs*, No. 111). Copyright of his Grace the Duke of Devonshire.

this masque, but from this point they became particularly noteworthy. "The whole heaven opened and in a bright cloud were seene sitting five persons," while

from the upper part of the heaven was seene to follow this: Another more beautifull cloud, in which alone triumphant sat *Peace*. . . . When the five persons which first descended were come to the earth, the cloud that bare them was in an instant turned into a richly adorned Throne.

In the task of interpreting these descriptions several designs by Inigo Jones aid us considerably. Quite clearly from that made for the Roman atrium (Fig. 39), the Serlian angled wings, three on each side, were being employed. It is strongly to be suspected that the second scene of the forum was presented merely by changing the back-shutters, without altering the wings on each side, and that the 'triumph' of Albanactus was shown by means of cut-out wooden figures drawn from one side of the stage to the other. Serlio refers to these,[1] and no doubt the design (Fig. 41) which seems to have been intended for this spectacle was planned for such a purpose.

To change the scene from the forum to the amphitheatre a plain flat was utilized. Inigo Jones's sketch (Fig. 42) demonstrates clearly that nothing more than that was planned. Presumably when

[1] Sir E. K. Chambers, *The Elizabethan Stage*, iv, 365.

90

this flat or shutter was removed the audience saw the grove and the temple, and perhaps the grove wings were not removed when the back-shutters changed for the view of Whitehall.

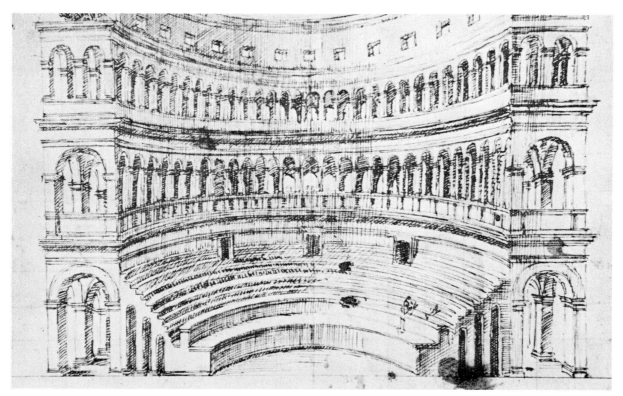

Fig. 42. An Amphitheatre in "Albion's Triumph" (1632)
Inigo Jones. Chatsworth (*Designs*, No. 112). Copyright of his Grace the Duke of Devonshire.

"Tempe Restored"

Townsend's second masque, *Tempe Restored*, was equally elaborate. The 'ornament' has been already described :[1] within this appeared the first scene, a "Lightsome" one,

> shewing a delicious place by nature and art, where in a Valley inviron'd with Hils a farre off was seated a prospect of curious Arbours of various formes. The first order of marble Pillasters. Betweene which were neeces [niches] of rocke worke and Statues: some spurting water received into vazes beneath them and others standing on Pedestals. On the returnes of these Pillasters run slender Cornishments, from which was raised a second order of gratious termes with womens faces which beare up the ornaments. Under this to a leaning height was a Ballestrata inricht. All this second story seem'd of silver worke mixt with fresh Verdures which on the tops of these arbours covered some of the returnes, in the forme of tipes with tender branches dangling downe; others were cover'd flatt and had flower pots of gold for finishing. Behind these appear'd the tops of slender trees whose leaves seem'de to move with a gentle breath comming from the farre off Hills.

Inigo Jones's design (Fig. 43) shows that this effect was achieved by means of the familiar three pairs of wings and back-shutters, closely imitated from another of the settings in *Il Giudizio di Paride* (Fig. 44). "Then," we are informed,

[1] *Supra*, p. 47.

the further part of the Sceane opening there appeares seated on the side of a fruitfull hill a sumptuous Palace, with an open Tarras before it and a great ſtaire of returne, descending into the lower grounds; the upper part environ'd with walles of Marble, alongſt which were planted *Cypreſſe* trees.

Fig. 43. ARBOURS IN "TEMPE RESTORED" (1632)
Inigo Jones. Chatsworth (*Designs*, No. 139). Copyright of his Grace the
Duke of Devonshire.

Townsend's comment leaves us in no doubt: the side-wings here remained unaltered; only the shutters were removed to reveal the palace, and these once more were drawn back to make the scene return "into the vale of TEMPE."   The aċtion proceeds:

Then the *Scene* is changed into an orientall skye, such as appeares at the Sun rising, and a far off is seene a Landscipt and a calme Sea which did terminate the Horizon; in the hither part was a Haven with a Citadell and opposite to that were broken grounds and craggey rocks.

In the midſt of the ayre the eight *Spheares* in rich habites were seated on a Cloud, which in a circular forme was on each side continued unto the higheſt part of the Heaven and seem'd to have let them downe as in a Chaine.

To the Musicke of these Spheares there appear'd two other Clouds descending & in them were discovered eight Stars; these being come to the middle Region of the skie, another greater Cloud came downe above them, which by little and little descending discovered other gliſtering Stars to the number of sixe; and above all in a Chariot of goldsmithes workes richly adorned with precious Iemmes sat Divine Beauty.

92

We may readily credit Townsend's remark that "this sight altogether was for the difficulty of the Ingining and number of the persons the greatest that hath beene seene here in our time."

The set itself is revealed in one of Jones's designs;[1] it must have been executed by a complete change of both side-wings and shutters. For the dawn effect Sabbatini has left elaborate instructions,[2] although his device presupposes not a mere change in the colour of the clouds, but the actual

GIARDINO DI CALIPSO INTERMEDIO TERZO

Fig. 44. THE GARDEN OF CALYPSO IN "IL GIUDIZIO DI PARIDE" (FLORENCE, 1608)
Giulio Parigi.

rising of a figure dressed to represent Aurora. How precisely the cloud machines were managed here we cannot tell. It seems probable that the circular frame was lowered directly from the heavens, and that the others were made to come down from the sides by means of the lever-engine already noted. Not satisfied with all these wonders, however, Jones attempted one further effect:

> The *Scene* is againe changed into a shady wood and a new Heaven appeares differing in shape and colour from the other. In the midst of which *Iove* sitting on an Eagle is seene hovering in the ayre with a glory beyond him. And at that instant *Cupid* from another part of the Heaven comes flying forth and, having past the *Scene*, turnes soaring about like a bird.

The appearance of Jove has been preserved for us (Fig. 45). For the glory Sabbatini has his directions.[3] This, it seems, was made of concentric rings with lights placed behind, the whole being set in an opening of the heavens (Fig. 46 and frontispiece). Cupid apparently was supported on a wire operated from a beam running crosswise from side to side of the stage.

[1] *Designs*, No. 155; E. Welsford, p. 336. [2] ii, 55.
[3] ii, 54. The glory is also dealt with by Furttenbach in *Mannhafter Kunstspiegel*, p. 134.

Fig. 45. Jove on an Eagle in "Tempe Restored" (1632)

Inigo Jones.   Chatsworth (*Designs*, No. 162).   Copyright of his Grace the Duke of Devonshire.

Fig. 46. THE PALACE OF APOLLO IN "VENERE GELOSA" (VENICE, 1644)
Giacomo Torelli.

"THE SHEPHERD'S PARADISE"

The experimentation in scenery was in the year 1633 applied to an ordinary play, *The Shepherd's Paradise*, by Walter Montague. "The scenes," noted Sir Henry Herbert in his diary, "were fitted to the paſtorall, and made, by Mr Inigo Jones." Turning to the printed text, we find only one vague mention of a set—"a wood called Love's Cabinet"; one manuscript [1] omits this, but gives another —"The Shepherds Paradice"; while a second manuscript [2] has four ſtage directions which demonſtrably refer to the scenes—"A front of a pallas seene through trees," "The Sheaperds Paradise," and "a woode" twice. How far such ſtage directions lack in exactitude is demonſtrated when we turn to the extant designs. Fig. 12 shows what Jones has marked as "The ſtanding sceane," together with the proscenium frame. Four wings of rocks and trees enclose the prospect of the palace. Alongside of this another design is marked "The Queenes Throne . . . Act yᵉ 2 : sceane yᵉ 4th changed into yᵉ Shapheards Paradise." The scene itself is not given, but three separate elevations of a richly ornamented throne indicate the elaborate nature of this production (Fig. 47). Only a brief allusion to a temple occurs in the dialogue of the play, but that this temple was set immediately before the eyes of the spectators is proved by a third sketch (Fig. 48), which is inscribed "The 8th sceane a Temple of Releiue." The word "relieve" indicates that here was a cut-out with a view of the shutter beyond. Still a fourth design, inscribed "Loves Cabinett of Relieve" (Fig. 49), shows us what, in the texts, was called variously a wood and a "cabinet." In all probability moſt of the altered effects were secured here by means of shifting the shutters; it is likely

[1] British Museum, MS. Sloane 3649.　　[2] British Museum, MS. Stowe 976.

Fig. 47. The Queen's Throne in "The Shepherd's
Paradise" (1633)

Inigo Jones. Chatsworth (*Designs*, No. 164). Inscribed: "The Queenes Throne
. . . Act y^e 2: sceane y^e 4th changed into y^e Shapheards Paradise." Copyright of his Grace the Duke of Devonshire.

Fig. 48. A Temple in "The Shepherd's Paradise" (1633)

Inigo Jones. Chatsworth (*Designs*, No. 166). Inscribed: "The 8th sceane a
Temple of Releive. . . . The toombes to [be] of whight marble wth ornamentes
of Brass guilte. A scelleton on each side in a shroud houlding torches."
Copyright of his Grace the Duke of Devonshire.

that throughout the play the tree wings remained unaltered—such at least seems indicated by Jones's note on Fig. 12.

Fig. 49. LOVE'S CABINET IN "THE SHEPHERD'S
PARADISE" (1633)

Inigo Jones. Chatsworth (*Designs*, No. 167). Inscribed, "Loves Cabinett of
Relieve." Copyright of his Grace the Duke of Devonshire.

"THE TRIUMPH OF PEACE"

The following year came James Shirley's scenically magnificent *The Triumph of Peace*.[1] The stage and proscenium are fully described for us, and happily shown, too, in several designs.[2] The curtain raised, there appeared

> a large streete with Sumptuous Pallaces, Lodges, Portico's and other noble peeces of Architecture, with pleasant Trees and grounds; this going farre from the eye, opens it selfe into a spacious place, adorn'd with publique and private buildings seene a far of, representing the *Forum* or *Piazza* of Peace. Over all was a cleare skie with transparent clouds, which enlightened all the Scene.

The original designs for this too have been preserved.[3] From these it seems as if Jones and his assistant, Webb, had been engaged in some considerable experimentation before finally a satisfactory setting was arrived at. That the means of securing the effect was that of the usual angle wings (apparently three pairs in all) and back-shutters is proved by Fig. 51.

[1] For a description of the procession and the chariots see Bulstrode Whitelocke, *Memorials of the English Affairs* (Oxford, 1853), i, 53–61.

[2] *Designs*, Nos. 180–182.   [3] *Id.*, Nos. 181–185. See the notes on these, pp. 80–81.

Suddenly the setting changed into a tavern. One thinks here of a front scene, painted in the flat, like the amphitheatre of *Albion's Triumph*. If this is correct, then there was prepared behind it

> a woody Landschape with low grounds proper for hunting, the furthest part more desert, with bushes and by waies representing a place fit for purse-taking. In the furthest part of the Scene is seene an Ivy-bush, out of which comes an Owle.

Fig. 50. A Forest Scene

Inigo Jones. Chatsworth (*Designs*, No. 396). Inscribed, "Wood of a new forme being a shutter" ("wood of Releive 6 sceane" deleted). Copyright of his Grace the Duke of Devonshire.

From the heavens descends a whitish cloud bearing a chariot, followed by an "orient" coloured cloud, also with a chariot, and by a third, "of a various colour from the other two"; after which

> the Scene is changed, and the Masquers appeare setting on the ascent of an Hill, cut out like the degrees of a Theater, and over them a delicious Arbor, with termes of young Men, their Armes converted into Scrowles and under their wasts a foliage with other carvings to cover the ioyning of the terme from the naked, all fained of Silver. These bore up an Architrave, from which was raised a light covering arched and interwoven with Branches through which the sky beyond was seene.

A sketch by Inigo Jones indicates the arrangement of this set, and from a note on it—"not to draw yᵉ upper shuters but yᵉ masqu[er]s form yᵉ under being draw[n]e"—it seems that here the back-shutters were divided horizontally, so that the lower or the upper pair could be removed at will (Fig. 54). Once more the Scene is changed into a plaine Champion Country, which terminates with the Horizon, and above a darkish skie with dusky clouds through which appeared the new Moone, but with a fainte light by the approach of the morning. From the furthest part of this ground arose by little and little a great

Fig. 51. THE FORUM OF PEACE IN "THE TRIUMPH OF PEACE" (1634)

Inigo Jones. Chatsworth (*Designs*, No. 183). Inscribed, "Forum of peace 1 sceane." Copyright of his Grace the Duke of Devonshire.

vapour, which, being come about the middle of the Scene, it slackens its motion and begins to fall downeward to the earth from whence it came; and out of this rose another cloud of a strange shape and colour, on which sate a young Maide, with a dimme Torch in her hand.

The effect of the vapour, we may readily believe, was secured by the use of gauze or thin silk.

Fig. 52. A CITY SQUARE

Inigo Jones. Chatsworth (*Designs*, No. 185). Copyright of his Grace the
Duke of Devonshire.

Fig. 53. A WOODY LANDSCAPE

Inigo Jones. Chatsworth (*Designs*, No. 187). Copyright of his Grace the Duke of Devonshire.

Fig. 54. PLAN FOR SEATING THE MASQUERS
IN "THE TRIUMPH OF PEACE" (1634)
Inigo Jones. Chatsworth (*Designs*, No. 188). Copyright
of his Grace the Duke of Devonshire.

"CŒLUM BRITANNICUM"

Cœlum Britannicum, by Thomas Carew, carried on the same spectacular tradition. Within the boldly ornamented proscenium frame appeared a

> *Scæne*, representing old Arches, old Palaces, decayed walls, parts of Temples, Theaters, Basilica's and Therme, with confused heaps of broken Columnes, Bases, Coronices and Statues, lying as under ground, and altogether resembling the ruines of some great City of the ancient Romans or civiliz'd Britaines.

Two of Jones's designs seem to have been prepared for this set (Fig. 55),[1] which was based on a third scene in *Il Giudizio di Paride* (Fig. 56). After the first antimasque the ruins give way to the appearance of

> a Spheare, with Stars placed in their several Images, born up by a huge naked Figure (only a piece of Drapery hanging over his thigh) kneeling and bowing forwards, as if the great weight lying on his shoulders opprest him, upon his head a Crown, by all which he might easily be known to be *Atlas*.

From the extant sketch (Fig. 60) it is to be deemed that this, the second scene, was a front one, painted in the flat. The globe probably had some illuminant behind it, for later in the masque we are informed that the "Sphear" was "darkned." Eventually it, with Atlas, vanishes, "and a new

[1] *Designs*, Nos. 192, 193 (Pl. XXIII). See also Nos. 194 (Pl. XXIV, A), 195 (Pl. XXIV, B).

Scæne appears of mountaines, whose eminent height exceed the Clouds which paſt beneath them; the lower parts were wild and woody." [1]   Here another antimasque was enacted, and, when that was over,

> there began to arise out of the earth the top of a hill which by little and little grew to be a huge mountain that covered all the Scæne; the underpart was wild and craggy, and above somewhat more pleasant and flourishing.

Fig. 55. A Ruined City in "Cœlum Britannicum" (1634)
Inigo Jones.   Chatsworth (*Designs*, No. 192).   Copyright of his Grace the Duke of Devonshire.

On the mountain were seated four characters.   Presently "the under-part of the Rock opens, and out of a cave are seen to come the Masquers."   A cloud descends from on high, and the mountain sinks again.   "This ſtrange spectacle gave great cause of admiration but especially how so huge a machine, and of that great height, could come from under the Stage, which was but six foot high."   The only possible solution is that the whole mountain muſt have been made in sections with, probably, a masking piece for the firſt of these.

Once more the scene

> varied into a new and pleasant prospect, clean differing from all the other, the nearest part shewing a delicious garden with several walks and per-terra's set round with low trees and on the sides againſt

[1] This seems to be *Designs*, No. 401 (Pl. LI).   To it belong the side-wings shown in Nos. 390 (Pl. L, A), 391 (Pl. L, B).

these walkes were fountaines and grots, and in the furthest part a Palace from whence went high walkes upon Arches, and above them open Tarraces planted with Cypresse trees, and all this together was composed of such Ornaments as might expresse a Princely Villa.

"For Conclusion to this Masque," we are informed,

there appeares coming forth from one of the sides, as moving by a gentle wind, a great Cloud which, arriving at the middle of the heaven, stayeth. This was of severall colours and so great that it covered the whole Scæne. Out of the further part of the heaven beginnes to breake forth two other Clouds,

PALAZZO DELLA FAMA INTERMEDIO PRIMO

Fig. 56. The Palace of Fame in "Il Giudizio di Paride" (Florence, 1608)
Giulio Parigi. Etching by Remigio Cantagallina.

differing in colour and shape. . . . These being come downe in an equall distance to the middle part of the Ayre, the great Cloud beganne to breake open, out of which stroke beames of light.

The design shown in Fig. 61 preserves its appearance. One may note that the rising mountain used in the midst of this masque served much the same purpose as the flats introduced in earlier entertainments; during the period that it remained on stage the setting of the rocks was changed into "a new and pleasant prospect." The huge cloud machine at the end no doubt followed the plan set down by Sabbatini in his chapter on "How to make a cloud divide into parts and become one again."[1] To achieve this effect a machine was made of the kind already described,[2] with the exception that to the main supporting arm were added two shorter arms designed to hold the other clouds. By a

[1] ii, 49.   [2] *Supra*, pp. 74-75.

complicated system of ropes and pulleys operated from beneath the stage floor the side clouds could then be made to swing in and out as desired (Fig. 62).

The descriptions given above might tend to make us believe that a new system of scenic method was being tried here. The wording seems to suggest the utilization of flat wings rather than the somewhat awkward angled wings of Serlian type. On the other hand, it may be that the old

SECONDO INTERMEDIO DOVE SI VIDE ARMARSI L INFERNO PER FAR VENDETTA DI CIRCE CONTRO TIRRENO

Fig. 57. Hell Scene in "Il Solimano" (Florence, 1619)
Giulio Parigi. Etching by Jacques Callot.

practice was still in service. When precisely the flat wing was made to supersede the other we cannot tell with absolute certainty; perhaps the two devices overlapped before finally the former was made standard.

"Comus" and "The Temple of Love"

We may rest assured, however, that only the older and tried forms were utilized when a young poet, John Milton, brought forth a masque called *Comus* at Ludlow Castle on September 29, 1634. Maybe there, in the great hall of the castle, only back-shutters were used; if more was attempted Serlian side-wings would have been all that might be required. That there was a curtain may be surmised from the fact that the first scene was a 'discovery'—"a wild wood." Next came "a stately

Fig. 58. A RUINED CASTLE

Inigo Jones.   Chatsworth (*Designs*, No. 407).   Copyright of his Grace the Duke of Devonshire.

Fig. 59. A DISTANT PROSPECT

Design by an unknown artist, probably Italian.   Chatsworth (*Designs*, No. 5*).   Copyright of his Grace the Duke of Devonshire.

Palace, set out with all manner of deliciousnesse," the change being effected, apparently, to the accompaniment of "soft musicke." A third (and final) set presented a view of "Ludlow towne and the Presidents Castle," in conception no doubt inspired by perspectives at Whitehall of London's houses.

Sir William D'Avenant was the next court masque-maker, starting his career with *The Temple of Love* in 1635. He too was sympathetic towards Inigo Jones, and there is every likelihood that the elaborate descriptions here and in *Salmacida Spolia* were written by the latter. The proscenium has already been dealt with ;[1] in this frame, when the curtain went 'flying up,' there

Fig. 60. Atlas in "Cœlum Britannicum" (1634)
Inigo Jones. Chatsworth (*Designs*, No. 197). Copyright of his Grace the Duke of Devonshire.

Fig. 61. The Great Cloud
Inigo Jones. Chatsworth (*Designs*, No. 209). Copyright of his Grace the Duke of Devonshire.

appeared a spacious grove of shady trees, and afar off on a Mount with a winding way to the top was seated a pleasant bower environed with young Trees and in the lower part walkes planted with Cypress, representing the place where the Soules of the Anciant Poets are feigned to reside.

Presently "out of the heaven by little and little broke forth a great Cloud of a Rosie Colour, which, being come down some little way, began to open and in it was seen sitting a beautiful woman." This cloud, having lowered its burden to the stage, closed again as it ascended.

The second scene was all "Mists and Clouds, through which some glimpse of a Temple is here and there scarcely discern'd." Evidently there were "Caves . . . underground" here; from them issued forth three magicians. After the entry and dance of the masquers

the mist and Clouds at an instant disappear and the Scene is all changed into a Sea somewhat calm where the billows, moving sometimes whole and sometimes breaking, beat gently on the land, which

[1] *Supra*, pp. 50–51.

represented a new and strange prospect. The nearest part was broken grounds and Rocks, with a mountainous Countrey, but of a pleasant aspect, in which were trees of strange form and colour, and here and there were placed in the bottom several Arbors like Cottages and strange beasts and birds, far unlike the Countrey of these parts, expressing an Indian Landschape. In the Sea were several Islands and a far off a Continent terminating with the Horizon.

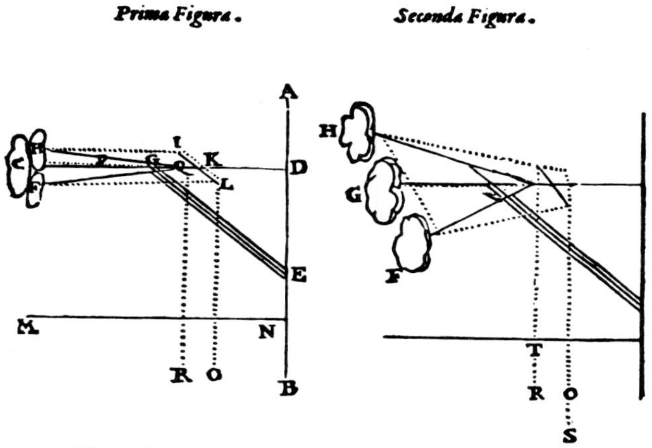

Fortunately, a fair amount of pictorial evidence remains to show us how all this appeared to the Whitehall audience of 1635, and before proceeding with the other scenes it may be well to glance at these designs. The first set, showing the grove with its bower,[1] demonstrates that four wings were used on each side and that the bower itself was painted on the back-shutters. Another design (Fig. 63) evidently was drawn to represent the huge cloud which descended with the figure of Divine Poesy. Particularly interesting is this because of the clear indication it gives of the rectangular frame, set in grooves, which bore the cloud and the goddess. Several sketches, too, seem to be associated with the scene of an Indian landscape.[2]

Prima Figura.   *Seconda Figura.*

Fig. 62. A Cloud Machine (1638)
Nicolà Sabbatini. Diagram in *Pratica di fabricar scene e machine.* The clouds F, G, H are shown first grouped together and then opened out.

One of these[3] is specifically marked "3 Sceane. Sceane of an India[n] shore and a sea for ye Quens masq of Indamora 1634." Here, too, four wings were employed, evidently now flat wings instead of angled in the Serlian style, shaped like crags and cliffs with palm-trees growing upon them. Italian influence was strong in this masque. The name Indamora and the Brahmin priests were taken directly from a pageant tournament held at Florence in 1615.[4] That show, designed by Giulio Parigi, introduced an "Indamoro" who was "King of Narsinga"; this hero was in love with an Indian queen, Lucinda, who arrived in a chariot escorted by "damsels of her court" and "Brahmin priests" (*Sacerdoti Bramanni*). No surprise need be felt when we find that for his

Fig. 63. A Cloud Machine in "The Temple of Love"
(1635)
Inigo Jones. Chatsworth (*Designs*, No. 212). Copyright of his Grace the Duke of Devonshire.

Indian scene Jones turned to other Italian sources. This was unquestionably taken from a volume which already had stood the English artist in good stead—*Il Giudizio di Paride* (Fig. 64). The way in which such designs were made to serve over and over again is well illustrated by the

---

[1] *Designs*, No. 211 (Pl. XXV, A).   [2] *Id.*, Nos. 227–230.   [3] *Id.*, No. 229 (Pl. XXV, B).
[4] *Gverra d' amore Festa del Serenissimo Gran Dvca di Toscana Cosimo Secondo, Fatta in Firenze il Carneuale del 1615* (Florence, 1615), pp. 8, 29.

fact that Giulio Parigi's setting clearly gave Alfonso Parigi the suggestion for his "Scena di Mare" in *Le Nozze degli dei* (Fig. 65), while its proportions, with the central rock motive, gave the same artist the idea for another scene in *Flora* (Fig. 66).

The design referred to above was definitely made for *The Temple of Love*, but puzzlement enters in when we compare this with two associated sketches.[1] Both of these show rocks, with a large arched central opening and a bank of clouds over which the Indian landscape is revealed in a kind

Fig. 64. The Fleet of Amerigo Vespucci in "Il Giudizio di Paride"
(Florence, 1608)
Giulio Parigi. Etching by Remigio Cantagallina.

of separate arch; the arch in the former is, indeed, practically a proscenium frame, with figures and cartouches reminiscent of the description of the 'ornament' in *Cælum Britannicum*. It seems quite impossible to suppose that a distinct inner proscenium was used for the presentation of the sea scene: nothing of the kind is introduced into any extant masque, and if there were an exception here we may be sure that word of it would have appeared in the libretto. One is, therefore, forced to the opinion that, although the rocks and the lower arched opening seem to be very deep, we have here a projected design for a stage in which the front was covered with craggy forms and an arch left below the acting area to permit the introduction of a small set. Such would have been possible with a stage about 10 feet high. That these two designs were actually used, however, we have no

[1] *Designs*, Nos. 227 (Pl. XXVI), 228 (Pl. XXVII, A).

assurance, although the former is, like so many of Inigo Jones's drawings, splashed with scene-painters' diſtemper. It may, perhaps, reasonably be supposed that they were trial essays, set aside in favour of the ſtraightforward set already noted and definitely inscribed with the name of this masque. The rocks from which the magicians entered would, then, be the lower parts of the formal wings. From between one pair of these, too,

> came waving forth a Barque of an Antique design, adorn'd with Sculpture finishing in Scrowles; that

QARTA SCENA DI MARE

Fig. 65. A Sea Scene in "Le Nozze degli dei" (Florence, 1637)
Alfonso Parigi. Etching by Stefano della Bella.

> on the Poope had for Ornament a great masque head of a Sea-God; and all the reſt enrich'd with emboſt work touch'd with silver and gold.

This ship, almoſt certainly, is shown in Fig. 67.[1]

"The Barque having taken port," the masquers next appeared

> in a Maratime Chariot, made of a spungie Rockſtuff mixt with shels, Sea-weeds, Corral and Pearl, born upon an Axletree with golden wheels without a rimme, with flat spokes like the blade of an Ore comming out of the Naves. This Chariot was drawn by Seamonſters and floated with a sweet motion in the Sea.

No sketch of the chariot is extant, but the editors of the Jones *Designs* have drawn attention to the

---

[1] The ship on wheels was, of course, a relic from medieval pageantry. At Modena in 1494 there was "a boat on wheels which was drawn by a horse over the square" (A. D'Ancona, i, 296).

faȼt that a kind of maritime bower, with palms,[1] corresponds to a similar 'machine' shown in the second of the two associated designs discussed above; and one might, perhaps, be warranted in hazarding the suggestion that here again we have record of an earlier plan for the staging of *The Temple of Love*.

AVVISO DI MERCVRIO A BERECINTIA DEA DELLA TERRA ET ALLE NINFE DE CAMPI

Fig. 66. A Wooded Shore in "La Flora" (Florence, 1628)
Alfonso Parigi.

Soon the sea vanished, turning in an instant to dry land, when

the Sceæn was changed into the true temple of Chast Love. This Temple instead of Columnes had terms of young Satyrs bearing up the returns of Architrave, Freeze and Coronice, all enrich'd of Gold-Smiths work. The farther part of the Temple running far from the eye was design'd of another kind of Architeȼture, with Pillasters, Neeches and Statues, and in the midst a stately gate adorn'd with Colomns and their Ornaments, and a Frontispiece on the top, all which seemed to be of burnish'd Gold.

The descent of a cloud closed this "Masque which, for the newness of the invention, variety of Scænes, Apparitions and richness of habits was generally approved to be one of the most magnificent that hath been done in *England*."

[1] *Designs*, No. 234 (Pl. XXVII, B).

Fig. 67. The Barge of Orpheus in "The Temple of Love" (1635)

Inigo Jones. Chatsworth (*Designs*, No. 231). Copyright of his Grace the Duke of Devonshire.

Fig. 68. Cupid's Palace

Inigo Jones. Chatsworth (*Designs*, No. 405). Inscribed, "Cupids Pallas." Copyright of his Grace the Duke of Devonshire.

"FLORIMÈNE"

D'Avenant's success was so great that he was commissioned to prepare the following entertainment of this kind, *The Triumphs of the Prince d'Amour*, but before that appeared a French pastoral,

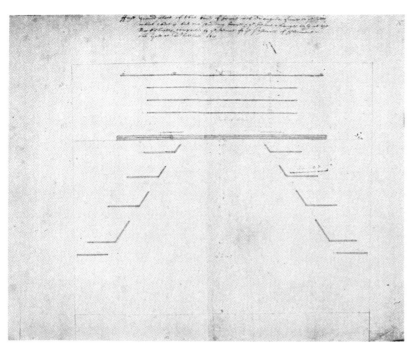

Fig. 69. GROUND-PLAN OF THE STAGE FOR "FLORIMÈNE"
(1635)
John Webb. British Museum, MS. Lansdowne, 1171, ff. 15*b*–16.

Florimène, had been produced at court, on the last day of the preceding year. This pastoral is important, for the plan of the hall, together with the cross-section of the stage, demonstrates the continued use of the Serlian angled wings. The first of these plans (Fig. 4) shows clearly the arrangement of the auditorium, with the state, the tiers of benches, and, interestingly, two "boxes," one for "yᵉ lady marquis" and the other for the Countess of Arundel. On stage the proscenium frame is set a little over 7 feet back from the front, and there are, behind it, four angled wings, a trifle over 2 feet distant from each other. Farther back still are three "relieves" and a final rear-shutter. The second design (Fig. 69) is devoted to "that kind of sceane with triangular frames on yᵉ sydes where there is but one standing sceane and

yᵉ sceane changes only at the Backshutters"—that is to say, with fixed wings; while the third is a section "for yᵉ standing sceane with Triangular frames" (Fig. 32). These two seem to have been prepared by Jones's assistant, John Webb.

The "border," or proscenium arch, and the standing scene of pastoral wings has frequently been reproduced.[1] It follows fairly exactly the description given in the *Argument* of the play, published in 1635—groves, hills, and plains, with a prospect of the sea. While the trees and cottage wings remained unaltered, the shutters changed several times. First appeared a "stately Temple" of Diana. For this a design is extant (Fig. 70), inscribed "The first Releive" and "only an Architrave and yᵉ Celing in squares." This formed the "Introduction." At the beginning of the play the scene returned to the first set, altering, when "The first Intermedium" arrived, into "a snowy Land-schipe," representing winter. This too is shown to us,[2] the design again being marked as a "Releive." "The second Intermedium" changed to "a spacious Garden," symbolic of spring. In two of Jones's designs is this scene displayed. One reveals the entire flat;[3] the other shows the centre of the set.[4] For "The third Intermedium the Sceene is turned into fields of Corne."[5] From that summer vision we next turn to a view of autumn;[6] while, finally, at the opening of

---

[1] *Designs*, No. 243 (Pl. XXVIII); *The Portfolio*, 1889, p. 90; W. J. Lawrence, *The Elizabethan Playhouse*, i, 48; A. H. Thorndike, *Shakespeare's Theater* (New York, 1916), p. 194. See also *Designs*, No. 244 (Pl. XXIX).
[2] *Designs*, No. 246 (Pl. XXX, A).   [3] *Id.*, No. 247 (Pl. XXXI).   [4] *Id.*, No. 248.   [5] *Id.*, No. 249 (Pl. XXX, B).
[6] *Id.*, No. 250 (Pl. XXXII, A).

the fifth act a new appearance of Diana's temple is provided.[1]   This is inscribed, "6th sceane the 2nd Temple of Diana a shutter."   "Here the Heavens open and there appear many deities."

"The Triumphs of the Prince d'Amour"

The Triumphs of the Prince d'Amour seems to have been moderately elaborate in its embellishments. The rise of the curtain here revealed

> a Village consisting of *Ale-houses* and *Tobacco-shops*, each fronted with a red Lettice, on which black Indian Boyes sate bestriding Roles of Tobacco, and in the place of Signes, Globes hung up, stuck up full of broken Pipes.   Before each door were seen old Logs and Trunks of hollow Trees.

This is Jonson's "shop with slyding windowes and false lights a'top," for which he girded at Jones in "To Inigo Marquesse Would-bee."[2]   "On the sudden" this changed to

> a Camp of Tents, distinguished by their several Colours: and in the midst was discover'd the Temple of *Mars*, the form being square and of the Dorick Order, with Trophies of Arms on the Front. Within the middle of the Temple stood the Statue of *Mars*, of a Copper, upon a Pedestal.

The masquers entered and Cupid descended "in a bright cloud," when once more the scene changed to reveal "a square Piazza, resembling that of *Venice*, and 'tis compos'd of Pallaces and lesser Fabricks, with Courtizans looking out of Windows and Balconees, fantastically adorn'd,

Fig. 70. The Temple of Diana in "Florimène" (1635)
Inigo Jones.   Chatsworth (*Designs*, No. 245).   Copyright of his Grace the Duke of Devonshire.

some in Italian, others in a Turkish dress."   A fourth scene alteration carried the spectators to a

> Grove of Cypress intermingled with Mirtle Trees, [and] the Temple of *Venus*, being an eight square of the Corinthian order;   within the Temple her Statue of Silver, standing in a Neech, with *Cupid* by her, to whom she seems to deliver an Arrow.   The Pilasters and Ornaments were heightned with Silver.

As a final spectacle

> strait was perceiv'd in a Grove of Lawrel Trees the Temple of *Apollo*, being round and transparent, of the order of Composita, the Columnes and Ornaments being heightned with Gold, his Statue of Gold standing in the middle of the Temple upon a round Pedestal.   Behind and between the Columnes did appear a prospect of Landskap.

According to the diary kept by Sir Henry Herbert,[3] all the scenes for this masque were prepared by a certain "Mr Corseilles," but one of Inigo Jones's designs, inscribed by him "The Temple of

---

[1] *Designs*, No. 251.   [2] *Poems*, ed. B. H. Newdigate, p. 298.
[3] *The Dramatic Records of Sir Henry Herbert* (New Haven, Connecticut, 1917), p. 56.

Apollo," [1] agrees in all essentials with the contemporary description. Though Jones seems to have had but a slight association, if any, with this masque, he was active about this time in connexion with the scenes used in Heywood's *Love's Mistress*.[2] "That admirable Artist," we are informed, "to every Act, nay almost to every Sceane, by his excellent Inventions gave . . . [an] extraordinary Luster, upon every occasion changing the Stage to the admiration of all the Spectators."

"BRITANNIA TRIUMPHANS"

What designer was responsible for *Prince Charles' Masque at Richmond* we do not know. It had as a first scene a view of "a pleasant Country for the most part champain," followed by "a well

PRIMA SCENA RAPRESENTANTE FIORENZA

FIG. 71. A VIEW OF FLORENCE IN "LE NOZZE DEGLI DEI" (FLORENCE, 1637)
Alfonso Parigi. Etching by Stefano della Bella.

ordered Campe, in which were seene severall tents, carriages, all kind of warlike ammunition and a trench cast round it." Later "on a suddaine the *Scene* flew open and five Knights Adventurers were discovered afarre off sitting on an arch Triumphant." Jones certainly was the artist in charge of *Britannia Triumphans*, D'Avenant's next effort in masque-making. The curtain ascended here to

---

[1] *Designs*, No. 252; E. Welsford, p. 366.

[2] This was printed in 1636, and may have been produced as early as 1633 or 1634. The theatre used was that in Denmark House, although later the play was "Publikely Acted. . . . At the *Phœnix* in *Drury-Lane*." Hardly any traces remain in the stage directions of scenic effects. Cupid, speaking the prologue, descends in a cloud and points "to the severall Plannets" in the epilogue. A practicable rock is referred to in Act I.

show a view of "English houses of the old and newer formes, intermixt with trees, and a farre off a prospect of the Citie of London and the River of Thames." Jones's original design for this has been preserved,[1] and another sketch seems to have been an earlier study for the same set. Presently "the whole Scene was transformed into a horrid Hell, the further part terminating in a flaming precipice, and the neerer parts expressing the Suburbs." Of this too we possess the original design (Fig. 72).

The antimasque over, this "Hell suddainly vanisheth, and there appeared a vast Forest in which stood part of an old Castle kept by a Giant, proper for the Scene of the Mock *Romansa* which

Fig. 72. A Horrid Hell in "Britannia Triumphans" (1638)
Inigo Jones. Chatsworth (*Designs*, No. 260). Copyright of his Grace the Duke of Devonshire.

followed." A sketch by Inigo Jones, since it is inscribed "3 sceane a forest & Gyants Castell," certainly gives us the original appearance of the scene.[2] Suddenly

> in the further part of the Scene the earth open'd and there rose up a richly adorn'd Palace, seeming all of Goldsmiths worke, with *Portico's* vaulted on Pillasters running farre in. The Pillasters were silver of rusticke worke, their bases and capitels of gold. In the midst was the principall entrance and a gate; the doores leaves with figures of Basse-relieve, with Jambs and frontispice all of gold. Above these ran an Architrave, Freese and Coronis of the same, the Freese enricht with Jewels. This bore up a Ballestrata, in the midst of which, upon an high Tower with many windowes, stood Fame.

Apparently, if we are to accept the terms of the description, something more than a rear-shutter opening was attempted here: it seems as if a cloth painted in the semblance of Fame's palace

[1] *Designs*, No. 258 (Pl. XXXIII).   [2] *Id.*, No. 290; another version is No. 291 (Pl. XXXVI, A).

(Fig. 73) were raised from the stage level. "When this Palace was arrived to the height," the description continues, "the whole Scene was changed into a Peristilium of two orders, Dorick and Ionick, with their severall Ornaments seeming of white marble, the Bases and Capitals of gold." This result was secured by an alteration in the three angled wings on each side of the stage.[1]

Fig. 73. The Palace of Fame in "Britannia Triumphans" (1638)

Inigo Jones. Chatsworth (*Designs*, No. 299). Copyright of his Grace the Duke of Devonshire.

That the palace actually did rise from below stage is proved definitely by the statement that, when its use was over, "The Palace sinkes" — apparently leaving the wings unchanged. Interesting is it to observe that for the outlines of this palace Jones returned to a design in *Il Giudizio di Paride* of which already he had made use (Fig. 56). For some reason that particular palace form was popular in the Renaissance; its features may be traced in the unidentified Italian design shown in Fig. 74 and in the castle of *Il Dono del re dell' Alpi* (Fig. 75).

The wings were altered, however, when

> the Scene changed and in the farthest part the sea was seene, terminating the sight with the Horizon. On the one side was a Haven with a Citadell, and on the other broken grounds and Rocks; from whence the sea-Nimph *Galatea* came waving forth, riding on the back of a Dolphin.

This scene also showed "some ships . . . sayling afar off severall wayes and in the end a great Fleet . . . which, passing by with a side wind, tackt about and with a prosperous gale entred into the Haven." An extant sketch displays this sea prospect, and a variant in the hand of Webb[2] no doubt was made on the same occasion.

"LUMINALIA"

The masques were now nearing their end. Only two, both written by D'Avenant, remained to be produced. The first of these, *Luminalia*, must have been a lovely show. The Queen, we are informed, had bidden Inigo Jones to devise something

> that with high and hearty invention might give occasion for variety of Scenes, strange aparitions, Songs, Musick and dancing of severall kinds; from whence doth result the true pleasure peculiar to our English Masques, which by strangers and travellers of judgement are held to be as noble and ingenious as those of any other nations.[3]

---

[1] *Designs*, No. 300 (Pl. XXXVI, B).   [2] *Id.*, Nos. 306, 307.

[3] E. Welsford, p. 236, draws attention to the fact that the idea of this masque was drawn from *La Notte d'amore*, by Francesco Cini, performed at Florence in 1608. There are connexions also with a Florentine pageant of 1565.

To satisfy this royal command Jones created "a Scene all of darknesse." "The first sceane of Night," he inscribed his design for the set,[1] where tree wings, drawn in the style of Rubens, frame a dark river beyond. From "the hollow caverns of the earth," no doubt concealed by a border, rose a "duskie cloud," bearing a chariot. Presently "a new and strange Prospect of Chimeras appear'd"

—once more happily preserved in a sketch marked "The Citty of Sleepe. Of Releive placed on a Rainebow."[2] Being a "releive," presumably this flat was shown with the wings unaltered.

After a time the sunrise dappled the sky and a gracious garden was shown; that, opening, revealed the masquers placed on a noble throne, while in the heavens floated rows of gods and goddesses.

> The figure of the seat was halfe an Ovall, about which were Termes, the upper parts like *Cupids* and the under part enricht with leaves. At the two ends of this seat were figures of women like Syrens converted into Foliage and Scrowles, all which seemed to be enchased of Gold-smiths worke. . . . In the further part of the Scene appeared a heaven full of Deities or second causes, with instruments and voices.

In all probability the design shown in Fig. 77 was connected with these

Fig. 74. THE PALACE OF FAME

Design by an unknown artist, probably Italian. Chatsworth (*Designs*, No. 23*). Copyright of his Grace the Duke of Devonshire.

apparitions, indication being given that the line of deities was a piece of painted scenery, no doubt lowered from behind the upper part of the heavens.

"SALMACIDA SPOLIA"

Then came the end. With *Salmacida Spolia* closed the magnificent array of masques which had glorified the courts of James and Charles, and characteristically this was the most splendid of them all. For it, we know from a ground-plan and section,[3] the later form of side-wings instead of the angled frames was employed (Figs. 78, 79). The former is lettered by John Webb "Ground platt of a sceane where ye side peeces of ye sceane doe altogither change with ye back shutters," while on the latter he wrote, "Profyle of ye sceane when ye sceane doth wholy change as well on ye sydes as at ye back shutters, & when ye syde peeces are made to change by running in groues [grooves]." These grooves (B) were four in number, set a little over three and a half feet from each other. At each side, in their centre, were posts with ropes (C), the "Engynes by which Deityes ascend and

[1] *Designs*, Nos. 308 (Pl. XXXVIII), 309 (Pl. XXXIX).   [2] *Id.*, No. 310 (Pl. XL, A).
[3] *Id.*, Nos. 321, 322; P. Reyher, Pls. II, III. Reyher's illustrations are redrawings; the originals are here reproduced for the first time.

117

Fig. 75. A Castle in "Il Dono del re dell' Alpi" (Turin, 1645)
Biblioteca Nazionale, Turin.

Fig. 76. A Temple
Design by an unknown artist, probably Italian. Chatsworth (*Designs*, No. 4*). Copyright of
his Grace the Duke of Devonshire.

discend." Behind them come the back-shutters (D), long frames apparently constructed in three portions. Three feet ten inches beyond were the masquers' seats (E), set in a great machine composed of two stout uprights (F)— "great vpright gr[ou]es by which yᵉ seates were lett vpp and downe"—in which was set (at G) "a crosse peece of tymber which went in yᵉ groues to which yᵉ seate was fastened and was made camb[er] in yᵉ middle for greater strength." It was possible to bring the seats completely below stage, and when that was done there remained (at I) a "space for Releiues betwixt yᵉ back-shutters & backcloth"—this back-cloth (H) being the rearmost piece of scenery, supported by four up-rights (L). Above each side-wing was a sky border (R), "peeces of Clouds which came downe from yᵉ roofe before yᵉ vpper part of yᵉ syde shutters"; these ran in upper grooves (S). Across the heavens, too, were (at T) "Clouds . . . which went crosse yᵉ sceane & were hung betwixt the Clouds of yᵉ sydes whereby it appeared but one sole heaven."

Here obviously is a system vastly differing from what has hitherto been described, and one wonders whether perhaps this flat-wing system had not already been introduced before 1640. That is a question which, unfortunately, is never likely to be answered, although from the design drawn for *The Temple of Love* one might hazard the suggestion that by 1635 at least it had been introduced

Fig. 77. Cloud Machines in "Luminalia" (1638)
Inigo Jones. Chatsworth (*Designs*, No. 311). Copyright of his Grace the Duke of Devonshire.

into England. It is difficult now to understand why the Serlian wings, both in England and in Italy, persisted so long, although we must recognize that, childish and cumbersome as they may seem, they did succeed in providing the means of securing some remarkable effects. Sabbatini knew of no better method, and quite clearly many of the settings in the Turin operas produced between 1645 and 1655 were carried out in this style. Yet the flat wing had been invented a full half-century earlier. There is every reason to believe that Aleotti used them in the theatre which he built for the Accademia degli Intrepidi at Ferrara in 1606,[1] while three years before that, in 1603, a public theatre at Venice had scenes "which could be drawn apart and put together." [2] So far as

[1] Franz Rapp, *Ein Theater-Bauplan des Giovanni Battista Aleotti* (*Neues Archiv für Theatergeschichte*, ii (1930), 79–125).

[2] "Portate divisamente dovransi metter insieme": A. Saviotti, *Feste e spettacoli nel seicento* (*Giornale storico della letteratura italiana*, xli (1903), 55). For Aleotti's work at the Teatro Farnese see Glauco Lombardi, *Il Teatro Farnesiano di Parma* (*Archivio storico per le province Parmensi*, N.S., ix (1909), 1–51).

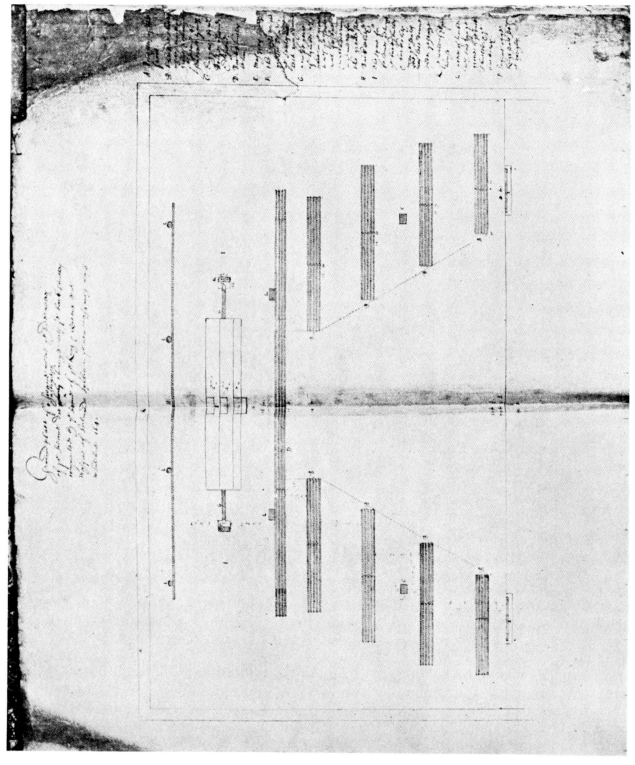

Fig. 78. Ground-plan of the Stage for "Salmacida Spolia" (1640)
John Webb. British Museum, MS. Lansdowne, 1171, ff. 3b-4.

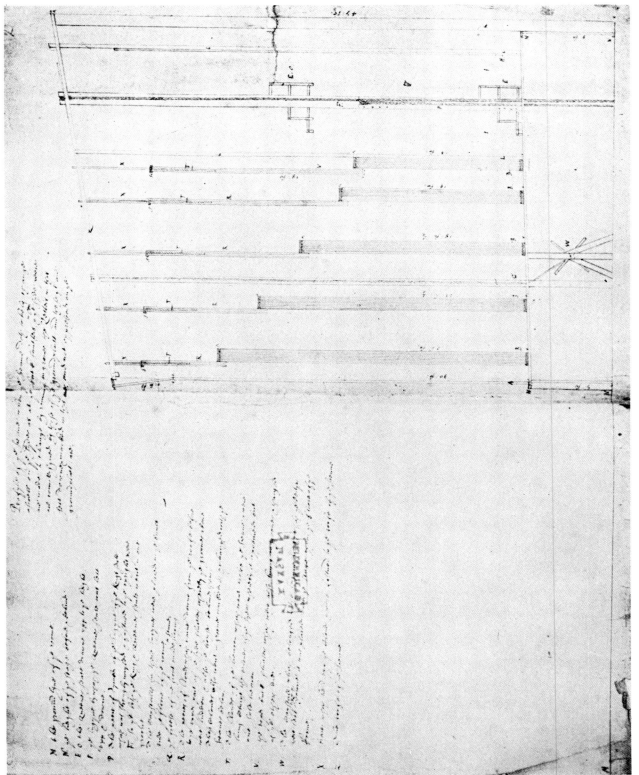

Fig. 79. SECTION OF THE STAGE FOR "SALMACIDA SPOLIA" (1640)
John Webb. British Museum, MS. Lansdowne, 1171, ff. 1b-2.

the masques are concerned, all we may say is that several descriptions of scenic changes between 1635 and 1640 seem to suggest the employment of this more flexible system.

On the stage of *Salmacida Spolia* first appeared

a horrid Sceane of storme and tempest; no glimpse of the Sun was seene as if darkenesse, confusion and deformity had possest the world and driven light to Heaven, the trees bending, as forced by a gust of winde, their branches rent from their trunkes and some torne up by the roots. A farre off was a

TEMPESTA COMMOSSA DA AMORE NE CAMPI TOSCANI

Fig. 80. A Tempest Scene in "La Flora" (Florence, 1628)
Alfonso Parigi.

darke wrought sea, with rowling billowes, breaking against the rockes, with rayne, lightning and thunder.

The design for this scene [1] follows the description exactly; on each side are four wings of rocks and trees, while the sea is painted on the shutter behind. In general terms, it seems to have been inspired by a setting of "Tempesta" by Alfonso Parigi in *Flora* (Fig. 80). Presently

the Sceane changed into a calme, the skie serene. A farre off *Zephyrus* appeared breathing a gentle gale. In the Landskip were Corne fields and pleasant Trees, sustayning Vines fraught with grapes and in some of the furthest parts Villages, with all such things as might expresse a Country in peace, rich and fruitfull.

From the heavens descended "a silver Chariot," lowered between the two foremost posts. Suddenly all this

[1] *Designs*, No. 323 (Pl. XLII, A).

was changed into craggy rockes and inaccessible mountaynes. In the upper parts where any earth could fasten were some trees, but of strange formes such as only grow in remote parts of the Alpes and in desolate places. The furthest of these was hollow in the middest and seemed to be cut through by art . . . and so high as the top pierced the clouds.

Of this too we possess pictorial record; one design is by Inigo Jones,[1] the other is a copy in the hand of John Webb. Here a new source of inspiration has been found in *Le Nozze degli dei*. Clearly

Fig. 81. Vulcan's Grotto in "Le Nozze degli dei" (Florence, 1637)
Alfonso Parigi. Etching by Stefano della Bella.

Vulcan's grotto there has inspired Jones's present effort (Fig. 81). During the progress of this scene "the further part . . . disappear'd" (by removing the upper shutters),

and the King's Majesty and the rest of the Masquers were discovered, sitting in the Throne of Honour. This throne was adorned with Palme trees, betweene which stood statues of the ancient Heroes. In the under parts on each side lay captives bound in severall postures, lying on trophees of armours, shields and Antique weapons; all his Throne being fayned of Goldsmiths worke.

[1] *Designs*, No. 339 (Pl. XLII, B), No. 340.

"A huge cloud of various colours" next

came softly from the upper part of the Heavens, . . . which discending to the midst of the Sceane open'd and within it was a transparent brightnes of thin exhalations, such as the Gods are feigned to

descend in: in the most eminent place of which her Majesty sate . . . environed with her martiall Ladies; and from over her head were darted lightsome Rayes that illuminated her seat.

A sketch-plan [1] indicates clearly the position of this cloud. The masquers are seated on the throne of honour, their chairs being attached to the two upright posts at the rear of the stage, so that they are seen above the cut-out shutters. Descending on the same grooves comes the great cloud, in three parts. At the back are platforms for the Queen's attendants, with a central throne for herself. Surrounding these are the cloud frames which, descending, concealed the "seat of honour." The cloud itself is displayed in two of Jones's designs (Fig. 82), [2] on one of which he has written memoranda—"to trye yf this great cloude may com dou[n]e betwene the groufes and then bee drawne open . . . and whether yᵉ shutters and this great cloude may not bee drawne a way boath togeather." The second notes the "raies of tinsell ou[e]r yᵉ Queene."

Finally, at the close of the masque,

the Sceane was changed into magnificent buildings composed of severall selected peeces of Architecture. In the furthest part was a Bridge over a River, where many people, coaches, horses and such like were seene to passe to and fro; beyond this, on the shore, were build-

Fig. 82. Two Cloud Machines in "Salmacida Spolia"
(1640)

Inigo Jones. Chatsworth (*Designs*, No. 350). Copyright of his Grace
the Duke of Devonshire.

ings in Prospective which, shooting far from the eye shewed as the suburbs of a great City. From the highest part of the Heavens came forth a cloud far in the Sceane, in which were eight persons

[1] *Designs*, No. 351 (reproduced at p. 129). [2] See also *id.*, No. 349.

Fig. 83. THE BRIDGE IN "SALMACIDA SPOLIA" (1640)

Inigo Jones. Chatsworth (*Designs*, No. 357). Copyright of his Grace the Duke of Devonshire.

Fig. 84. THE DEITIES IN "SALMACIDA SPOLIA" (1640)

Inigo Jones. Chatsworth (*Designs*, No. 359). Copyright of his Grace the Duke of Devonshire.

richly attired representing the spheares; this, joyning with two other clouds which appeard at that instant full of Musicke, covered all the upper part of the Sceane and, at that instant beyond all these, a Heaven opened full of Deities, which celestiall Prospect with the Chorus below filled all the whole Sceane with apparitions and harmony.

What happened scenically we can but guess. Presumably the masquers' seats sank below the stage level, room thus being made for a "relieve" of the bridge. The sky beyond would be displayed on the farthest back-cloth. Using the machine already employed for the descent of the Queen and her ladies, Jones then caused the eight deities to come from the heavens, while two other rows of clouds, with painted figures, made the whole sky seem full of gods. To the appearance of this scene there is considerable testimony.[1] The entire set is shown to us,[2] while several studies are devoted to the bridge (Fig. 83). Two sketches indicate the outlines of the cloud machine (Fig. 84).

Thus the masques ended their career in a blaze of splendour amid the heavens, music from the enskied deities sounding in swan notes beautiful and sad. To hundreds of courtiers they had given delight, and made wondering the poets by their loveliness. Inigo Jones's magic was magic indeed, increased rather than dissipated for those privileged to move behind the scenes, there to view the arrays of grooves, capstans, ropes, and platforms necessary for calling into being the mysteries of cloud palaces and of enchanted seas. When he came to Mantua in 1608 for the festivities arranged in honour of the marriage of Francesco Gonzaga and Margherita of Savoy, Federico Zuccaro described in rapturous terms the marvellous *intermezzi* which accompanied the performance of Guarini's *L'Idropica*, "but not less pleasure," he adds,

did I get from seeing the huge engines, the windlasses, the stout cables, the ropes, and the cords by which the machines are manipulated; and the enormous number of men necessary for working them, each at his post ready at a signal to lower or raise, to move or stay motionless—more than three hundred of these stage hands are employed, all requiring experience, skill, and ability, together with dexterity, acuteness, and judgment, so that they may cope with unexpected accidents and mishaps. One spark from a lamp, be it remembered, might bring all to ruin. Truly it was extraordinary that no disaster occurred, even although care was taken to provide huge jars, vessels, tubs, and pails of water ready for any emergency.[3]

Zuccaro's experience must have been duplicated by that of many another granted access to Jones's back-stage world. There the ropes, the windlasses, and the "huge engines" can have been no less imposing than those which operated the scenes and machines of Mantua.

---

[1] *Designs*, Nos. 355–360. [2] *Id.*, No. 355 (Pl. XL, B).
[3] *Il Passagio per Italia* (Bologna, 1608), section "La Dimora di Parma," p. 27.

IV

CHARIOTS OF TRIUMPH AND DIAPHANAL GLASSES

PAGEANT-WAGONS were the masque's original 'settings,' and to the end of its career this type of court entertainment displayed a fond and almost nostaglic passion for triumphal chairs and chariots which, if denuded of their original significance, at least preserved some features of their more important predecessors. Occasionally, even in the later masques, they played such a part in the production that only with difficulty can we distinguish between the scenery proper and these accompaniments of deities, lords, and their ladies.

A few properties of this kind have already been described and illustrated, but the passing references in preceding chapters but faintly indicate the manner in which the chariot contributed to the wonder and magnificence of the stage spectacle, or whetted an appetite for later glories by moving, like the wagons of a modern circus, in formal procession immediately before the opening of the show. The processional technique is well exemplified in the masque of the Middle Temple in 1613. On this occasion the performers apparelled themselves at the house of Sir Edward Philips, and thence set forth on their journey through London's streets. In the vanguard came two triumphal chariots, "adorned with great Maske heads, Festons, scroules and antick leaves, every part inricht with silver and golde," while at the rear of the troupe was seen another even more richly embellished. This "had his whole frame fill'd with moulded worke, mixt with paintings and glittering scarffings of silver, over which was cast a Canopie of golde borne up with antick figures, and all compos'd *a la Grotesca.*" Similarly, before the presentation of *The Masque of Queens* a procession was organized in which the twelve masquers were driven in three "triumphant *Chariots.*" "The first foure," we are informed, "were drawne with *Eagles. . . .* Then followed the second, drawne by *Griffons. . . .* Then the last, which was drawne by *Lions.*" Processional chariots too played a part in *The Triumph of Peace.* Each had "a glorious Canopy over their heads, all bordered with silver Fringe and beautified with Plumes of Feathers on the top." They were wrought "all after the Romane forme, adorned with much embossed and carved workes, and each of them wrought with Silver and his severall colour"—the several colours being orange, watchet, crimson, and white.

TRIUMPHAL CHARIOTS

These cars can have differed in but small degree from those which were introduced in the midst of the performances. The lions, griffins, and eagles find their counterpart in the two white bears which in *Oberon* pulled in a chariot "to a lowd triumphant musique," and the description of rich scroll-work and leaves may be paralleled by many similar records of stage cars. Sometimes they were lowered from the heavens. Cupid descended thus in *Love Restored*, Pallas in *The Golden Age Restored*, and Night in *The Vision of Delight.* Two of this sort, together with images of deities in clouds, are shown in Fig. 86; one of these appears delineated in greater detail in Fig. 87. Of Diana's glorious chariot, too, in *Albion's Triumph* we possess the original sketch (Fig. 88). In *Tempe Restored* the chariot of Divine Beauty was "of gold-smithes workes richly adorned with precious Iemmes" and surmounted by "a brightnesse, full of small starres that inviron'd the top of the Chariot, striking a light round about it." Two similar cars entered in *Luminalia*: the first

127

was of Night, "enricht and drawne by two great owles," and the second of Aurora, "touch'd with gold, borne up by a rosie coloured cloud." While the cloud-supported chariot was the most

common, wheeled thrones were of frequent occurrence. The car of Comus, showing that deity riding in triumph, is represented in one of Jones's sketches (Fig. 85); this was prepared for *Pleasure reconciled to Virtue*, and no doubt was similar to the car of Bacchus in *Cupid's Banishment*, "hunge all with vine-leaves and grapes" "and drawne by a goate." Sea monsters pulled in a wondrous "Maratime Chariot" in *The Temple of Love*. Sea monsters, owls, eagles —of these and others use was made to make more surprising and effective the entries of cars which, glittering with heavily chased gold-work, added still further embellishment to scenes already enriched by all the scene-painter's art.

In appearing thus the English deities were in no wise different from the Italian. In most of the

Fig. 86. CLOUD MACHINES AND CHARIOTS

scenic designs which have come down to us from the Renaissance we see, in the sky or on the waves, figures fundamentally similar and similarly presented. There, too, Juno was seated in her cloud-borne chariot, drawn by a pair of peacocks (Fig. 90), Jove appeared enthroned on his eagle (Fig. 91), and sea deities were drawn ashore to the music of wreathed horns (Fig. 92).

LIGHTING EFFECTS

Not the least element contributing to the beauty of these visions was the "glory" which played about them. "Let the *Scenes* abound with *Light*, specially *Coloured* and *Varied*," counselled Bacon,"[1] and one may imagine, from the many references in contemporary literature, that his admonition was strictly heeded. Perhaps to us who are familiar with stages glaring fiercely in the light of electric 'floods' and 'spots' the Renaissance theatre would appear but misty and dim, but maybe even we should be able to appreciate its loveliness. Although no thousand-watt instruments bathed the scenes in vivid illumination, the placing of the myriad lamps and candles, with their rays reflected by the glittering costumes of the masquers

Fig. 87. A Chariot

Inigo Jones. Chatsworth (*Designs*, No. 110). Copyright of his Grace the Duke of Devonshire.

and of the audience, must have produced a flickering wonder by no means in ill accord with the spirit of these courtly entertainments. A clever contrasting of dark scenes and of light, the sudden descent of a cloud chariot flaming in splendour, the rush of torch-bearers over a stage upon which the masquers have been discovered—all these would have contributed to startle and gratify the spectators, the light itself adding to the transitory delight of the evening's show.

The instruments were few and simple. Candles and lamps were all that the age could provide in this way, and much ingenuity had to be exerted ere they could be made to brighten and diversify the scenic spectacle. Sabbatini[2] is a trifle uncertain whether oil-lamps or candles of white wax are better for his purposes, but few shared his indecision. Candles certainly were used, especially for the illumination of the auditorium, but there seems to be little doubt that lamps were more conveniently adapted for back-stage work. Of these there were probably various kinds. Sabbatini's is shaped like the peasant's "cruze," a relic from ancient Rome, but probably the kind of lamp described by Furttenbach[3] was the most familiar. Simply blown of glass, this consisted of a round container with a small handle below, the wick being set in a tiny metal holder so wrought as to fit the aperture at the top. Such lamps are still to be seen in the Teatro Olimpico at Vicenza (Fig. 93), and we can readily agree that they were well fitted for their duties. The projecting glass handle allowed them to be placed securely in metal rings or else arranged in rows upon boards or battens drilled with suitable holes. Nor did their usefulness end there. When filled with coloured liquid and placed in front of other lamps they might serve, as occasion demanded, to modify the quality of the stage's illumination.[1] To increase the light cast from the diminutive wicks, reflectors seem regularly to have been employed.[2] Sometimes these were separate and placed where required behind individual lamps; sometimes the lamp itself was built into a box with reflecting sides, so becoming a definitely contrived stage instrument; and occasionally at least regular battens were constructed in the manner of footlight containers.

In the auditorium Sabbatini recommended the placing of the instruments close to the sides of the stage in order that the scenes might be the more brightly lit. Against this advice Leone di Somi entered a caveat.[3] From his own observation, he argued, a man who stood in the dark could see

Fig. 88. The Chariot of Diana
Inigo Jones.   Chatsworth (*Designs*, No. 120).   Copyright of his Grace the Duke of Devonshire.

more clearly a bright object than could a man who himself was placed in an illuminated spot. Hence in his opinion the hall should be kept as dark as was convenient, and those lamps or candles which were definitely necessary should be placed at the rear of the auditorium. In reading these remarks one must, of course, bear in mind the practical difficulties confronting a theatre worker of that age who desired in any wise to control the fore-stage lighting. Because of this, problems arose of a kind unknown to directors able at a moment's notice to control every single instrument set in auditorium or stage. To kindle many candles rapidly, it is true, Bernardo Buontalenti had invented a device in 1585 [4]—a simple affair, consisting of a string, soaked in spirits or other inflammable material, which ran from wick to wick—but it may easily be realized that considerable danger might attend its operation and that there could be but small assurance of its successfully accomplishing its purpose.

[1] See *infra*, pp. 134–135.
[2] It is to be noted that in medieval Italian plays a 'glory' was often secured by means of a barber's basin well burnished: see Virginia Galante Garrone, *L'Apparato scenico del dramma sacro in Italia* (Turin, 1935), p. 112.
[3] *The Development of the Theatre* (second edition), p. 253.
[4] F. Baldinucci, *Notizie de' professori del disegno* (*Opere* (Florence, 1774), viii, 41–70).

Hardly more assurance could there be from Sabbatini's method for darkening the candles. Here numerous metal cylinders were made, to be set over the instruments of illumination and controlled

Fig. 89. THE CHARIOT OF MERCURY IN "LA MASCHERATA DELLA GENEALOGIA DEGLI DEI" (FLORENCE, 1565)

Giorgio Vasari. Biblioteca Nazionale, Florence (C. B. 3. 53; i, 85–86).

by a series of strings and pulleys.[1] The difficulties and dangers were such that in general the Renaissance auditorium must have been left illuminated throughout the entirety of the production.[2]

[1] ii, 12.

[2] Although there is reason to believe that normally the auditorium in England remained lit during the performance, it is to be noted that "the Hall" was "darkened" before a performance of *Loyola* at Trinity College, Cambridge, in 1623 (see T. Birch and R. F. Williams, *The Court and Times of James I* (1849), ii, 375–376).

Fig. 90. THE CHARIOT OF JUNO IN "L'UNIONE PERLA PEREGRINA"
(TURIN, 1660)

Biblioteca Nazionale, Turin.

Fig. 91. JOVE, HERCULES, JUNO, AND NEPTUNE IN "L'UNIONE PERLA
PEREGRINA" (TURIN, 1660)

Biblioteca Nazionale, Turin.

For the stage itself Sabbatini demanded a row of lights immediately behind the upper part of the proscenium arch [1] and behind the various side-scenes. In order to keep the latter from being disturbed by the movement of the dancers, he counselled the making of supports which, let down through holes in the stage-floor, might be fixed firmly to the solid floor of the hall. The parapet too came in useful, for behind it might be placed a row of candles calculated to produce the effect of footlights. [2] Here, however, there entered in a difficulty. Since, remarks Sabbatini, fairly large wicks had to be used to obtain adequate illumination, frequently "such dense smoke is sent forth as to make it seem that a mist has risen before the eyes of the spectators, thus preventing their seeing the scene on stage." "Besides which," he adds, "there is a bad smell emanating from these oil-

Fig. 92. A SEA-GODDESS IN "L'UNIONE PERLA PEREGRINA" (TURIN, 1660)
Biblioteca Nazionale, Turin.

lamps, especially when they are placed so low"; and Leone di Somi too referred to the smoke screen thus engendered. Even without that the stage must oftentimes have been but dimly visible—not, of course, that that dimness did not at times contribute a loveliness of its own. "Let the Masquers," says Bacon,[3]

> or any other that are to come down from the *Scene* have some Motions upon the *Scene* it selfe before their Comming down: For it drawes the Eye strangely and makes it with great pleasure to desire to see that it cannot perfectly discerne.

Similar instructions regarding the placing of the lights appear in a discourse of Angelo Ingegnieri.[4] "There remains," says this author,

> one matter of supreme theatrical importance—the lighting. Lighting in a theatre ought to be pleasing and clear, and the instruments should be so placed that the spectators' view of the stage is not interrupted by hanging chandeliers or lamps; nor should the spectators go in any fear of wax or oil dropping upon them. Moreover, care should be taken to see that there is no bad smell coming from the lamps, and no danger of their causing a fire or of creating disturbance and confusion among the actors behind the scenes. The man who is able to arrange this illumination so that only its splendour is seen, and its

---

[1] i, 39.   [2] See also J. Furttenbach, *Mannhafter Kunstspiegel*, p. 119.

[3] *A Harmony of the Essays*, ed. Edward Arber (1871), p. 539.

[4] *Della Poesia rappresentativa e del modo di rappresentare le favole sceniche* (Ferrara, 1598; reprinted in *Delle Opere del Cavalier Battista Guarini* (Verona, 1738), iii, 526–527).

effect created without any member of the audience being in a position to say whence or how it is obtained, unquestionably does much to add to the magnificence of a show. Especially is this true if the lights are placed so as to illuminate the faces of the actors. To those who may have charge of theatre illumination, it may be pointed out that the method of securing this result is by no means difficult, nor does it call for any very great expense. The method, which I now wish to demonstrate so that it may be of general service in all future productions, consists in hanging up a valance between the stage heavens and the roof of the auditorium, without, of course, bringing it so low as to cut off too much of the set. On the inner side facing the stage it is to be fitted with many lighted lamps, having tinsel reflectors to direct the beams upon the actors. These lamps ought to be firmly fixed at the top and lit before being drawn up to the positions they are to occupy. Naturally, the whole business must be carried out back-stage before the curtain is drawn. . . . The set will thus glow with light, and yet no one will see the source of that light or at least discern how it has been made so resplendent. Lastly, take care —especially when a valance of this kind cannot be employed—to contrive that the whole of the light falls on the stage, the setting, and the proscenium, and does not become diffused over the auditorium. The darker the auditorium is, the brighter the stage will appear; contrariwise, the brighter the auditorium, the more confused will be the spectators' view of the stage, for then that which ought to have been distinctly and easily seen will be rendered obscure and consequently less pleasing. Hence, at the fall of the curtain I recommend that every lamp in the auditorium set there to show the spectators to their seats should be removed. Still further, the less illumination there has been up to that point,

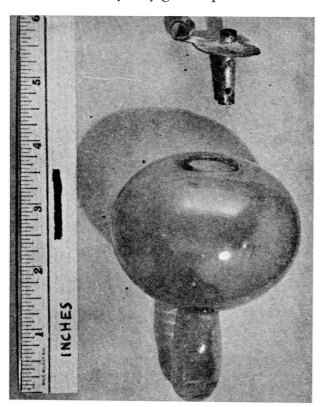

Fig. 93. A Sixteenth-century Glass Lamp from the Teatro Olimpico, Vicenza

the better it will be, for when the curtain falls the light on stage will seem more powerful and accordingly will produce a more lovely effect.

From various other sources we may glean information regarding devices and effects. Leone di Somi stands forward as the earliest exponent of what may be styled symbolic lighting; for a scene of tragedy and gloom he would have a dark stage, and to harmonize the appearance of the stage and a scene of joy he would flood the setting with light. From Sebastiano Serlio[1] we learn the use of bottles filled with various coloured liquids. Set in holes cut from a flat board, these might be placed in an opening of one of the 'houses,' with a row of lamps behind. As has already been noted, it is probable that the same glass globes which served for the lamps were utilized for this purpose. They seem to have been known technically as *bozze*,[2] and one may imagine, from the numbers required, that the glass-workers at Venice found themselves busily occupied in their manufacture. Malespini records how, for a production at Mantua, orders had been placed there for "a great quantity of glasses [*vetri*] to be used for illuminating the scenes." The workmen, however, knowing that the orders had been sent rather late, "demanded as much for them as if they had been fashioned of

---

[1] Sir E. K. Chambers, *The Elizabethan Stage*, iv, 363–365.
[2] This word is used by Leone di Somi and by Serlio. These *feux ou verres de couleur* were employed for plays given at Bayonne in 1565.

silver." As a result the architect-director was forced to journey post-haste to Milan, happily having recalled that his friend Malespini had "several hundreds" in his house.[1]

All the evidence that remains convinces us that the system of lighting which Inigo Jones employed was based fundamentally upon this Italian practice. How closely the London stage followed the Florentine and the Mantuan is shown by the references to those globes we have just been discussing. "Glasses for yᵉ Rocke" were ordered in 1609, as a manuscript note on the back of one of the Chatsworth designs testifies.[2] More specific allusion is made to them in the *Entertainment at Theobalds*; in the "Lararium" of that masque "were placed divers Diaphanall glasses, fill'd with severall waters that shew'd like so many stones of orient and transparent hiewes." The reference to "stones" demonstrates that the arrangement was of the Serlian kind; indeed, some of the masque descriptions read almost as if they were direct translations of the *Architettura*. Serlio had alluded to lights shining like sapphires, emeralds, rubies, and topaz. Turning to the text of *Tethys' Festival*, we are informed that "above the Skallop and round about the sides was a resplendent freeze of iewell glasses or lights, which shewed like Diamonds, Rubies, Saphires, Emralds and such like." The House of Fame which figured in *Queens* had friezes "fill'd with several-colour'd lights, like *Emeralds, Rubies, Saphyres, Carbuncles*, &c., the reflexe of which, with other lights placed in the Concave, upon the *Masquers* habits was

Fig. 94. A Throne of Light

Inigo Jones. Chatsworth (*Designs*, No. 381). Copyright of his Grace the Duke of Devonshire.

full of glory." Two pyramids in *Flowers* similarly were all "glistering with transparent lights resembling *Carbuncles, Saphires* and *Rubies*," and the golden pillars of *Lords* were "set with Rubies, Saphyrs, Emeralds, Opals, and such like." The "several coloured lights" which adorned the pillars in *Beauty* no doubt were of the same kind, as were "the lights of severall colours" in the obelisk of *Lords*. Two designs by Inigo Jones, that for the House of Fame [3] and another representing an unidentified scenic object (Fig. 94), demonstrate clearly how these were placed in position—sometimes in straight lines, sometimes in geometrical forms. Such lights contributed much to the masque's glory, and even a simple production like the *Knowsley Masque* had to have its "Temple . . . full of lights."

Perhaps glasses of a similar kind were utilized for the interesting device employed in *Tethys' Festival*. "First," we are told,

---

[1] Celio Malespini, *Ducento Novelle* (Venice, 1609), ii, 29, novella xi.   [2] *Designs*, No. 15.   [3] *Id.*, No. 14 (Pl. IV).

at the opening of the Heavens appeared 3 circles of lights and glasses, one within another, and came downe in a ſtraight motion five foote and then began to moove circularly; which lights and motion so occupied the eyes of the speƈtators that the manner of altering the Scene was scarcely discerned.

"Severall circles of lights in continuall motion" also appeared in *Lords*, but not for the same purpose. These moving spheres were certainly not of Jones's invention. Writing of Francesco d'Angelo, familiarly named Il Cecca, a Florentine engineer who died in 1488, Vasari[1] describes various devices invented for processional shows sponsored by civic fraternities. At the Church of the Carmine in Florence was ereƈted a high heaven

in which were large wheels shaped like windlasses that moved, from the centre to the circumference, ten circles representing the ten heavens, all full of small lights to indicate the ſtars; this was accomplished by means of tiny copper lamps set on swivels, so that, though the sphere revolved, they remained upright.

A favourite device of Inigo Jones was to present a 'concave' made dazzling by light; in these, without a doubt, the lamps were concealed and the rays refleƈted so as to create a glory. The "great concave shell, like mother of pearle," which was one of the principal features of *Blackness* "was ſtuck with a *chev'ron* of lights which, indented to the proportion of the shell, ſtruck a glorious beame upon" the masquers. Akin to this was the "mine of several metals" in *Hymenæi*, where "the lights were so placed as no one was seene, but seemed as if only REASON, with the splendor of her crowne, illumin'd the whole Grot." The 'concave' of *Hue and Cry after Cupid* was likewise "fill'd with an ample and gliſtering light," while in *Middle Temple* "a rich and refulgent mine of gold" had

lights . . . so ordred that, though none were seene, yet had their luſtre such vertue that by it the leaſt spangle or sparke of the Maskers rich habites might with ease and cleerenesse be discerned as far off as the seate.

For *Flowers* "certaine lights" were "shadowed" by "great pottes of Illiflowers," thus making "a resplendent and admirable luſtre," and additional "luſtre" was provided by "secret lights" placed behind "great tufts of severall kindes of Flowers." *Pan's Anniversary* had a huge Fountain of Light, and *Tempe Reſtored* a lovely "Lightsome Scene." A "Scene of light," too, was "discovered" in *The Golden Age Reſtored*.

The effeƈt of the concave was oftentimes reproduced in cloud forms. The clouds in *Hymenæi* "were of relievo, embossed and tralucent as naturals"; this means that they were cut out so that one flat showed through an opening of that in front while the material of which they were made allowed the light behind to filter through. Two materials Jones seems to have used for this purpose— calico and oiled paper. The firſt is mentioned by John Aubrey,[2] who was informed by Emmanuel De Critz, serjeant painter to Charles I, that Jones had used "drapery of . . . white Callico" for certain caryatides, "which was very handsome and very cheap and shewed as well as if they had been cutt out of white marble." The oiled paper comes in for an attack by Jonson. "Now, Sir," says the burlesque mechanic in *A Tale of a Tub*, "This Tub I will have capt with paper: A fine oild Lantern-paper, that we use." Intereſting is it to note that the Banqueting House was consumed by fire in 1619 because "the device of the Masque, all of oiled paper and dry fir," got ignited.[3] This lantern-paper may, of course, have sometimes been subſtituted for the glasses of coloured liquid, but its general use muſt have been for the conſtruƈtion of certain scenic effeƈts. Of it may have been made the "pleasant Cloud" of *Cælum Britannicum* which was "bright and transparent." There was, too, a "bright cloud" in *Chloridia*, while in *Tempe Reſtored* "appear'd a brightnesse, full of small ſtarres, that inviron'd the top of the Chariot, ſtriking a light round about it." The description of *Salmacida Spolia* specifically mentions the glory surrounding the queen: "From over her head were

[1] *Vite de' più eccellenti pittori, scultori, e architetti* (Milan, 1809), vi, 60–61.
[2] *Brief Lives*, ed. Andrew Clark (Oxford, 1898), ii, 10.   [3] J. Nichols, *The Progresses of James the Firſt*, iii, 523.

darted lightsome Rayes that illuminated her seat and all the Ladies about her participated more or lesse of that light."

Moon effects, of course, were closely associated with these. "The Moone began to shew" at one corner of the scene in *Oberon*; in *The Vision of Delight*, too, it rises; in *Beauty*, personified, it rode in the clouds; and in *The Triumph of Peace* a "new moon" appeared, "but with a faint light by the approach of the morning." The sunrise was shown in *Tempe Restored*, while in *Luminalia* "the Heaven began to bee enlightned as before the Sunne rising." A sunset similarly was simulated in *Middle Temple*. Presumably the "sodaine flash of lightning" which startled the characters in *Tethys' Festival* was contrived by the means referred to in Serlio's *Architettura*.[1] This consisted of a bowl filled with sulphur; the top of the bowl had many small holes in it, and in the centre a large one wherein a candle was fixed; by shaking this instrument up and down the sulphur was made to fly out and ignite. Another device mentioned by Serlio demanded the drawing of a thin wire over part of the stage; down this might be run a squib covered with gold foil.

The calico and oiled paper, naturally, were used for other things than clouds. In *Beauty* there was "a tralucent *Pillar*, shining with severall colour'd lights." This was, in all probability, transparent, although in Ongaro's *L'Alceo* (1613) the columns gleamed like rubies and diamonds "because of the mirrors and talc"—evidently attached to them. We definitely know, however, that the "gates and walls" of Oberon's palace "were transparent."

From the evidence before us we must believe that the majority of the lights in the English masques were concealed from the eyes of the audience. It is true that in *Lord Hay's Masque* "flowrie branches with lights in them" adorned Flora's bower, and that "every personage and beast" set to embellish the scene of *Flowers* "did hold a torchet burning that gave light and lustre to the whole fabrique"; but these were no doubt exceptions. Save for the lights carried by the torch-bearers the illumination seems to have been "secret." [2]

That it was not ineffective is proved by the comment of the Venetian ambassador after he had attended *The Masque of Beauty*, but by what strange miracle the stage-hands, Italian and English alike, contrived to prevent conflagrations among their wooden frames and oiled paper baffles the imagination. When we think of the hundreds of flimsy glass lamps, of the flaring torches, and of the ambitious effects aimed at, we can only wonder that any of these spectacles reached a happy conclusion. "One spark from a lamp," as Zuccaro declared, "might bring all to ruin." The stage-directors were daring, and the audiences certainly were more phlegmatic than audiences of to-day would be likely to prove if confronted by the same conditions. In his life of G. L. Bernini a characteristic anecdote is related by the historian Baldinucci.[3] The artist was directing a play and, for comic relief, caused a clown to come on stage behind a *carro carnevalesco*. This clown carried a torch,

> which repeatedly he beat against one of the wings. . . . Those who were not in the know cried out loudly to him to stop lest he should set fire to the whole scene, and, just when the audience had become frightened both by his actions and the cries, suddenly the setting was caused, by artifice, to burst into flame. Such terror seized upon the spectators that they had to be prevented (by the exposing of the trick) from immediately dashing out of the theatre. When this was over, another noble and lovely scene took its place.

One might hardly dare to hope that in a modern playhouse such an easy solution would have been found for a similar "trick." A Renaissance audience was familiarized to dangers and avid of all things strange or beautiful; for inconvenience and hazards endured it counted "a noble and lovely scene" full recompense.

---

[1] Sir E. K. Chambers, *The Elizabethan Stage*, iv, 365.   [2] *Supra*, p. 136.
[3] F. Baldinucci, *Notizie de' professori del disegno* (Florence, 1774), xx, 147.

V

THE GAUDY SCENES

THE masque was, of course, a highly specialized and peculiar form of entertainment, strictly associated with princely diversions and sponsored by a royal treasury. In so far the scenic methods which have been described and analysed above remain outside the sphere of that playhouse which produced and encouraged Shakespeare and his fellows. A connexion, however, does exist between the courtly and the popular. The actors themselves were frequently called upon to share in Whitehall's spectacles, and some at least of the courtiers were part of London's regular theatre-going public. In view of this, it becomes important to inquire whether those devices which Inigo Jones had made familiar in the Banqueting House succeeded in finding their way within the walls of the commercial theatres of that time. That literary elements of the masque were taken over and incorporated in ordinary plays we know; [1] was there a corresponding utilization of scenic elements derived from the same source?

Already it has been observed that the preparation of scenery was not confined to masque productions. Among the court performances already examined several were of plays—a French pastoral, *Florimène*, and *The Shepherd's Paradise*. At Oxford, too, it was a drama which gave occasion for what seems to have been the first introduction of *periaktoi* to the English stage. These few references are by no means all that may be brought forward, and it is imperative now to pass briefly in review the further evidence adducible concerning the utilization of settings for entertainments of a directly dramatic kind and particularly of such as were displayed in the public playhouses.

STRODE AND CARTWRIGHT

If Oxford aided us in 1604 by presenting a record of a play in which turning scenes were employed, in 1636 it again comes to our assistance with description of a performance wherein is to be found the earliest certain reference to flat wings. The play was William Strode's *The Floating Island*, presented on August 29, 1636, and the account of it we owe to Anthony à Wood. The stage, says this memorialist,

> had on it three or four openings on each side thereof, and partitions between them, much resembling the desks or studies in a Library, out of which the Actors issued forth. The said partitions they could draw in and out at their pleasure upon a sudden, and thrust out new in their places according to the nature of the Screen, whereon were represented Churches, Dwelling-houses, Palaces, etc. which for its variety bred very great admiration. Over all was delicate painting, resembling the Sky, Clouds, etc. At the upper end a great fair shut[ter?] of two leaves that opened and shut without any visible help. Within which was set forth the emblem of the whole Play in a very sumptuous manner. Therein was the perfect resemblance of the billows of the Sea rolling, and an artificial Island, with Churches and Houses waving up and down and floating, as also rocks, trees and hills. Many other fine pieces of work and Landscapes did also appear at sundry openings thereof, and a Chair also seen to come gliding on the Stage without any visible help.[2]

[1] P. Reyer, pp. 497–498, gives a long list of the chief plays in which masques were inserted. The influence of the masque on literature forms a major part of Enid Welsford's study. Alfred Harbage, in *Cavalier Drama* (New York, 1936), discusses briefly the introduction of scenery in productions of plays between 1630 and 1640.

[2] *The History and Antiquities of the University of Oxford*, ed. J. Gutch (1796), II, i, 409.

With this description may be compared the (unfortunately scanty) stage directions in the printed text of the play itself. Wood's artificial island was evidently the scene set for the prologue. This changed to "the Court of Prudentius" for Act I, and in the second act to "Fancies Court." The first of these probably showed an inner room, since, we are informed, Prudentius enters "from the Bedchamber." For the beginning of the third act there is no indicative scene direction, although here was introduced a short inset masque presenting Morpheus and six dreams. At Scene v, however, "The Scene turns to feilds, walkes & scattered houses," followed in Act V by "the house of Despair." Apparently towards the end of the play there was a return to "Prudentius his Court" and a final vision of the island.

"All these representations," remarks Wood, were "the first (as I have been informed) that were used on the English stage." His information undoubtedly was mistaken, but the facts that he records have paramount importance. A careful examination of his words demonstrates clearly that the effects must have been secured by means of the regular flat wings already referred to. The old-type Serlian wings were not drawn 'in and out,' and hardly would have been likely to suggest to Wood's mind study desks. Obviously the model he thought of was Duke Humphrey's Library, in the Bodleian. Standing at the entrance and looking down, one may even to-day see the likeness to a stage with rows of wings at each side and maybe an inner room at the rear.

On the same occasion as when *The Floating Island* was performed students of Christ Church undertook the production of another drama—*The Royal Slave*, by William Cartwright. This too had scenic embellishments; "within the shuts," Wood tells us,[1] "were seen a curious Temple, and the Sun shining over it, delightful forests also and other prospects." Within these "great shuts . . . were seen villages and men visibly appearing in them, going up and down, here and there about their business." Inigo Jones in this apparently displayed to the full his "great wit." The printed text of the play happily preserves some record of the scenery thus displayed. In it Cartwright has noted eight "Appearances," a word which seemingly is related to the Spanish *apariencia*, technically employed for a scenic perspective.[2] The first of these, designed for the prologue, was " a Temple of the Sun," the second (for Act I) "a City in the front and a Prison on the side," the third (for Act II) "a stately Palace," evidently practicable in part since during the action Atossa appears "above." Another change of scene does not occur until the third scene of Act IV, when "a Wood" is shown, followed at the beginning of Act V by "A Castle," on the walls of which several characters are "discover'd." "The Court again" is shown for Act V, Scene v, and at Scene vii "the Temple" is "again discover'd" with "an Altar"; while the final "appearance" is "the Sun eclipsed and a showr of rain dashing out the fire."

That Cartwright was deliberately writing with scenery in mind is made evident by an examination of his play, and another drama, *The Lady-Errant*, probably never acted, equally shows him conscious of the possibilities inherent in the new method. This tragi-comedy had a scene of a "Myrtle Grove," which featured, as later stage directions show, a number of separate trees, no doubt presented in the form of wings. The interest of these two productions, however, is not exhausted when we have outlined the sets designed for each. Well known is the fact that the Queen so admired Jones's scenery that she asked the Chancellor to cause the stage equipment to be forwarded to her in London, "Whereupon the Chancellor caused the Cloaths and Perspectives of the Stage to be sent to Hampton Court in a Waggon," at the same time desiring of the King and Queen "that neither the Play, or Cloaths, nor Stage, might come into the hands and use of the common Players abroad." The proviso is definite in its terms, and demonstrates immediately that some public

---

[1] II, i, 413.

[2] Furttenbach frequently uses the term *aparenza* in this sense; the adjectival form, *apparentes*, is employed by Guido Ubaldo in his Latin treatise on perspective (*Perspectivæ libri sex* (Pesaro, 1600)) in the sense of 'perspectively depicted.'

theatres at least possessed stages which might on occasion be suited to the presentation thereon of painted scenery. In our further examination of various plays it must be our endeavour to find out how far such possibilities had been realized.

Nabbes and Brome

Among the most interesting plays for our present purpose are those of Thomas Nabbes. His *Covent Garden*, acted by the Queen's company in 1632, specifically mentions "The Scœne COVENT-GARDEN," and throughout the text the characters are bidden to enter or leave "by the right SCŒNE," "by the left SCŒNE," or "by the middle SCŒNE." What precisely this signifies we cannot tell. It may be that the reference to Covent Garden means nothing, and that the various "Scœnes" were nothing but the entrance to the inner stage and the two side-doors. Stage directions of the kind, however, are peculiar, and when we find Nabbes definitely making use of the new scenery in later plays we wonder whether perhaps he had not in view here something in the nature of a painted setting. His *Hannibal and Scipio*, performed by the Queen's company at Drury Lane in 1635, leaves no doubt in our minds. Definitely the prologue informs us that

> The places sometimes chang'd too for the Scene,
> Which is translated as the music playes
> Betwixt the acts.

The five sections of the play are duly headed "The Scene *Capua*," "The Scene, the Court of *Syphax* in *Cyrtha*," "The Scene *Vtica*," "The Scene *Carthage*," and "The Scene *Bythinia*."

This interest in scenery finds expression about the same time in a masque-like play which Nabbes had performed at the private theatre in Salisbury Court.[1] *Microcosmus* boasted a "Front" or proscenium arch just like the masque at court—

> of a workmanship proper to the fancy of the rest, adorn'd with brasse figures of Angels and Divels, with severall inscriptions: The Title in an Escocheon supported by an Angell and a Divell. Within the arch a continuing perspective of ruines, which is drawne still before the other scenes whilst they are varied.

This verb "drawne" has been taken by several to indicate that there was a curtain with ruins painted upon it, the curtain being drawn to conceal changes of scene. Such an interpretation is extremely doubtful. In the first place, no other instance of a similar use of the front curtain is known to us, and, secondly, no first scene is described as being revealed by the removing of the curtain. We are, it seems, forced to believe that the scene of ruins was made up of Serlian wings which remained in position throughout the course of the performance. It was, in fact, the same as the "standing scene" in *Florimène*. The next stage direction is, accordingly, for "The second Scene . . . a perspective of clouds." Later, "during the following Song . . . the third Scene is discover'd, being a pleasant arbour, with perspectives behind it, of a magnifique building." A fourth scene "is suddainly discover'd, being a Rock, with a spring of water issuing out of it; at the foot thereof a cave." Finally, "a glorious throne" is revealed as a "last Scene."[2]

Perhaps Nabbes was the first playwright consciously to write with scenery in view. At any rate, his next drama, *The Unfortunate Mother*, published in 1640 but never acted, contains directions indicative of the author's desires:

---

[1] *Microcosmus* was printed in 1637, and had been entered in the Stationers' Register on August 6 of the preceding year. Some slight doubt exists concerning the scenery for this production. The title-page states that the play was "presented with generall liking at the private house in Salisbury Court" and that it was now being printed "according to the intentions of the Authour." The second phrase might apply either to the text or to the stage directions noted above.

[2] On the introduction of the masque to the public theatres see W. J. Lawrence's essay in *Pre-Restoration Stage Studies*, pp. 325–339. There he argues that these were originally brought on during Lent by actors other than the regular companies of comedians.

THE GAUDY SCENES

The first Act, and first Scene: The Scene being the Presence.
The Scene being the Dutchesse Chamber.
The Scene being the Presence.
The Scene being the Gallery.
The Scene the Grove.

This evidence presented in the plays of Nabbes finds corroboration in those of Richard Brome. In 1638 Brome, in producing *The Court Beggar*, caused his prologue to declare that

> no gaudy Sceane
> Shall give instructions what his plot doth meane—

a certain indication that scenery was at that time known in other dramas, and one, too, that does not stand alone.

William Prynne, writing his *Histriomastix* in 1633, varies Richard Brome's phrase in speaking of the "Pompous and stately Showes and Scenes" used by the actors, while Newcastle a few years later referred in *The Country Captain* (Blackfriars, 1640) to "a glorious painted Scene with various doores" as if that were a thing by no means unfamiliar to contemporary audiences. The word 'scene,' of course, held a variety of senses in the seventeenth century. Generally it meant simply a piece of stage action; sometimes, as in *The White Ætheopian*,[1] it meant no more than 'stage.' Brome's "gaudy Sceane," however, is sufficiently explicit. It can signify nothing but a painted setting. In the prologue written for the same author's *The Antipodes*, performed at Salisbury Court in 1638, the utilization of such settings is again referred to:

> Opinion, which our *Author* cannot court
>   (For the deare daintinesse of it), has, of late,
> From the old way of *Playes* possest a Sort
>   Only to run to those that carry state
> In Scene magnificent and language high,
>   And Cloathes worth all the rest.

The "Scene magnificent," we may believe, was something not uncommon. Perhaps Brome himself had to fall. At least, in *A Jovial Crew*, acted at Drury Lane in 1641, Springlove "opens the Scene; the Beggars are discovered in their Postures"; and later "Randal opens the Scene. The Beggars discovered at their Feast." It is possible, however, that here "scene" indicates only a curtain.[2]

STAGE DIRECTIONS IN PLAYS

With these indications before us, conclusive and definite in their terms, many other stage directions in scattered plays assume specific importance. Even in Beaumont and Fletcher's early *The Maid's Tragedy*, acted at Blackfriars about 1611, an inserted masque makes Eolus enter "out of a Rock." One may suspect that "the Black-house" and "the Whitehouse" of Middleton's *A Game at Chess* (Globe, 1624) were not left entirely to the imagination; the same play introduces "An Altar . . . with Tapers on it, and Images about it," these images later moving "in a Dance." Unfortunately, there is no way of discovering when or where appeared Beaumont's *Four Plays, or Moral Representations, in One*, among the most interesting scenically of all seventeenth-century dramas. There can be no doubt that this play, printed in the folio of 1647, was written and performed considerably over twenty years before the date of publication.[3] That the theatre used was a public playhouse

---

[1] Although in this play (Harl. MS. 7313) there was evidently a "city gate" and a "cave."
[2] See Ashley H. Thorndike, *Shakespeare's Theater* (New York, 1916), p. 80.
[3] W. J. Lawrence, *The Date of Four Plays in One* (*Times Literary Supplement*, December 11, 1919), argues that it was composed about 1613. This may be true, but the evidence adduced is inconclusive.

seems indicated by several references to doors and by stage directions calling for the entry of characters "above." On the other hand, scenic display of a masque-like nature is freely called for. "A mist riseth" and "the rocks remove" towards the beginning of the first drama. Later this rock reappears when "They carry *Anthropos* to a Rock and fall a digging"; "*Plutus* strikes" it, "and flames flie out." A trap is used when "*Plutus* stamps" and "*Labour* rises," while several deities—Diana, Jupiter, Mercury, and Cupid—descend. During the course of the action two chariots are brought in, one "drawn by two Moors" and the other "with the person of *Time* sitting in it, drawn by four persons, representing Hours." Most significant of all is a stage direction at the close, reading, "One half of a cloud drawn. Singers are discovered: then the other half drawn. *Jupiter* seen in glory." If nothing else, these references prove conclusively that on occasion the ordinary public stages were capable of introducing something of that scenic display which had been made familiar in the productions at Whitehall. *The Two Noble Kinsmen*, acted at Blackfriars in 1613, brings in a certain amount of similar material. There characters "exeunt towards the Temple," Palamon and Arcite "enter . . . in prison," Palamon comes "from the Bush," and at the end an altar is introduced; under this altar a hind vanishes "and in the place ascends a Rose-Tree." A manuscript play, *The Queen of Corsica* (1642), has two references to "A Wood," and several plays refer to the use of an "arbour."

Several references to a "Cave" occur in *The Jew's Tragedy* (c. 1638), by William Hemings, where too are "an Alter and Tapers set." In this play occurs a stage direction—"The Temple fir'd"—which recalls those conflagration scenes so beloved of the Italian Renaissance. "An Altar covered with white" figures in Ford's *The Broken Heart* (Blackfriars, c. 1629), while in Shirley's *St Patrick for Ireland* (Dublin, 1637) there are an altar and "two Idolls," one of which is caused to move. *The Sun's Darling* (Whitehall and Drury Lane, 1624), by Ford and Dekker, introduced another altar and presented a scene where the sun became "clowded." In the dialogue of Henry Killigrew's *The Conspiracy* (Blackfriars, 1635) a temple is mentioned.

With such references may be taken a sentence from Heywood's *The Royal King and Loyal Subject*. The prologue to this play declares:

> To give content to this most curious Age
> The gods themselves we have brought downe to the Stage
> And figur'd them in Planets.

"Plannets," we recall, were also used in the same author's *Love's Mistress* (c. 1634). They may have been cut-outs or else have had something to do with effects of illumination. The use of light, as is well known, was not by any means neglected on the public stage, even at an early period. Peele's *The Battle of Alcazar* (1589) had its blazing star, and in *The True Tragedie* (c. 1590) "three sunnes" appeared "in the air." "Artificial lightning in their Heavens" was an old love of the professional actors.[1]

When we survey this evidence relating to the introduction of scenery on public stages we may turn with renewed interest to those settings which were given to similar plays at court. For a particular reason the designs prepared by Inigo Jones for *The Shepherd's Paradise* in 1633 have been already dealt with;[2] here may be noted the fact that for this pastoral is also extant an interesting series of costume sketches (Figs. 95–100). Whether *The Faithful Shepherdess*, when acted before

---

[1] In view of doubts concerning the performance of William Percy's plays, these are not dealt with here. On their stage directions see G. F. Reynolds, *William Percy and his Plays* (Modern Philology, xii (1914), 241–250), and various articles by Madeleine Hope Dodds—*William Percy and Charles Fitzjeffrey* (Notes and Queries, clx (1931), 420–422), *William Percy and James I* (id., clxi (1931), 13–14), *William Percy's "Aphrodysial"* (id., 237–240, 257–261), *A Dreame of a Drye Yeare* (Journal of English and Germanic Philology, xxxii (1933), 172–195). In these articles evidence is brought forward to demonstrate that Percy's peculiar dramas actually did receive professional performance.

[2] See the reference to these in Sir Henry Herbert's office-book (ed. J. Q. Adams, New Haven, 1917). The costume designs for this performance are noted in *Designs*, Nos. 168–179 (Pl. XXII, A).

Fig. 95. BASILINO IN "THE
SHEPHERD'S PARADISE" (1633)
Inigo Jones. Chatsworth (*Designs*, No. 171).
Copyright of his Grace the Duke of Devonshire.

Fig. 96. BELLESA IN "THE
SHEPHERD'S PARADISE" (1633)
Inigo Jones. Chatsworth (*Designs*, No. 169).
Copyright of his Grace the Duke of Devonshire.

Fig. 97. AGENOR DISGUISED AS A
PILGRIM IN "THE SHEPHERD'S
PARADISE" (1633)
Inigo Jones. Chatsworth (*Designs*, No. 172).
Copyright of his Grace the Duke of Devonshire.

Fig. 98. THE KING OF VAL-
ENTIA IN "THE SHEP-
HERD'S PARADISE" (1633)
Inigo Jones. Chatsworth (*Designs*,
No. 177). Copyright of his Grace
the Duke of Devonshire.

royalty on January 6, 1634, was similarly adorned with scenes we do not know, but certainly the actors wore "the clothes the Queene had given Taylor the year before" from the stock prepared for Montague's pastoral.[1]

Fig. 99. FIDAMIRA IN "THE SHEPHERD'S PARADISE" (1633)

Inigo Jones. Chatsworth (*Designs*, No. 176).
Copyright of his Grace the Duke of Devonshire.

Fig. 100. THE HIGH PRIEST IN "THE SHEPHERD'S PARADISE"

Inigo Jones. Chatsworth (*Designs*, No. 179).
Copyright of his Grace the Duke of Devonshire.

"THE QUEEN OF ARAGON" AND "THE PASSIONATE LOVERS"

Another note by Herbert records the presentation of Habington's *Cleodora* or *The Queen of Aragon* at Whitehall: "It was performed by my lord's servants out of his own family and his charge in the cloathes and sceanes, which were very rich and curious."[2]   This was in 1640.   Three designs in the Inigo Jones collection unquestionably belong to this production.   The first (Fig. 101) is inscribed, "Cleodora . . . first sceane a shutter of a fortified Towne & a Campe a farr off."   The second, by John Webb, has a similar inscription, "Cleodora . . . 2 sceane of Releive."[3]   Apparently, from the use of the word "relieve," we have here a cut-out with the hall seen through pillars.   The dimensions are given as 13 feet by 11½ feet.   By John Webb also is the third design (Fig. 102), inscribed, "3 sceane.   A shutter with statues & figures a farr of."   This too has pillars at each side with a low terrace and balustrade in front; beyond is the perspective of a large loggia or gallery.

The design [4] originally assumed to have been executed for the proscenium and first scene of this

[1] J. Q. Adams, *The Dramatic Records of Sir Henry Herbert*, p. 53.   [2] *Id.*, p. 58.
[3] *Designs*, No. 363.   [4] No. 361; reproduced in *British Drama* (1932), p. 106.

Fig. 101. A Fortified Town in "The Queen of Aragon" (1640)

Inigo Jones. Chatsworth (*Designs*, No. 362). Inscribed, "Cleodora . . . firſt ſceane a shutter of a fortified Towne & a Campe a farr off." Copyright of his Grace the Duke of Devonshire.

Fig. 102. A Courtyard in "The Queen of Aragon" (1640)

John Webb. Chatsworth (*Designs*, No. 364). Inscribed, "3 ſceane. A shutter with ſtatues & figures a farr of."

play must, it seems, be denied to it. Jones has written on this "for yᵉ cockpitt for my lo Chãaberalin 1639." One might assume that the Cockpit referred to was the Cockpit-in-Court, but the sketch hardly agrees with the plan, recently discovered at Worcester College,[1] evidently made by John Webb. Here there is a Palladian façade, modelled on that of the Teatro Olimpico, with five door-ways, none of which would prove large enough for the introduction of scenery. The "Cockpit" drawing must belong to another theatre. That theatre may have been the one shown in a second plan preserved at Worcester College and certainly the work of Inigo Jones himself.[2] This shows a stage 43 feet wide, with a façade likewise reminiscent of the Teatro Olimpico, but with a large, arched central opening (24 feet by 15 feet 6 inches) allowing for the introduction of pairs of Serlian wings.

Fig. 103. A Wood in "The Passionate Lovers"
(1638)

Inigo Jones. Chatsworth (*Designs*, No. 319). Inscribed, "The Wood 6 sceane
. . . the wood a shutter in yᵉ 2ᵈ part of Mr Lodowicks play." Copyright
of his Grace the Duke of Devonshire.

The connexion between the arched proscenium of the "Cockpit" design and this seems likely, and, if so, might not the suggestion be hazarded that the theatre plan may have been executed for the Cockpit in Drury Lane, D'Avenant's playhouse? Assuredly it is a puzzle to determine what association the Lord Chamberlain should have had with a public theatre; but plays were given with scenes at Drury Lane, and in 1661, when the French actors presented there *Le mariage d'Orphée et d'Eurydice*, the effects seem to have been of a very spectacular sort, proving that the stage had scenic possibilities.

One other play is represented among the entertainments for which Jones executed scenery. *The Passionate Lovers*, by Lodowick Carlell, was presented at court in the year 1638. Fig. 103,

---

[1] W. G. Keith, *John Webb and the Court Theatre of Charles II* (*Architectural Review*, lvii (1925), 50–55), argues that this was the work of John Webb after the Restoration. The plan was originally published by Hamilton Bell in *The Architectural Record* (New York, xxxiii (1913), 258–264). There is a reproduction of it in *The Development of the Theatre*, Fig. 149. Eleanore Boswell, *The Restoration Court Stage (1660–1702)* (1932), pp. 11–12, accepts the attribution to Webb, but deems it must be pre-Restoration in date. See also J. Q. Adams, *Shakespearean Playhouses* (New York, 1917), pp. 393–396.

[2] Reproduced in *The Development of the Theatre*, Fig. 150. W. G. Keith, *A Theatre Project of Inigo Jones* (*The Burlington Magazine*, xxxi (1917), 61–70).

showing a grove, is inscribed, "The Wood 6 sceane . . . the wood a shutter in ye 2^d part of Mr Lodowicks play." [1]

SETTINGS FOR A PLAY AT COURT

Reviewing this record of scenic display, unquestionably only a tithe of the material which has been irretrievably lost, we must find an added interest in several unidentified designs in the Chatsworth collection. The first of these is the well-known "Tragic Scene," [2] named so on the sketch

Fig. 104. A Palace
Inigo Jones. Chatsworth (*Designs*, No. 371). Inscribed, "i A Pallas."
Copyright of his Grace the Duke of Devonshire.

Fig. 105. An Army
Inigo Jones. Chatsworth (*Designs*, No. 372). Inscribed, "An Army."
Copyright of his Grace the Duke of Devonshire.

itself—"The Tragick a standing seene y^e first sceane"—clearly inspired by Italian efforts to create a "Vitruvian" set. For what purpose this was made we cannot tell, but evident care was bestowed on it, as testimony remains in a set of four studies for the figures represented on the proscenium frame [3] and also in a sketch which evidently presents a variant of the scene itself. [4] With these in some way are associated eight or nine other designs. [5] The connexion seems established by a list which appears on the *verso* of one of the "Tragic Scene" studies; [6] this reads:

[1] One wonders whether *Designs*, No. 396, and the other sketch, marked "the seventh sceane" (No. 397 (Pl. XXXII, B)), may not have some connexion with this production.
[2] *Designs*, No. 365 (Pl. XLVIII).   [3] *Id.*, Nos. 366–369.   [4] *Id.*, No. 370.   [5] *Id.*, Nos. 371–378.   [6] No. 366.

shuters: the comon sceane

a wrak & port, 1.	cabinett, 1.
prinses hir cha[m]ber, 1.	the dreame, 1.
a desart, 1.	cabinett varied, 1.
too campes, 1.	a cattafalk.
prinses cha[m]ber, 1.	
the kinges cha[m]ber or prospectt, 1.	

This list clearly finds association with some of the other sketches referred to. Three of these go together, since each is framed in a similar arched proscenium. The first (Fig. 104) recalls the central

Fig. 106. A Prison
Inigo Jones. Chatsworth (*Designs*, No. 373). Inscribed, " 3 A Prison."
Copyright of his Grace the Duke of Devonshire.

structure of the "Tragic Scene," but the resemblance may not be of any significance. It represents "A Pallas" (palace). "An Army" is shown in the second (Fig. 105), and "A prison" in the third (Fig. 106). It is to be observed that these, save possibly for the "army," do not correspond with the entries in the list. The suggestion might be made that they belong to the same series as that represented in the "Cockpit" drawing.[1]

[1] Eleanore Boswell, *The Restoration Court Stage*, p. 55, suggests that they may belong to the original set of scenes painted for the Cockpit-in-Court in 1632–33.

Fig. 107. A Court Room

Design by an unknown artist, probably Italian.   Chatsworth (*Designs*, No. 6*).
Copyright of his Grace the Duke of Devonshire.

Fig. 108. A Bedchamber

Inigo Jones.   Chatsworth (*Designs*, No. 374).   Inscribed, "the bed in the
inner cha[m]br."   Copyright of his Grace the Duke of Devonshire.

Something different enters in with Fig. 108. This slight sketch, executed in black lead, displays an interior, described as "the bed in the inner cha[m]br." That it, like those which follow, was intended for a rectangular proscenium is obvious. A second sketch [1] is closely allied, although it has not the bed; its inscription reads "ye 4th sceane a Chamber—a shutter sett back & so y^t one might passe by." "A desert place" is revealed in Fig. 109, a design which must be taken together with another which reproduces some of the same details.[2] Finally, one comes to Fig. 112, which is "the dreame of relievo 5 sceane" with deities "of past bord finto," including "pallas on a Whight

Fig. 109. A DESERT PLACE

Inigo Jones. Chatsworth (*Designs*, No. 376). Inscribed, "a desert place." Copyright of his Grace the Duke of Devonshire.

Cloude wch turnes to a roke, a laurell in hir hande." Of the entries in the list we have thus represented two chambers, a desert, and a dream.

Presumably these were made for the performance of some play, but to determine which particular drama is now almost impossible. One suggestion might very tentatively be put forward— that these scenes fit rather well the localities of *Cymbeline*. A king's chamber would be required there, a princess's bedchamber where one might pass by, two camps, and a dream scene when Posthumus has his vision.[3] No record exists of any production of *Cymbeline* with scenery at this time, but Herbert has recorded in his office book a court performance of the play just about the time when spectacular productions of *The Faithful Shepherdess* and *The Shepherd's Paradise* were delighting audiences at court.[4] Whether or not we indeed possess here the first recorded scenery prepared for

[1] *Designs*, No. 375.   [2] *Id.*, No. 377.

[3] Although, of course, it is Jupiter, not Pallas, who appears in the vision; the locality in *Cymbeline* is a prison, whereas the design shows an open place with trees at the sides.

[4] J. Q. Adams, *The Dramatic Records of Sir Henry Herbert*, p. 53.

150

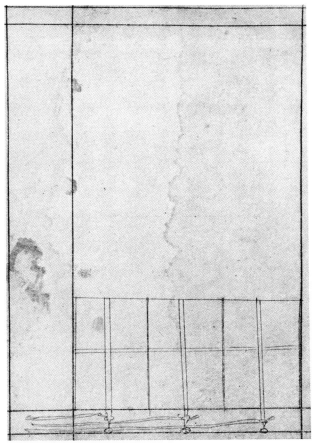

Fig. 110. Section of the Stage for
"Candy Restored" (1641)
Henry E. Huntington Library.

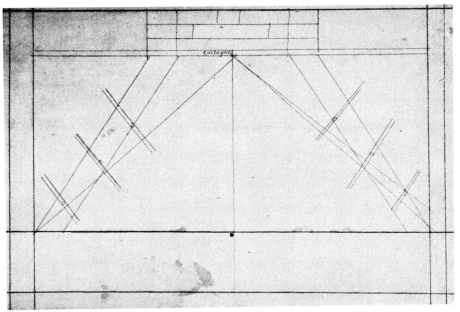

Fig. 111. Ground-plan of the Stage for
"Candy Restored" (1641)
Henry E. Huntington Library.

the performance of a Shakespearian drama, at least in these designs we have a series of sketches which are among the most interesting the seventeenth century has to give us.

Not the least part of their interest derives from their subjects. A fact not always fully recognized is that practically all the scenes presented in the theatres between 1600 and 1650 were outdoor settings. The tradition, of course, was set in the mid-sixteenth century by the Serlian tragic, comic, and pastoral scenes. True, the medieval theatre had made fairly plentiful use of 'interiors,' and during the early days of Renaissance enthusiasm for the drama at Ferrara and at Rome the little curtained

Fig. 112. A Dream

Inigo Jones. Chatsworth (*Designs*, No. 378). Inscribed, "the dreame of relievo 5 sceane . . . pallas on a Whight Cloude wch turnes to a roke, a laurell in hir hande . . . of past bord finto." Copyright of his Grace the Duke of Devonshire.

alcoves which corresponded to the medieval 'houses' frequently were opened to reveal furniture and windows within.[1] Since 1550, however, much had happened in the realm of scenic display; ideals of a unified perspective vista, of verisimilitude, and of classical imitation, coalesced to produce the stock outdoor sets. Two or three countries in Europe alone retained the interiors. Spain had them, revealed by the drawing of traverse curtains;[2] in Portugal, too, Leone di Somi had become acquainted with the practice, and, familiar as he was with Italian example, saw fit to condemn it. In his *Dialogues* the problem of the fourth wall is, for the first time, brought to our notice.[3] Above all, they were known in England. Faust's study and Prospero's cave were both presented by the drawing of a traverse in front of the inner stage. Perhaps we should not err in assuming that the early appearance of interiors among the designs of Inigo Jones was due to that artist's familiarity with the current stage practice of his own time and land. In any event, it is important to recognize that we have here some of the earliest interior settings which the modern stage has to offer us.

The Elizabethan inner stage comes once more into the picture when we turn to a stage-plan and cross-section which forms part of a manuscript play, *Candy Restored*, now preserved in the Henry E. Huntington Library (Figs. 110, 111).[4] These show an interesting arrangement of three pairs of flat wings with, in place of the familiar shutters, a curtain or traverse concealing the 'scene.' The plan suggests nothing so much as the typical Elizabethan stage roughly adapted for the new scenic devices. The side-wings are peculiarly placed, and it is somewhat difficult to determine precisely how they were originally set. Luckily an almost contemporary illustration of a Prodigal Son play seems to give us aid (Fig. 113). We may believe that the three wings were set almost in one straight line on each side of the stage, leading the eye back to the 'scene'[5] in the rear—a practice hardly differing from that in *Florimène*, where the shutters changed while the front wings remained unaltered. The pivots permitted the wings, of course, to present two separate appearances, although, strangely enough, similar utilization of combined flats and *periaktoi* is exceedingly rare in this period. Only

[1] See *The Development of the Theatre* (second edition), pp. 83–84.
[2] H. A. Rennert, *The Spanish Stage in the Time of Lope de Vega* (New York, 1909), pp. 84–86.
[3] See *The Development of the Theatre* (second edition), p. 254.
[4] My attention was drawn to these by Mr Clifford Leech. See *The Times Literary Supplement*, August 15, 1936.
[5] It is interesting to note that a similar division of the stage seems to have been made in *Microcosmus*. In Act II some characters "descend from the Scene," evidently on to the fore-stage.

one author seems to have referred to the stage method used in *Candy Restored*.   Jean Dubreuil, in his *Perspective pratique* (1642–49),[1] indicates that the device was not unknown in France during the mid-years of the seventeenth century.

[1] Vol. iii, Pratique XI, 103.

Fig. 113.   A Seventeenth-century Stage

Engraving in Johan Amos Comenius, *Orbis sensualium pictus*, translated by Charles Hoole (London, 1658).

VI

COURT HIEROGLYPHICKS

IN the description of the proscenium prepared for D'Avenant's *Salmacida Spolia* it was indicated that various figures were presented "with significant signes to expresse their severall qualities."

"Significant signes"—the phrase is a key by which we may unlock the true secrets of those spectacles which so delighted the courtiers and their lords. This vast effort of the poets and the painters was more than a thing of immediate delight, a trivial titillation of the senses, to be forgotten when the last candles guttered and the palace halls had grown still. The masques enshrined a philosophy of life; in them the conceptions of poetry took visible form, and the symbols through which current ideas became manifest assumed shapes of material loveliness.

EMBLEMS AND IMPRESE

This was the age of the emblem-book and the *impresa*. From Alciati to Quarles men delighted in devising or in looking upon allegorical designs with their appropriate mottoes. For Francis Manners, Earl of Rutland, an *impresa* borne at a tourney in 1613 was conceived by no less persons than William Shakespeare and the actor Richard Burbage,[1] while Ben Jonson carried out a similar service for Prince Charles.[2] Intellectual ingenuity was expended on these things, and to them was attached a peculiar emotional significance. The courtly gentlemen took delight in recognizing ideas expressed in symbolic forms and in truncated quotations from classical authors; the attributes of the gods they knew, and of the common personifications; in the motto, Anglicized as the 'word,'[3] they saw either an explanation of the design or else another symbol, not expository, but suggestive of further implications. Hamlet was a typical prince of the Renaissance, and in a moment of crisis nothing seemed to him more fitting than to pull out his table-book and, making as it were an *impresa* of his experience, write down that the "word," or motto, was "Remember me."[4]

It were by no means too much to say that in the masque the fashion for the courtly *impresa* and for the emblem-book reached its completest expression. In the figures which stepped out before Inigo Jones's fantastic settings was incorporated—to use the phrase of Scipione Ammirato—a kind of "cavalier's philosophy."[5] Such things were "Images . . . Representatives of our Notions,"

---

[1] Sir E. K. Chambers, *William Shakespeare* (Oxford, 1930), ii, 253. The tourney took place on March 24, 1613.

[2] *The Works of Ben Jonson*, i, 83.

[3] The Italian *motto* and French *mot* were both used in England. On Hamlet's "word" see *Hamlet*, ed. J. Dover Wilson (Cambridge, 1934), pp. 162–163.

[4] On the emblem literature of this age in general see Mario Praz, *Studi sul concettismo* (Milan, 1934). For the *impresa* may be consulted Abd-el-Kader Salza, *La Letteratura delle 'Imprese' e la fortuna di esse nel 500* (appendix to *Luca Contile, uomo di lettere e negozj del secolo xvi* (Florence, 1903)), G. F. Barwick, *Impresas* (*The Library*, Ser. II, vii (1906), 140–148), and F. Brie, *Shakespeare und die Impresa-Kunst seiner Zeit* (*Shakespeare-Jahrbuch*, l (1914), 9). See also Henry Green, *Shakespeare and the Emblem Writers* (1870). The distinction between the emblem and *impresa* is summarized in the preface to Samuel Daniel's *The Worthy Tract of Paulus Iouius, contayning a Discourse of rare inventions* (1585), sig. * 6 verso and 7 recto: "The mot of an *Impresa* may not exceede three wordes. Emblemes are interpreted by many verses. An *Impresa* is not garnished with many different Images, *Emblemes* are not limited. . . . In *Emblems* is more libertie and fewer laws. *Impreses* manifest the special purpose of Gentlemen in warlike combats or chamber tournaments. *Emblems* are generall conceiptes rather of moral matters then perticulare deliberations."

[5] "Una filosofia del cavaliere," quoted by Mario Praz, p. 38, from *Rota, ovvero dell' imprese* (Naples, 1562).

154

under which were "ingeniously conceal'd the Mysteries of Nature and Philosophy."[1]   In the *impresa* and in the masque alike the quality of *meraviglia*, or wonder, was called for—the exciting of that admiration aimed at in the entire spectacle.   Paolo Giovio[2] legislated learnedly on the proper qualities of these things in terms which might, with but few variations, be applied to the painted figures on the ornaments and to the costumes worn by the actors in Whitehall's entertainments. Beauty above all things was obligatory, for of beauty the Renaissance mind was intoxicate.   Beauty alone, however, might not serve; with it must be borne two elements—a due proportion and an intellectual appeal.   In the *impresa* must reside a harmony of body and soul, emblem and motto evenly balanced in accord.   In it, too, must be a due infusion of thought.   The symbols had to be such as would interest and excite a cultured intelligence—neither obscurely demanding a sibyl's interpretation nor childishly addressing an untutored understanding.   Because Inigo Jones (bereft of the poet's aid) erred in this, Jonson saw fit to gird against his practice of so attiring his "persons as no thought can teach sense what they are."[3]

The audience gathered at Whitehall, trained in the study of emblem and *impresa*, alive to all the "significant signes," can have looked upon the masques as nothing but a series of living emblems or have listened to their verses as aught else than a string of mottoes.   How close the emblem came to the masque is demonstrated in *The Vision of the Twelve Goddesses* when Sibylla takes the "Prospective" glass to look upon the deities.   "Well have mortall men apparelled all the vertues," she is told, "all the graces, all blessings, with that shape wherewith themselves are most delighted and which worke the best motions and best represent the beauty of heavenly powers."   Thereupon the goddesses appear in the guise of living pictures taken from Alciati or another, with a four-line motto appended to each.[4]   In association with the procession of masquers in *Blackness*, too, was directly introduced a series of *imprese*, while Campion's "squares" in *Lords* were equally emblem-like."[5]

These things were, to use Jonson's words, "Court Hieroglyphicks."[6]   Part of the audience's delight in watching the scenes unfold undoubtedly arose from an immediate recognition of certain figures presented in painted form on the 'ornaments' or incorporated materially in the masquers' costumes—part, too, from eager guessing at the purpose of newly invented signs, hitherto unutilized.   When the spectators assembled for D'Avenant's *Britannia Triumphans* and saw at the side of the proscenium

> a woman in a watchet drapery, heightned with silver, on her head a *Corona Rostrata*, with one hand holding the rudder of a ship and in the other a little winged figure with a branch of Palme and a Girland,

how proud and delighted must have been those who, having read Cesare Ripa's *Iconologia*,[7] were able to identify the figure for their neighbours.   In Ripa they would have read that "Vittoria Navale"—naval victory personified—was to be figured as "a winged woman, standing upon the

[1] *Iconologia : or Morall Emblems*, by Cæsar Ripa (1709), "To the Reader."

[2] *Dialogo dell' imprese militari et amorose* (Rome, 1555).   Camden paraphrased these judgments in his *Remains concerning Britain* (1605), ed. 1636, pp. 341–359.   See also *The Art of Making Devises done into English by Tho: Blount Gent.* (1648), translated from Henri Estienne, *L'Art de faire les devises* (Paris, 1645).

[3] *An Expostulation with Inigo Jones* (*Poems*, ed. B. H. Newdigate, p. 296).

[4] In view of the emblematic character of this episode, it is interesting to note the picture in Hermann Hugo's *Pia desideria* (Antwerp, 1624), I, iv, which shows a woman looking through a similar "prospective" glass at figures beyond.   A like emblem was used by Francis Quarles (*Emblemes* (1635), III, iv, 177).   Hugo (III, vi) has another design showing a globe somewhat reminiscent of that in *Hymenæi*. My attention was drawn to these engravings by Mr Gordon Haight, of Yale University.

[5] *Supra*, p. 73.

[6] *An Expostulation with Inigo Jones* (*Poems*, ed. B. H. Newdigate, p. 296).   Jonson, of course, uses the phrase here satirically in allusion to Daniel's remarks in *The Vision of the Twelve Goddesses*.

[7] References to this work are given from the edition published at Rome in 1603.   The English translation (*supra*, note 1) is referred to as *Iconologia* (1709).

prow of a ship, holding a crown in her right hand and a palm in the left." [1] Culture was to be displayed by quickness in appreciation of these things, by the rapid association of symbols elsewhere displayed with those here made manifest. "And who," says Ongaro in his *L'Alceo*, after describing a figure clad in silver, "and who would be so stupid and obtuse as not to recognize, from this pure white dress unmixed with any other colour, that the person is Faith?" For the stupid and obtuse— or, rather, for those without the courtly training—the masques were not intended. Ongaro's sentiment finds echo in one of Dekker's remarks.[2] "Having told you," he says, "that her name was Justice, I hope you will not put me to describe what properties she held in her hands, sithence every painted cloath can informe you."

Many—indeed, most—of the significant signs were derived from classical sources, for humanism had laid its spell upon the world. Jonson and others tire not in quoting authorities for their various devices; anxiously the ancients were ransacked in search of material which might with propriety be wrought into the fabric of the masque. These poets and artists, however, were not humanists only; they were children of the Renaissance whom contemporary invention pleased no less than classic authority. Daniel drew the attention of his auditors to the fact that all his figures were "not drawn in all proportion to the life of antiquity," and boldly declared that he saw no reason why he and his companions might not emancipate their inventions from the "tyrannie" of the ancients and be as free as they to use their own images.[3] From the current emblem-books they selected much, and on their desks lay well-thumbed copies of volumes concerned with the *impresa*. To Ripa's *Iconologia* even Jonson, proudest of all in his classical learning, acknowledged indebtedness, and as we survey the figures introduced into the masques between 1604 and 1640 we encounter instance after instance, not merely of suggestions taken from that book, but of direct and literal borrowings. Thus the proscenium of Townsend's *Tempe Restored* included two statues, representing a man and a woman.[4] The descriptions given of these are almost literal translations from the passages in Ripa relating to "Inventione" (Invention) and "Sapienza" (Knowledge)—"a beautiful woman who bears a pair of wings on her head like Mercury" and "a young man . . . holding in his right hand a burning lamp filled with oil and in his left a book." [5] Similarly in *Salmacida Spolia* we see an old man in a purple robe, "with a heart of gold in a chayne about his necke, figured for Counsell," and immediately recognize Ripa's "Consiglio," "an old man dressed in a dignified costume, dark red in colour, bearing a gold chain from which hangs a heart." [6]

In this world of significant signs every smallest thing bears its message. Material objects assume symbolic value, and in colours secrets are enclosed. A sword, a palm-branch, a crown, a star—these and others indicate specific qualities, while blue and red and green are used with precise significance. Sometimes, it is true, deviations from precise paths were demanded by the necessities of the stage, but in general such erratic procedure can easily be detected. Francis Bacon suggests one reason for departure from stricter ways when he notes that the colours which "shew best by Candlelight are White, Carnation and a kinde of Sea-Water-Greene, and *Oes* or *Spangs* [spangles], as they are of no great Cost, so they are of most Glory." [7] The costumes worn in these masques are to be viewed in the light of a thousand candles, the candlelight itself oftentimes determining the choice of this shade or of that, and always demanding a rich show of spangles to glitter in their reflected rays. Occasionally, too, a queen's complexion may have demanded modification of an artist's conception. In submitting for the eyes of majesty a design representing the dress of Chloris, Inigo Jones

---

[1] Pp. 516–517. "Donna, alata, in piedi sopra un rostro di Nave, nella destra mano tiene una corona e nella sinistra una palma."
[2] *Description of the Entertainment* of 1604 (J. Nichols, *The Progresses of James the First*, i, 369).
[3] *Tethys' Festival.*　　　　　　　　[4] *Supra*, p. 47.
[5] Pp. 240, 441. See *Iconologia* (1709), pp. 42, 67. The wings indicate "*Elevation* of Intellect," while the lamp signifies "the *Light* of the Understanding." "The Book is the *Bible*, where perfect Wisdom is to be learned."
[6] P. 85.　　　　　　　　[7] *A Harmony of the Essays*, ed. Edward Arber (1871), p. 539.

saw fit to append a note declaring that if the Queen desired "to add or alter any thinge" he desired to receive her command. Above all, "the collors ar in hir ma[jesty's] choyse but my oppinion is that severall fresh greenes mixt with gould and siller will bee most propper."[1] Examination of descriptions and designs, however, definitely proves that such variations from established principle were rare. A "cavalier's philosophy" is here—the metaphysics of a court wherein pleasure and virtue occupied twin thrones and Platonic visions vied with the material loveliness of Venus—and its symbolic images demanded, and received, a reverend attention and were carefully adapted to theatrical needs. For such costumes C. F. Ménestrier demanded the satisfaction of four conditions—that they should be symbolically or historically significant, that they should show variety, that the several "entries" of characters should display well-blended colourings, and that the costumes themselves should not hinder the actors' movements—and these, after all, are the essential ideals of the designer of stage costumes.[2]

Fig. 114. Eternity in "La Fenice rinovata" (Fossano, 1644)
Biblioteca Nazionale, Turin.

Eternity and the Stars

Over all the trivial evening's entertainment, flimsy and evanescent yet strangely thoughtful— the brief amusement of a passing hour, yet that to which highest wits and noblest courtiers devoted their energy and their time—stood Eternity, "in a long blew Taffata robe, painted with Starres, and on her head a Crowne"[3]—generally, too, with "a Serpent bent into a circle, with his taile in his mouth,"[4] an emblem noted by Ripa (Fig. 114). The blue of the dress was symbolic, for it represented the infinitude of the heavens. To all airy nymphs this colour was granted, and by a transference of thought it passed on to those figures which revealed the soaring of the spirit into realms metaphysical or the mystic contemplation of the universe.[5] The significance of the painted stars is obvious; the crown testifies to the majesty of this person; while the serpent emblem is one which for generations has denoted the unendingness of time.

Eternity's companion was Saturn,[6] holder, too, of the mystic circle,[7] a heavy old man, slow of

---

[1] *Designs*, No. 97.

[2] *Des Ballets anciens et modernes selon les règles du théâtre* (Paris, 1682), pp. 250–253. He gives suggestions for the costuming of the Seasons, the Winds, Time, Night, Fortune, Destiny, and Love (pp. 254–256).

[3] *Somerset's Masque*. In *Cælum Britannicum* "her Garment was long, of a light blue, wrought over with Stars of gold."

[4] *Cælum Britannicum*.

[5] On the significance of colours during this period see Margaritha Turmann, *Die Farbenbezeichnungen in der Dichtung der englischen Renaissance* (Reval, 1934); blue is discussed at pp. 51–52. Don Cameron Allen has an essay on *Symbolic Color in the Literature of the English Renaissance* (*Philological Quarterly*, xv (1936), 81–90); blue he finds symbolic of truth, hope, and fidelity in love. Notes on colour meanings appear also in M. Channing Linthicum, *Costume in the Drama of Shakespeare and his Contemporaries* (Cambridge, 1936). C. F. Ménestrier, *La Philosophie des images énigmatiques* (Paris, 1694), p. 238, notes that blue was a colour given to many nymphs as well as to figures associated with the sky and serenity.

[6] *Time Vindicated*.

[7] Vincenzo Cartari, *Le Imagini de gli dei de gli antichi* (Venice, 1625), p. 25. This work appeared originally at Venice in 1566. C. Ripa, p. 53.

movement, with a cloth drawn over his head. Grimly he advanced as the unconquerable image of Time.

Of all times, the masque was an affair of night, a thing of darkness made glorious by many lamps and glittering jewels; no spirit of day is represented here, but Night treads these boards, accompanied by her train of Stars—

> Night, like a masque, is entered heaven's great hall
> With thousand torches ushering the way.[1]

From below she rose in *The Vision of the Twelve Goddesses* "in a black vesture set with Starres." "A close robe of blacke silk and gold," together with "a blacke mantle embrodered with starres," graced her in *Lord Hay's Masque*— "a crowne of starres on her head, her haire blacke and spangled with gold, her face blacke, her buskins blacke and painted with starres." Seated in a chariot, she advanced in *The Vision of Delight*; and in *Luminalia*, set on "a Chariot enricht and drawne by two great owles," she appeared as "a matron in a purple robe, with starres of gold and large black wings displaied, her browne haire loose, and on her head a vaile of russet cipresse with a picked [peaked] crowne and a golden Scepter in her hand." Here Ripa was followed:[2] his Night, too, was a "matrona," "clad in an azure robe all set with stars; two great wings at her shoulders spread as if for flight." In Ripa she was accompanied by the "four Vigils of the night" (*quattro vigilie della notte*), and these also figure in *Luminalia*:

> The first vigill in a robe of blue, with a red mantle, her haire hanging downe in locks, and a bat sitting before.
> The second habited as the former, but the colours somewhat darker, on her head a scritch-owle.
> The third in purple and black, on her head a dormouse.
> The fourth in watchet and carnation, her haire mixt with silver like dew, and a little Swan on her head.

These in the main correspond with Ripa's vigils, the first "clad in a grey colour" with a "bat in flight," the second "clad in a dim colour,"[3] the third "clad in black in an obscure night" with "various animals sleeping," and the fourth "clad in mixed colours, white and blue," with a "cock by her side."[4] No doubt in Ripa a common source was found by the contrivers of the masque and by Francesco Cini, whose *Notte d'amore* (1608) has been noted in this connexion.[5]

With the Vigils are to be associated the nocturnal Hours which appeared in *Lord Hay's Masque*, nine in number, "apparrelled in large robes of black taffatie, painted thicke with starres, their haires long, blacke, and spangled with gold, on their heads coronets of stars, and their faces blacke."[6]

The stars themselves, Hesperus and Phosphorus, made their entries, too. The former, in *Lord Hay's Masque*, had

> a close robe of a deep crimson Taffatie mingled with skye colour, and over that a large loose robe of a lighter crimson taffatie; on his head he wore a wreathed band of gold, with a starre in the front thereof; his haire and beard red, and buskins yellow.

---

[1] John Marston, *The Insatiate Countess* (1613).

[2] Pp. 59, 360: "vestita d'un manto azzurro tutto pieno di stelle, & habbia alle spalle due grandi ali in atto di volare."

[3] Her emblem "a peacock with tail outspread" (*un pavone che con la coda faccia una bella rota*).

[4] "Una donna vestita di color bertino, vedendosi sopra la sua testa alcune stelle, & per l'aria una nottola volante. . . . Una donna vestita di color lionato. . . . Una donna vestita di nero in una notte oscura . . . accanto diversi animali dormendo. . . . Donna vestita di cangiante, cioè bianche, è torchino."

[5] E. Welsford, pp. 235–237.

[6] It may perhaps be well to note here that, in the masque descriptions, 'hair' regularly signified 'wig' and that 'face' similarly referred to a mask.

COURT HIEROGLYPHICKS

By 1638, however, in *Luminalia*, the mantle had turned to "watchet cipresse"—transparent silk of a pale blue shade [1]—covering the body of "a beautifull youth naked."

SLEEP AND DREAMS

Night brings with her her great gift of Sleep, as he seems in *Luminalia*, "a fat man in a blacke robe, and over it a white mantle; on his head a garland of Grapes, with a Dormouse sitting before; in his hand a golden wand"—or else, as Somnus in *The Vision of the Twelve Goddesses*, in

> a white thin Vesture cast over a blacke, to signifie both the day and the night, with wings of the same colour, a Garland of Poppy on his head; and in stead of his yuorie and transparent horne, hee was shewed bearing a blacke Wand in the left hand and a white in the other.

Fig. 115. SILENCE IN "LA MASCHE-RATA DELLA GENEALOGIA DEGLI DEI" (FLORENCE, 1565)

Giorgio Vasari. Biblioteca Nazionale, Florence (C. B. 3. 53; i, 19).

Fig. 116. AN AIRY SPIRIT, MEREFOOL, SKOGAN, AND SKELTON IN "THE FORTUNATE ISLES" (1625)

Inigo Jones. Chatsworth (*Designs*, No. 66). Inscribed, "Aery spirrit Scoga[n] Skelton A Brother of the Rosicros." Copyright of his Grace the Duke of Devonshire.

The horn here referred to is Ripa's "cornucopia"; there too his dress is black and white, and he is bidden to carry a wand in his left hand.

Sleep comes in the twilight, twilight symbolized in Amphiluche,[2] with "Olive-colour" face, breast, and arms: "Her garment was transparent, the ground darke blue and sprinkled with silver spangles, her Buskins white trim'd with gold." And here, too, is Silence, "an old man in a skin

[1] M. Channing Linthicum, pp. 118–119, 28–29. "Blew or watchet" is referred to in Holland's translation of Pliny, while Browne speaks of a "watchet deep'ned with a blew." [2] *The Triumph of Peace.*

coat close to his body set full of eyes, his mantle tawny, and a girland of Peach-tree about his head."[1] Tawny was the colour of sadness or solemnity, and peach seems to have indicated inactivity.[2] The fantasies of dreams attend. In *The Triumph of Peace* Fancy is clad "in a sute of severall coloured Feathers, hooded, a paire of Bats-wings on his shoulders," and hence akin to Iceles, spirit "of fearfull visions," in *Luminalia*, "in a brownish flesh colour close to him, like the naked, a red mantle, great Bats wings on his shoulders." The airy lightness of feathers no doubt caused their

Fig. 117. Past Time in "La Fenice rinovata" (Fossano, 1644)
Biblioteca Nazionale, Turin.

association with all things fantastical, a supposition justified by Livebyhope's words in William Strode's *The Floating Island* when he brings to Fancy's court "a Crown of all colour'd feathers":

> *Liveby* a Crown of Feathers here presents,
> To represent the light and easy yoak
> Which all the Passions hope.

Similarly was clad the Phantaste of *Luminalia*, "in a white robe of cloth of silver, a greene mantle, and on his head a dressing of severall coloured feathers." [3]

The companion of Iceles was Morpheus, "the presenter of humane shapes," who had "a robe of cloth of gold, his mantle Blue, on his head a girland of Poppy." The poppy emblem, which accompanied Morpheus also in *The Floating Island*, is readily appreciated. The robe's colour apparently suggested the richness of dreams, gold being used to signify both wealth and perfection, while in the blue mantle was enshrined the idea that dreams come in the serenity of the night. Viewing these two figures, we realize that, where the colours used for Morpheus betoken calm and joy, those given to Iceles indicate tormented emotion. The brown tights provided a darkness allied to evil, while red was a hue regularly associated with passion of an extravagant sort.[4] Wrath for this period was "red tyrannizing," shame was "crimson," and lust "scarlet." [5]

---

[1] *Luminalia.*   [2] M. C. Linthicum, pp. 46–47, 40.   D. C. Allen, p. 89, notes that tawny also indicates humility.
[3] There were also Phantasms in *The Vision of Delight.*
[4] *Cf.* C. F. Ménestrier, *La Philosophie des images énigmatiques* (Paris, 1694), p. 234, associates red with anger and zeal; *cf.* also M. Turmann, pp. 44–47.
[5] It is noticeable that Sonno (Sleep), Icelo (Iceles), and Morfeo (Morpheus) all appeared in a Florentine pageant of 1565: *Descrizione del canto de sogni* (Florence, 1566), pp. 4, 5, 17, 18.

COURT HIEROGLYPHICKS

THE ELEMENTS: AIRY SPIRITS

All of these figures, from the infinitude of eternity to the airy wraiths of night's dream-world, gained their significance because of their relationship to man, whose Five Senses, the source of his enjoyment, figured in *Cælum Britannicum*.[1] Ripa describes Sight as a man holding a mirror and a shield showing eagles staring at the sun, Hearing as a woman playing a lute with a hind near by, Taste as a woman holding a basket of fruit, Touch a woman holding a falcon, and Smell a youth standing in a stream of water. Next troop forth the four Humours [2] and the four Affections [3]— cardinal elements in man's make-up, according to contemporary opinion. The former, as presented in the "Complexions" of the English *Iconologia*,[4] showed the "Sanguin," "A jovial Spark with a Garland of various Flowers, with fair Hair, and a due Mixture of white and red in his Cheeks, playing on a Lute"; Choler, "A meagre Youth of a sallow Colour, with a haughty Look, being almost naked, holds a drawn Sword in his right Hand"; Melancholy,

> Of a brown Complexion, placing a Foot upon a Cube, holds, in his left Hand, a Book open, as if he would study; his Mouth is mufled; in his right Hand a Purse close shut, and, on his Head, a Sparrow;

Phlegm, "A gross Man, pale-fac'd, sitting in a Fur-Gown, clapping both Hands into his Bosom, his Head on one side bound up with a black Cloth, almost covering his Eyes, and a Tortoise by him."

Such humours or complexions, however, have a significance which succeeds in relating man directly to the universe around him. Man is a microcosm, as the emblem-writers knew. Symbolic of the masque, indeed, might stand Henry Peacham's design for "Homo microcosmus,"[5] and the humours are but human manifestations of elemental forces which, personified, find expression in the pagan deities of ancient Greece and of Rome. Above all, in anthropomorphic conception of the whole and complete man, is Jove,[6] a white-bearded monarch, thunderbolt in hand, seated usually upon an eagle and often "with a glory beyond him" (Fig. 91). Under his sway come others, each representative of some force which in turn associates itself with human emotions. First in rank and importance stands Juno, queen in a double right. As the mate of Jove she proved a popular figure; her peacock-drawn car was a familiar sight both in the masques and in Italian *intermezzi* (Fig. 90)—

> Imperiall Juno in her Chayre,
> With Scepter of command, for Kingdomes large,
> Descends, all clad in colours of the Ayre,
> Crown'd with bright Starres, to signifie her charge.

Her dress, because of the vagaries of feminine fashions, permitted of some variations. In 1604 she was clad "in a skie-colour mantle imbrodered with gold and figured with Peacocks feathers, wearing a Crowne of gold on her head." [7] " Sitting on a throne supported by two beautiful peacocks," she was discovered two years later in *Hymenæi*,

> her attyre rich and like a Queene, a white Diademe on her head from whence descended a Veyle and that bound with a *Fascia* of severall coloured silkes, set with all sorts of iewels and raysed in the top with *Lillies* and *Roses*. In her right hand she held a Scepter, in the other a timbrell. At her golden feete the hide of a lyon was placed.

---

[1] They likewise appeared in the *Entertainment* of 1604 and in the *Pageant* of 1613.
[2] *Hymenæi.*   [3] *Hymenæi* and *Love's Welcome.*   [4] *Iconologia* (1709), p. 15.
[5] *Minerva Britanna; or, A Garden of Heroical Devises* (1612), p. 190. He too presents figures of the humours, as Melancholia (p. 126), Sanguis (p. 127), Choller (p. 128), and Phlegma (p. 129).
[6] *World tost at Tennis, Augurs, Love's Triumph, Tempe Restored.*   [7] *The Vision of the Twelve Goddesses.*

This description, in its essential details, tallies with Ripa's; he also mentions "the white veil covering the head and bound by a fascia in the manner of an antique crown, full of jewels green and red and blue." In her right hand, he adds, "she holds a sceptre and in her left a timbrel." [1] How she appeared in *Love's Triumph* we do not know, but a design for her dress and that of Iris in *Chloridia* is happily extant. [2] A crown with projecting points and a sceptre indicate her majesty; the dress is simple, with puffed-up sleeves, and girded at the waist.

Juno is clad in colours of the air and crowned with stars to signify her charge, for, besides being the mate of Jove, she holds regal sway in her own right. She is mistress of the sky, and as such

Fig. 118. Winter and Boreas in "La Primavera trionfante" (Turin, 1657)
Biblioteca Nazionale, Turin.

wields large sovereignty; air is the first among the four elements, the counterparts of man's humours. These four elements of nature, spirits of Air, Water, Earth, and Fire, provide a considerable background for the masque's allegorical action, associated as they are with the deities of ancient Greece. If Juno, representing the Sanguine, rules on high, Vulcan is lord of choleric fire and Neptune master of the phlegmatic waters. Among these, naturally, in accordance with the airy substance of the masque, Juno is pre-eminent; her subjects are legion. *Hymenæi* surrounds her with aerial sprites "in severall colours, making musique," their attire

> wholy new for the invention and full of glorie, as having in it the most true impression of a celestiall figure: The upper part of *white* cloth of silver, wrought with Ivnoes birds and fruits, a loose under-garment, full gather'd, of *carnation* strip't with *silver* and parted with a golden *Zone*; Beneath that, another flowing garment of *watchet* cloth of silver lac'd with gold; Through all which, though they were round and swelling, there yet appeared some touch of their delicate *lineaments*, preserving the sweetenesse of *proportion* and expressing it selfe beyond expression. The *attyre* of their heads did answer if not exceed; their haire being carelesly (but yet with more art then if more affected) bound under the circle of a rare and rich *Coronet*, adorn'd with all varietie and choise of iewels; from the top of which flow'd a transparent *veile* downe to the ground, whose verge returning up was fastened to either side in most sprightly manner. Their shooes were *Azure* and gold, set with Rubies and Diamonds; so were all their garments; and everie part abounding in ornament.

[1] P. 57. "Con un velo bianco che gli cuopre il capo, il quale è circondato da una fascia, a uso di corona antica e reale, piena di gioie verde, rosse & azurre." See also *Descrizione delle pompe e delle feste* (Florence, 1584), sig. I4 *recto*.
[2] *Designs*, No. 102 (Pl. XIV, B).

162

The symbolic significance of the colours again is amply apparent. Watchet and azure immediately establish these figures as belonging to the world of air, the watchet suggesting further an element of dignity; [1] white by itself indicates purity, and in association with carnation desire; while silver and gold, being precious, betoken perfection and regal quality.

A male figure of Air appeared in *Somerset's Masque*, "in a skye-coloured skin-coat with a mantle painted with Fowle and on his head an Eagle," companioned by Johphiel, of *The Fortunate Isles*,

Fig. 119. ZEPHYRUS IN
"TETHYS' FESTIVAL" (1610)

Inigo Jones. Chatsworth (*Designs*, No. 36).
Copyright of his Grace the Duke of Devonshire.

Fig. 120. EOLUS IN "LA MASCHERATA
DELLA GENEALOGIA DEGLI DEI"
(FLORENCE, 1565)

Giorgio Vasari. Uffizi, Florence (copy of original).

"an aery spirit . . . attired in light silkes of severall colours, with wings of the same, a bright yellow haire, a chaplet of flowers, blew silke stockings and pumpes and gloves, with a silver fan in his hand" (Fig. 116). The appearance of the same figures, "Ayrely sprites" as Jones has marked them, in *The Temple of Love*, "with sanguine vizards, their Garments and Caps all of feathers," is indicated in two of the Chatsworth designs.[2] Closely allied is the realm of the Winds. The North Wind, Boreas, makes his boisterous entry in *Beauty*

in a robe of Russet and White mixt, full and bagg'd; his haire and beard rough and horride; his wings gray and full of snow and ycicles; his mantle borne from him with wyres and in severall puffes; his feet ending in Serpents tayles; and in his hand a leave-lesse Branch laden with ycicles.

By those in the audience who were familiar with contemporary emblem literature this costume must at once have been appreciated. Cartari [3] had declared that Boreas possessed serpents' tails instead

[1] M. C. Linthicum, pp. 38, 29.   [2] *Designs*, Nos. 217, 218.   None of these correspond to Ripa's figure of air, p. 121.
[3] P. 191: "Invece di piedi haveva code di serpenti . . . l' ali tutte coperte di neve."

of feet, and that his wings were all covered with snow; while Ripa [1] described him as a "horrid figure of a man, his beard, hair and wings all full of snow and his feet shaped like serpents' tails." The same person in *Somerset's Masque* bore "a grisled skin coate, with haire and wings accordingly" (Fig. 118, and *cf.* Fig. 122).[2] In *Beauty* figured, too, Volturnus or Vulturnus, wind of the south-east, "in a blue coloured robe and mantle, pufft . . . his face blacke and on his head a red Sunne, shewing he came from the *East*; his wings of severall colours; his buskins white and wrought

Fig. 121. Austro in "La Mascherata della Genealogia degli dei" (Florence, 1565)

Giorgio Vasari. Uffizi, Florence (copy of original).

Fig. 122. Euros in "La Mascherata della Genealogia degli dei" (Florence, 1565)

Giorgio Vasari. Uffizi, Florence (copy of original).

with gold." Presumably he is here thought of as the Eastern Wind, who, in *Somerset's Masque*, had "a skin coate of the colour of the Sun-rising, with a yellow haire, and wings both on his shoulders and feete." This was Ripa's Euro (Euros),[3] "a man with puffed-out cheeks, wings at his shoulders dark red in colour, and a red sun on his head" (Fig. 122). Both in *Chloridia* and *Somerset's Masque* appears the Western Wind, a figure in "a skin coate of darke crimson, with crimson haire and wings" (Fig. 121). Zephyrus was a more familiar figure, being introduced into six masques.[4] In *Lord Hay's Masque* he was graced with

---

[1] P. 497: "Huomo horrido, con la barba, i capelli & le ali tutte piene di neve, & con li piedi come code di serpi." The serpent-like feet were inspired by Pausanias. They are referred to also in the MS. note relating to the Boreas design for *La Mascherata della genealogia degli dei* (1565) (Biblioteca Nazionale, Florence, MS. Follini II, i, 142, f. 108 *verso*).   [2] He also appeared in *Chloridia*.

[3] P. 496: "Huomo con le gote gonfiate, con l'ali à gl' homeri, di carnagione moresca; haverà in capo un Sole rosso." Vergil's *igneus* inspired most of these conceptions; it is noted in the Follini MS., 107 *verso*.

[4] *Penates, Lord Hay's Masque, Tethys' Festival, Somerset's Masque, Chloridia, Luminalia.*

a white loose robe of sky coloured Taffatie, with a mantle of white silke, prop't with wyre, still waving behind him as he moved; on his head hee wore a wreath of Palme deckt with Primmeroses and Violets; the hayre of his head and beard were flaxen, and his buskins white and painted with flowers.

Three years later, in *Tethys' Festival*, his costume was

of greene satin imbrodered with golden flowers with a round wing made of lawnes on wyers, and hung down in labels. Behind his shoulders two silver wings. On his head a Garland of flowers, consisting of all colours, and on one Arme, which was out bare, he wore a bracelet of gold set with rich stones.

Fig. 123. Iris in "La Mascherata della genealogia degli dei" (Florence, 1565)

Giorgio Vasari. Biblioteca Nazionale, Florence (C. B. 3. 53; i, 115).

Fig. 124. Divine Beauty in "Tempe Restored" (1632)

Inigo Jones. Chatsworth (*Designs*, No. 161). Copyright of his Grace the Duke of Devonshire.

As such he is presented to us in one of Jones's designs (Fig. 119); another shows us the Zephyrus of *Chloridia*, set on a cloud and scattering flowers on the earth below.[1] These dresses tally with the descriptions of Cartari and Ripa: the former explains "that as he belongs to the spring he clothes the earth with green plants; he has a garland of diverse flowers on his head and his robe is similarly painted with flowers of various colours";[2] while the latter describes him as "a young man of pleasing aspect, with wings and puffed cheeks, on his head a garland of diverse flowers."[3]

[1] *Designs*, No. 84 (Pl. XIII, A).

[2] "Perciò di primavera veste la terra di verdi herbe . . . portava ghirlanda in capo di diversi fiori, & veste parimente tutta dipinta à fiori di colori diversi."

[3] "Vn Giovane di leggiadro aspetto, con l' ali, & con le gote gonfiate . . . haverà in capo una ghirlanda con testa di varij fiori." See also Follini MS., 106 *verso*.

That the puffed cheeks were duly indicated on the stage is proved by the pictures of the Winds in the ballets given at the Savoy court about the middle of the seventeenth century (Fig. 118).

Of Juno's train, too, were Aurora and Iris. The latter, messenger to the Queen of Heaven and symbolic of the rainbow, appears suitably clad in *Chloridia* and *Inner Temple*, "in a robe of dis-coloured [many-coloured] Taffita, figured in variable colours like the Raine-bowe, a cloudie wreath on her head." [1] In three masques [2] Aurora is introduced,

Fig. 125. One of the Spheres in "La Pellegrina" (Florence, 1589)

Bernardo Buontalenti. Biblioteca Nazionale, Florence (C. B. 3. 53; ii, 33 *verso*).

Fig. 126. Chloris at Florence, *c.* 1580

Biblioteca Nazionale, Florence (C. B. 3. 53; ii, 89).

her garment white trim'd with gold, loosely tuck'd about her, and cut downe on the sides; her armes bare with bracelets of gold, with a vaile of Carnation flying as blowne up by the winde; her wings white spotted with gold; her faire haire disheveled; and on her head a Girland of Roses.

This dress corresponds with that given by Ripa—"down to the waist white, thin and almost transparent; from the waist to the knees an overdress of scarlet . . . and from the knees down gold-colour." [3]

With Juno, too, may be grouped those Figures of the Zodiac which in *Cælum Britannicum* stepped down from on high, the Spheres [4] who sent forth their harmony to grace the occasion and the

[1] *Cf.* C. Ripa, p. 355; A. Cartari, p. 130. See Fig. 123.
[2] *Penates, The Vision of the Twelve Goddesses*, and *Luminalia*.
[3] P. 34: "Una veste sino alla cintura, candida, sottile e como trasparente, dalla cintura sino alle ginocchia una sopraveste di scarlatto, . . . dalle ginocchia sino à i piedi di color d' oro."
[4] *Tempe Restored* and *Twelve Months*.

Influences of the Stars who, in *Tempe Restored*, accompanied Divine Beauty.[1] "The description," says Townsend (or Inigo Jones), "of the severall Habites of the maine Masque would make a booke alone as big as this"; consequently there is presented

> onely thus much—the Queenes Maiestie was in a garment of watchet Sattine with Stars of silver imbrodered and imbost from the ground, and on her head a Crowne of Stars mixt with some small falls of white Feathers—

a silver-blue world this, with the faint light of Cinthia shining down (Fig. 124).   Cinthia herself was no stranger to these shows.   In *Huntingdon Masque* the Moon's dress was "blew satten, fairely embroidered with starres and cloudes," while in *Blackness* and *Beauty* silver formed the staple of her costume.   For the former "the dressing of her head" was "antique, and crown'd with a *Luminarie* or *Sphere* of light"—possibly that shown in a hitherto unidentified design by Inigo Jones.[2]

The essential standard of most of these dresses was that of the 'nymph,' a character whose attire formed the staple for nearly all these 'Greek' characters.[3]   According as they belonged to woods, rivers, or air their embellishments varied, but the basic features of their garments remained for the most part unchanged.   Closest to Juno were the Hyades and the Graces.   The former in *Inner Temple* were "apparelled in skie coloured Taffita robes, spangled like the Heavens, golden Tresses, and each a faire Starre on their head"; the latter in *The Vision of the Twelve Goddesses* had "silver Robes with white Torches," and in *Hue and Cry after Cupid* were "all attyr'd according to their antique figures."[4]

SPIRITS OF FIRE, EARTH, AND WATER

Opposed to and yet closely associated with the realm of air was that of fire, governed by Vulcan. The god himself, besides a burlesque entry in *Love's Welcome*, figured in two masques, *Hue and Cry after Cupid* and *Mercury Vindicated*.   For the former he was "attyr'd in a cassocke girt to him, with bare armes, his haire and beard rough; his hat of blue and ending in a *Cone*; in his hand a hammer and tongs,

Fig. 127.   A FIERY SPIRIT IN "THE TEMPLE OF LOVE" (1635)

Inigo Jones.   Chatsworth (*Designs*, No. 216).   Copyright of his Grace the Duke of Devonshire.

as comming from the Forge."   "Naked, brawny, smoky, lame," he was in Ripa's account,[5] "with a blue-coloured hat on his head, holding a hammer in his right hand and tongs in his left." [6]   Always flaming in dress leaped forth the

---

[1] *Designs*, Nos. 156–161.

[2] *Id.*, No. 422.   The Moon also appeared in *Twelve Months*.   See C. Ripa, p. 48.

[3] This subject of the nymph's dress is dealt with by A. Warburg (*supra*, p. 62) and by Oskar Fischel, *Inigo Jones und der Theaterstil der Renaissance* (*Vorträge der Bibliothek Warburg* (Leipzig, 1932), pp. 103–132).

[4] They appeared also in *Love freed from Ignorance*.   A. Cartari, p. 410, specifies their 'Greek' dress.

[5] P. 56: "Nudo, brutto, affumicato, zoppo, con un cappello di color celeste in capo, & che con una mano tenesse un martello, & con la sinistra una tenaglia."

[6] The Cyclops with Pyrcamon belong to his train: *Hue and Cry after Cupid*, *Mercury Vindicated*, *Love's Welcome*.

Element of Fire,[1] "with fierie Wings and Bases" and "Vizards of a Cholericke Complexion," or else "a skin coate and a mantle painted with flames" and "a cap of flames, with a Salamander in the midst thereof" (Fig. 127).[2]

Vulcan too held a certain sovereignty over the Element of Earth, which in *Somerset's Masque* wore "a skin coate of grasse greene, a mantle painted full of trees, plants, and flowers, and on his head an oke [oak] growing"; corresponding spirits in *The Temple of Love* "had their garments wrought all over with leaveless trees and bushes, with Serpents and other little Animals here and

Fig. 128. Neptune, Galatea, Nereids, and Tritons in "L'Unione perla peregrina"
(Turin, 1660)
Biblioteca Nazionale, Turin.

there about them, and on their heads barren rocks." To this description Inigo Jones added in a manuscript note:[3]

yearthy spirrit in blak a cloth carllesly & a rok wrapt abowt his head, long black haires uncurled and a thinn beard somewhat longe, the scincote [skin coat] coott [cut] open in many plases, dark fles [flesh] colour underneath.[4]

Over water Neptune held monarchy; he and his companions Nereus, Oceanus, and Amphitrite appeared in many masques (Fig. 128). The first, when he came forth in *Albion's Triumph*, no doubt seemed as he did in Ripa's description:[5] "An old man with hair and beard coloured like the sea

---

[1] *The Lords' Masque, Somerset's Masque, The Temple of Love.*

[2] C. Ripa, p. 120, notes the salamander emblem, although he treats this figure as a woman. For a Fiery Spirit in *The Lords' Masque* see *Designs*, frontispiece (No. 59).

[3] *Designs*, No. 223.

[4] C. Ripa, p. 121, makes this figure also a woman; he speaks of the "dress full of diverse trees and flowers" ("vestita d' habito pieno di varie herbe e fiori").

[5] P. 57: "Un vecchio con la barba & i capelli del colore dell' acqua marina & un panno indosso del medesmo colore; nella destra mano tiene un Tridente & sta detta figura sopra d'una conca marina con le rote, tirata da doi balene overo da due cavalli marini in mezzo del mare."

and a cloak of the same; a trident in his right hand; ſtanding on a sea-shell drawn by two whales or sea-horses." Nereus of *Love's Triumph* is not described for us, but his comrade Oceanus, who appeared in *Blackness*, had

> the colour of his flesh blue and shaddowed with a robe of sea-greene; his head grey and horned as he is described by the *Ancients*; his beard of the like mixt colour; hee was gyrlonded with *Alga* or sea-grasse; and in his hand a *Trident*.

In spite of the reference to the ancients, this particularization of his coſtume seems again derived from Ripa,[1] whose Oceanus was an old man of venerable aspeĉt, naked, of the colour of the sea; his hair and beard full of algæ and shells.[2]

Round these sported the Tritons, popular because of their ſtrangeness (Fig. 130). In *Blackness* "their upper parts" were "humane,[3] save that their haires were blue, as partaking of the sea-colour, their desinent parts fish"; "out of wreathed shells" they made music. A few years later Daniel's Tritons in *Tethys' Feſtival*

> wore skin-coates of watchet Taffata lightned with silver, to shew the Muscles of their bodies. From the waſte almoſt to the knee were finnes of silver in the manner of bases; a mantle of Sea-greene, laced and fringed with golde, tyed with a knot upon one shoulder and falling down in folds behinde, was faſtened to the contrary side; on their heads garlands of Sedge, with trumpets of writhen shels in their hand; Buskins of Sea-greene laid with silver lace.

Not unlike was the Spirit of Water in *Somerset's Masque*, "in a skin coate waved, with a mantle full of fishes, on his head a Dolphin." In *The Temple of Love* the same person was "all over wrought with scales, and had fishes heads and fins" (Fig. 129).[4]

Watery nymphs abounded, beloved for those sea-green coſtumes which showed so well by candle-light. Not, however, that green was confined entirely to the denizens of ocean, for essentially that colour expressed youth, joy, and vitality, thus being, as Méneſtrier noted, especially suited for all young maids and nymphs.[5] From Statius he quotes, "Ite deæ virides, liquidosque avertite vultus." Chief of the nymphs of water, Tethys appeared twice and gave her name to one masque.[6] Her mantle is described in 1604 as "Sea-greene, with a silver imbrodery of Waves and a dressing

Fig. 129. A Watery Spirit in "The Temple of Love" (1635)

Inigo Jones. Chatsworth (*Designs*, No. 220). Copyright of his Grace the Duke of Devonshire.

---

[1] P. 61: "Un vecchio ignudo di venerando aspetto, & del colore dell' acqua marina, con la barba & capelli longhi pieni d' alega & di chiocciolette."

[2] In William Percy's *Aphrodysial* (1602) Oceanus was "a grave old man with crown of Gold, long white Bearde and braided Haire. Crown white and blew ennamald."

[3] One of the earlieſt Renaissance descriptions of a Triton appears in *Apparato et feſte nelle noze dello illuſtrissimo Signor Duca di Firenze* (Florence, 1539), pp. 47–48. The occasion was the marriage of Cosmo de' Medici to Eleonora of Toledo. The Triton who appeared then had long hair and beard "with an extravagant headdress of sea-weeds and shells"; fish-scales and a forked tail completed his coſtume.

[4] Unparticularized sea-gods come into *Love's Triumph*, among them Proteus, who had already made his bow in *Neptune's Triumph* and *The Fortunate Isles*.

[5] *La Philosophie des images énigmatiques* (Paris), p. 238. *Cf.* also M. Turmann, pp. 49–50. D. C. Allen, pp. 85–86, ſtresses the significance of green as the colour of youth and joy.

[6] *The Vision of the Twelve Goddesses, Tethys' Feſtival.*

of Reedes"; in her hand she held a trident. Much more elaborate is the record of her appearance six years later, for on that occasion the goddess was impersonated by a queen (Anne of Denmark). To this record we may add two of Jones's designs, luckily preserved.[1] Her headdress was made up "of shels and corall" with a veil hanging down "from a great Muriake [murex] shell in forme of the creſt of an helme." The bodice was composed

of sky-colored taffataes for lightnes, all embrodered with maritime invention. Then had they a kinde of halfe skirts of cloth of silver imbrodered with golde, all the ground work cut out for lightnes, which

Fig. 130. A Triton in "La Mascherata della genealogia degli dei" (Florence, 1565)

Giorgio Vasari. Uffizi, Florence (copy of original).

Fig. 131. A Greek Nymph in "La Mascherata della genealogia degli dei" (Florence, 1565)

Giorgio Vasari. Uffizi, Florence (copy of original).

hung down ful and cut in points: underneath that came bases (of the same as was their bodies) beneath their knee. The long skirt was wrought with lace, waved round about like a River, and on the bankes sedge and Sea-weedes, all of gold. Their shoulders were all imbrodered with the worke of the short skirt of cloth of silver and had cypresse [2] spangled, ruffed out, and fell in a ruffe above the elbow. The under sleeves were all imbrodered as the bodies. Their shoes were of Satin, richly imbrodered with the worke of the short skirt.

Some conception of the richness of these masquing dresses may be gained from an examination of the account presented by "Mr Thomas Henshawe her Maieſties silkeman," detailing the material supplied by him for "The 14 Ladyes of the maske." These fourteen ladies, among whom was a queen, required no less than 2142 ounces of silk, amounting to 780 yards apiece. In all there were

[1] See *Designs*, Nos. 38, 39 (Pl. V).   [2] "A light, transparent material of silk and linen" (M. C. Linthicum, pp. 118–119).

2010 yards of "gold spangled bone Lace," 5270 yards of "gold spangled Loome Lace," 658 yards of "silver spangled bone Lace," and 2982 yards of "silver spangled Loome Lace," the total cost of these items alone coming to over £1071—at least, according to the computation of worthy Mr Henshawe. A note on his bill acknowledges receipt of the material, but, says the writer, "I referre the prices vnto the Lordes of his Maiesties Priuie Counsell," who, we trust, were able to judge.

Still another account [1] details the cost of embroidering the Queen's dress. In this it is stated that "the scewtts" were "of clothe a [of] sciluer, the pettecote of wachad [watchet] taffete" with sea-green sleeves; the embroidery cost £25. Besides, there was the cost of embroidering some "Copwebe lane withe vaynes of sciluer and segrene and sciluer oose [spangles] and Carnation scilke," together with a quarter of a yard of sea-green taffeta ornamented "vere Riche with goold oose and Carnation scilke." The accounts leave no doubt in our minds but that the description in the text was equalled in lavishness by the costumes themselves.[2] In all essentials the attire thus outlined agrees with that of Tethys in *L'Educatione d'Achille* (Turin, 1650), which was of "blue and white . . . with shells," the mantle adorned by sparkling waves.

Akin to Tethys and her nymphs of the rivers were the Naiades, impersonated by children in *Tethys' Festival*, "in light robes adorned with flowers, their haire hanging downe, and waving with Garlands of water ornaments on their heads." [3] *Inner Temple* showed the same characters "attired in long habits

Fig. 132. A Delphic Couple in "La Pellegrina" (Florence, 1589)

Bernardo Buontalenti. Biblioteca Nazionale, Florence (C. B. 3. 53; ii, 15).

of sea-greene Taffita, with bubbles of Christall intermixt with powdering of silver resembling drops of water, blewish Tresses, on their heads garlands of Water-Lillies." [4] To the same group belonged the Daughters of Oceanus in *Blackness*, described by Jonson and conceived in form by Inigo Jones. "Sea-greene" was their colour, "waved about the skirts with gold and silver; their hayre loose and flowing, gyrlanded with Sea-grasse and that stuck with branches of Corall." [5] These in turn remind us of the Nereids of *Browne's Masque*, "in sea greene robes, greenish haire hanging loose with leaves of corall and shelles intermixte upon it," [6] and of Galatea in *Britannia Triumphans*. This sea-nymph swam on stage seated on a dolphin. A "loose snow-white garment" environed her fair shape,

> about her neck chaines of Pearls and her armes adorn'd with bracelets of the same, her faire haire disheveled and mixt with silver and in some part covered with a veile which she with one hand graciously held up.

In *Browne's Masque* the Nereids were accompanied by four other nymphs "in white taffita robes, long tresses & chaplets of flowers, herbs & weeds on their heades, with little wicker baskets in their hands, neatly painted." Such were the nymphs of *Chloridia*, attendants of Chloris,

---

[1] Both of these are printed in P. Reyher, pp. 507–508.
[2] The carnation mentioned above was a colour associated with Tethys by C. Ripa, p. 354.
[3] See *Designs*, No. 37 (Pl. VI, B).
[4] Their appearance in *Chloridia* is recorded in one of Jones's sketches (*Designs*, No. 86 (Pl. XIV, C)).
[5] *Designs*, No. 4 (Pl. II).
[6] The greenish hair derives from Horace: "Et virides Nereidum comas."

their apparell white, embroydered with silver, trim'd at the shoulders with great leaves of greene, embroydered with gold, falling one under the other. And of the same worke were their bases; their head-tyres of flowers, mix'd with silver and gold, with some sprigs of Ægrets among, and from the top of their dressing a thin vayle hanging downe.[1]

These were lightsome maids and lovely, meet for pleasant places and association with virtue. Not all were such, for by their side moved the Mermaids of *Blackness* and the Sirens of *Browne's Masque*. The latter were "as they are described by Hyginus and Servius with their upper parts like woemen to the navell and the rest like a hen" (Fig. 133). Dangerous tempters these, whom only an astute Odysseus could reject:

> Which shewes to us, when Bewtie seekes to snare
> The carelesse man whoe dothe no daunger dreede,
> That he shoulde flie and shoulde in time beware,
> And not on lookes his fickle fancie feede:
> > Such Mairemaides live that promise onelie ioyes:
> > But hee that yeldes at length him selffe distroies.[2]

Near by too was Circe, the charmer, in *Browne's Masque* "quaintly attyr'd, her hair loose about her shoulders, an Anadem of flowers on her head, with a wand in her hand." How she appeared in *Tempe Restored* (Fig. 135, and *cf.* Fig. 134) several of Jones's designs give indication.[3]

Such ancient deities and poetically imaginative figures, calm and fiery, evil and good, set the general background for the masque, symbolizing the elemental forces against which man moved and out of which he had his being, and at the same time affording many opportunities for that not too subtle flattery in which these entertainments abounded. Neptune might be lord of the waters, and find entry primarily because of these general associations, but of his appearance advantage might well be taken to promise a boorish James or a courtly Charles the sovereignty of the seas.

Fig. 133. A Siren in "La Masche-rata della Genealogia degli dei" (Florence, 1565)
Giorgio Vasari. Uffizi, Florence (copy of original).

THE FORCES OF NATURE

The elements, of course, were all combined in Nature and her symbols. There was Ceres, "in a Strawe colour and Silver imbrodery, with eares of Corne and a dressing of the same," [4] and her daughter Proserpina, "in a blacke Mantle imbrodered with gold-flames, with a crowne of gold on her head":

> Next, plenteous *Ceres* in her Harvest weede,
> Crown'd with th' increase of what she gave to keepe
> To gratitude and faith in whom we read,
> Who sowes on Vertue shall with glory reape.

[1] See *Designs*, Nos. 94–101 (Pls. XVII, B; XVIII, A; XIX; XVII, A; XVIII, B). See also *The Works of Ben Jonson*, ii, frontispiece, 249. Other nymphs appeared in *Pan's Anniversary* and *The Triumph of Peace*. In *Cupid's Banishment* and *Tempe Restored* figured the Dryades.
[2] Geoffrey Whitney, *Choice of Emblemes* (1586), p. 10.
[3] *Designs*, Nos. 140–142.
[4] See A. Cartari, p. 163.

COURT HIEROGLYPHICKS

Next, rich *Proserpina* with flames of gold,
Whose ſtate, although within the earth, yet shee
Comes from above, and in her hand doth hold
The Myne of wealth, with cheereful Maieſty.[1]

Another goddess of fertility was Macaria, who in the same masque appeared "in a Mantle of purple and silver, imbrodered with the Figures of Plentie and Wisedome"; she held "a Cadaceum with

Fig. 134. Circe in "La Mascherata della genealogia degli
dei" (Florence, 1565)

Giorgio Vasari.   Uffizi, Florence (copy of original).

Fig. 135. Circe in "Tempe Restored" (1632)

Inigo Jones.   Chatsworth (*Designs*, No. 141).   Copyright of
his Grace the Duke of Devonshire.

the Figure of abundance."   Perhaps the designer went directly here to Cartari, who describes this deity "with the caduceus and the horn of plenty in her hand."[2]

Materially Nature expressed herself in the four seasons.[3]   Winter hobbled on,

attired like an old man, in a short gowne of silke shagge like withered grasse all froſted and snowed over, and his Cappe, Gowne, Gamashes and Mittins furred crimson, with long white haire and beard, hung with Icecicles.[4]

Here too was Chriſtmas, "attir'd in round Hose, long Stockings, a close Doublet, a high crowned Hat with a Brooch, a long thin beard, a Truncheon, little Ruffes, white Shoes, his Scarffes and Garters tyed crosse."[5]   With him came January,[6]

in a throne of silver, his robe of ash-colour, long, fringed with silver; a white mantle; his wings white

[1] *The Vision of the Twelve Goddesses.*
[2] P. 357: "con il caduceo e il corno di dovitia in mano."
[3] *Mercury Vindicated* introduces Nature herself: the four seasons are in the masque of that name.
[4] *The Masque of Flowers.*   New Year and the months appeared in the *Knowsley Masque.*
[5] Chriſtmas was "an old gent" in the *Knowsley Masque.*   [6] *Beauty.*

173

and his buskins; in his hand a Lawrell bough; upon his head an *Anademe* of Lawrell fronted with the sign *Aquarius*,

precisely as Ripa had described him.[1]   More pleasing was Spring,

attired like a *Nymph*, a high tire on her head, *Antike* with knottes of faire haire and Cobweb Lawnes rising one above an other, garnished with Flowers to some height and behinde falling downe in a pendant; an upper-body of cloth of silver storie; naked necke and breast, decked with Pearls; a kertle of yellow cloth of gold, brancht with leaves, a mantle of greene and silver stuffe cut out in leaves; white buskins tied with greene ribande fringed with flowers.[2]

Fig. 136. Flora in "La Primavera trionfante"
(Turin, 1657)
Biblioteca Nazionale, Turin.

A later vision of this spirit showed her as "a beautifull Maid, her upper garment greene, under it a white robe wrought with flowers" and a garland on her head [3]—

> Cheereful *Flora*, all adorn'd with flowers,
> Who cloathes the earth with beauty and delight
> In thousand sundry suits, whilst shining houres
> Will skarce afford a darknesse to the night.[4]

Variously she is clad "in a Mantle of divers colours imbrodered with all sorts of flowers," [5] or "in a changeable Taffatie Gowne, with a large vale embroidred with flowers, a Crowne of flowers, and white buskins painted with flowers." [6]

The masque was a thing of love, and love arrives when spring is come to town. Hymen truly rules here, although the actual appearance of this god occurs but twice, in *Love's Triumph* and in *Hymenæi*, when he boasted "a saffron-coloured robe, his under vestures white, his socks yellow, a yellow veile of silke on his left arme, his head crowned with *Roses* and *marioram*; in his right hand a *torch* of *pine tree*." [7]   The yellow and saffron derived from Pliny, who had noted it as a bridal colour, and the white spelt purity.   Perhaps, however, Hymen was too decorous and solemn for these occasions when love was free and Venus seized on all men's eyes.   That the Venus who appeared at Whitehall differed markedly from the Venus of antiquity is obvious, although at Milan in 1594 a commentator declares she came on stage "quite naked, very white, with a garland of roses in her golden hair," her loveliness set off by "a sky-blue veil." [8]   In England her mantle was of "Dove-colour and silver, imbroidred with Doves";[9] she was "crowned with her *starre*" and seated on a chariot drawn by doves and swans, "with silver geares" (Fig. 137).[10]   Cupids were her

[1] P. 320: "Giovane alato, & vestito di bianco, il quale terrà con ambe le mani il segno d' acquario."
[2] *Flowers*.   [3] *Chloridia*.
[4] *The Vision of the Twelve Goddesses*.   [5] *Penates*.
[6] *Lord Hay's Masque*.
[7] A full description of Hymen's costume in a Florentine masquerade of 1584 appears in *Descrizione delle pompe e delle feste* (Florence, 1584), Sig. I3 *recto*.
[8] A. D'Ancona, ii, 516: "Venere tutta ignuda, bianchissima . . . chioma d' oro, ghirlanda di rose . . . velo ceruleo."
[9] *The Vision of the Twelve Goddesses*.
[10] *Hue and Cry after Cupid*.   Venus appeared also in *Time Vindicated* and in *Love's Triumph*.

174

obvious attendants; these proved by far the most popular characters in the courtly entertainments of England and of Italy alike. Their precise costume is described only once, when in the course of Beaumont's *Inner Temple Masque* four Cupids enter from each side of the stage, "attired in flame coloured Taffita close to their body like naked Boyes, with Bowes, Arrowes and wings of gold: Chaplets of flowers on their heads, hoodwinckt with Tiffany scarfs."[1]

Not, of course, that the masques exploited sensual love exclusively; indeed, the main theme which runs through the entire series of courtly presentations is that of idealism and Platonic affection.

Fig. 137. VENUS AT FLORENCE,
c. 1580

Biblioteca Nazionale, Florence (C. B. 3. 53; ii, 87).

Fig. 138. DIANA

Inigo Jones. Chatsworth (*Designs*, No. 412). Copyright of his Grace the Duke of Devonshire.

If the Moon shone down on these festivities Diana descended on the rays and gave to the performance the impress of her chastity. Diana had been a familiar figure in Italian entertainments. Cartari[2] places the half-moon on her head and in her hands the traditional bow and quiver. At Milan in 1594 she was "dressed in a silver skirt, tucked up, with a golden bow in her hand and silver sandals on her feet; her hair silvery, loose, long, curled, falling to the shoulder, garlanded with diverse flowers amid which a moon; covered with a transparent black veil all covered with stars."[3] Daniel presents a slight variant by giving her "a greene Mantle imbrodered with silver halfe-Moones

---

[1] Their other entries were in *Hue and Cry after Cupid, Love freed from Ignorance, Love Restored, Christmas, Lethe, Cupid's Banishment, Love's Triumph, Chloridia, Le Prince d'Amour, Albion's Triumph,* and *Tempe Restored.* For the second of these masques Cupid was given "3 yeardes of flesh collored satten" costing a total of two guineas (P. Reyher, p. 509).

[2] P. 70. See also *Descrizione delle pompe e delle feste* (Florence, 1584), sig. I3 *verso.*

[3] A. D'Ancona, ii, 516: "Diana . . . abito d' argento succinto . . . arco d' oro in mano . . . stivaletti d'argento . . . chioma quasi d' argento folta, lunga, crespa, pendente al collo, ghirlanda di diversi fiori con luna, vesta di velo negro sopra trasparente, quasi tutta coperta di stelle." See also *Descrittione dell' intermedii fatti nel felicissimo palazo del Gran Duca Cosimo* (Florence, 1569), sig. A8 *recto.*

and a croissant of pearle on her head." [1]   An extant design by Inigo Jones almost certainly was made for *Time Vindicated* (Fig. 138).   Here she has a loose dress, tucked up at the waist and the hips, with a close-fitting bodice; a crescent is set on her head, and she carries her familiar bow and quiver.   With Diana, too, comes Vesta, clothed in *The Vision of the Twelve Goddesses* "in a white Mantle imbrodered with gold-flames, with a dressing like a Nun," a burning lamp and a book being her attributes.

Fig. 139.   Harmony in "La Pellegrina"
(Florence, 1589)
Bernardo Buontalenti.   Biblioteca Nazionale, Florence
(C. B. 3. 53; ii, 11).

> Next Holy *Vesta* with her flames of Zeale
> Presents her selfe, clad in white Purity,
> Whose booke the soules sweet comfort doth
>   reveale
> By the ever-burning Lampe of Piety.

Love, in this world of courtiers and their ladies, takes many forms, and beside Venus, Diana, and Vesta appear the images of Eros,[2] Anteros,[3] and Amianteros.   The last, Chaste Love, was a character in *The Temple of Love*, "clad all in Carnation and White, and two Garlands of Laurel in one hand, and crown'd with another of the same."   All these were figures of loveliness, and were caught up, as it were, in the personified Divine Beauty who, richly habited, dazzled men's eyes in *Tempe Restored*.[4]   Grace danced meetly in *The Vision of Delight*, and Harmony figured in five masques (*cf.* Fig. 139).[5]   Ripa had described the latter as "a lovely and fair lady, with a double lyre of fifteen strings, on her head a crown of seven even sized jewels; her dress of seven colours embroidered with gold and diverse gems."[6]   As she appeared in *Tempe Restored* she is shown in two of Jones's designs.[7]

After Harmony comes Innocence, in *Albion's Triumph*, "a woman in a pure white robe, with a garland of flowers on her head."

Delight and Pleasure are her handmaidens.   The former is a character in *The Vision of Delight*, the latter in *Pleasure reconciled to Virtue*, and, as Hedone, in *Cælum Britannicum*: "a young woman with a smiling face, in a light lascivious habit, adorn'd with Silver and Gold, her Temples crown'd with a garland of Roses and over that a Rainbow circling her head down to her shoulders," herein copied from Ripa's "Piacere" and "Allegrezza."   The first was "a youth about sixteen years old, of a pleasant smiling countenance, with a garland of roses on his head, clad in a green dress richly embroidered with a rainbow circling his head about his shoulders ";[8] the second a "young

[1] *The Vision of the Twelve Goddesses.*   She also appeared in *Cupid's Banishment* and *Albion's Triumph*.
[2] *Love's Welcome, Love freed from Ignorance,* and *The Vision of Delight.*
[3] *Love's Welcome.*
[4] See *supra*, p. 167.
[5] *Somerset's Masque, The Vision of Delight, Heroes, Neptune's Triumph,* and *Tempe Restored.*
[6] P. 16: "Una vaga & bella donna, con una lira doppia di quindici cordo in mano; in capo haverà una corona di sette gioie tutti uguali; il vestimento è di sette colori, guarnito d' oro & di diverse gioie."
[7] *Designs*, Nos. 153, 154 (Pl. XXII, B).
[8] P. 398: "Un Giovane di sedici anni in circa, di bello aspetto & ridente, con una ghirlanda di rose in capo, vestito di verde e molto ornato, con un' Iride che da una spalla all' altra gli circondi il capo."

176

woman with a large ruddy face, dressed in a white dress painted with green leaves and flowers red and yellow, with a garland of diverse flowers on her head." [1]

THE REVELLERS

The rougher pleasures flock in too, headed by Bacchus and his revellers. The god himself, set "in a chariot hung all over with vine leaves and grapes, drawn by a goat," trundles on stage in *Cupid's Banishment*. So also comes the Comus of *Pleasure reconciled to Virtue*, "his head crowned with *Roses* and other flowers, his haire curled." In Milton's masque he bore "a Charming rod in one hand" and "his Glasse in the other." Silenus in *The Masque of Flowers* was

> an old fat man, attired in a crimson Sattin Doublet, without wings, collar or skirts, a great paunch, so as his Dublet, though drawne with a lace, would not meete together by a handfull, sleeves of cloth of Golde, bases and gamashaes of the same, a red swolne face, with a bunched nose, grey beard, bald head, pricke eares and little hornes (Fig. 140).

Fig. 140. A SILENE AND TWO OF THE NATION OF FAIES IN "OBERON" (1611)

Inigo Jones. Chatsworth (*Designs*, No. 46). Copyright of his Grace the Duke of Devonshire.

His companions, by tradition, are the Satyrs (Fig. 141).[2] *Cœlum Britannicum* introduced Momus, god of mockery and son of Nyx, "in a long darkish robe all wrought over with ponyards, Serpents tongues, eyes and eares, his beard and hair party coloured, and upon his head a wreath stuck with Feathers, and a Porcupine in the forepart" (Figs. 142, 143). With them entered Laughter,[3] "in a long side Coate of severall colours, laughing Visards on his breast and backe, a Cap with two grinning faces and Feathers betweene." Here rolled in Jollity, dressed "in a flame-coloured Suite, but trick'd like a Morise dancer, with Scarfes and Napkins, his Hat fastened like a Cone with a little fall," [4] Revel,[5] Sport,[6] and all the accompaniments of a festive season— Carol, Baby-Cake, Gambol, Minced-Pie, Misrule, Mumming, New-Year's Gift, Offering, Post-and-Pair, Wassel,[7] and Viands.[8]

---

[1] P. 10: "Giovanetta con fronte carnosa, liscia & grande, sarà vestita di bianco & detto vestimento dipinto di verdi fronde & fiori rossi & gialli, con una ghirlanda in capo di varij fiori." Allegrezza was similarly dressed in a Florentine masquerade of 1584 (*Descrizione delle pompe a delle feste* (Florence, 1584), sig. I2).

[2] *The Vision of the Twelve Goddesses, The Masque at Althorpe, Oberon, Time Vindicated, Albion's Triumph, The Triumph of Peace.*

[3] *The Vision of Delight, The Triumph of Peace.*

[4] *The Triumph of Peace.*

[5] *The Vision of Delight.*

[6] *The Vision of Delight, Time Vindicated.*

[7] All in *The Masque of Christmas.*

[8] *Neptune's Triumph.*

Heroic Virtue

These occasions, however, were not only excuses for revelling; they had their heroic side, and Virtue [1] was their nominal genius, as Ripa describes her, "a gracious young woman, with

Fig. 141. A Satyr in "La Mascherata della genealogia degli dei" (Florence, 1565)

Giorgio Vasari. Uffizi, Florence (copy of original).

Fig. 142. Momus in "La Mascherata della genealogia degli dei" (Florence, 1565)

Giorgio Vasari. Uffizi, Florence (copy of original).

wings at her shoulders, holding in her right hand a spear and in her left a laurel crown; a sun on her breast." [2] This the English version of Ripa's work explains:

> Young, because she never grows *old*; her Actions commencing into Habits. The Wings signifie her *soaring* aloft far above the Vulgar. The Sun, that Virtue *inspires* Virtue to the whole Body. The Laurel, that she is ever *green*, being proof against *Vice*. The Spear, *Dignity*, ruling over Vice. [3]

The green of her dress and of her wreath here signified the eternal youthfulness which kept her spirit alive over generations, although at times her costume, as in the *Mascherata della genealogia degli dei* of 1565, might be of purple, that colour being given her by Alciati on account of her pride and nobility (Figs. 146, 147). [4]

---

[1] *Pleasure reconciled to Virtue.*

[2] P. 510: "Una giovane donna & gratiosa, con l' ali alle spallo, nella destra mano tenghi un' basta & con la sinistra una corona di lauro, & nel petto habbia il sole."

[3] P. 79, Fig. 315.

[4] It is so noted in the Follini MS., 87 *verso*.

178

Virtue's companion is Honour,[1] a figure in

> a rich full robe of blew silke girt about her, a mantle of silver worne overthwart, ful gathered and descending in folds behind, a vaile of net lawne embroidered with Oos and Spangl'd, her tresses in tucks, braided with silver, the hinder part shadowing in waves her shoulders.

So important is she that with her she brings her Herald, Phemis, and her "Virgin Priest," Eunomia. The former appears

> attyr'd in an Antique Curace of silver stuffe, with labells at the wings and basses; a short gowne of gold stuffe, with wide sleeves, cut in panes; a wreath of gould on his head and a Rod of gould in his hand.

With such figures several ancient gods naturally associated themselves. Pallas made four appearances between 1604 and 1632; but unfortunately no design of her costume by Inigo Jones is extant, and there is only one detailed description—that in *The Vision of the Twelve Goddesses*, where she "was attyred in a blew mantle with a silver imbrodery of all weapons and engines of war, with a helmet-dressing on her head," in her hands "a Launce and a Target."[2] Daniel's goddesses also include Concordia, who, as simple Concord, made a formal entry in three later masques.[3] Concerning her most fitting attire some doubt seemed to rest in the minds of contemporaries. In *The Vision of the Twelve Goddesses* she had "a party coloured Mantle of Crimson and White . . . imbrodered with silver hands in hand, with a dressing likewise of party coloured Roses";

Fig. 143. Momus in "Cœlum Britannicum" (1634)

Inigo Jones. Chatsworth (*Designs*, No. 196). Copyright of the Duke of Devonshire.

carnation (which may be the same as the earlier "crimson") was her colour in *Cælum Britannicum*, where she bore "in her hand a litle faggot of stickes bound together, and on the top of it a hart, and a garland of corne on her head." In *Salmacida Spolia*, on the other hand, she sported "a watchet garment, her dressing of silver mixt with bulrushes," while in *Albion's Triumph* she had changed her sex and came as "a man in a skie coloured Robe and a yellow Mantle; on his head a Garland of wheate and in his hand a bunch of arrowes tyed together with a white band." Whence derive the bulrushes is uncertain, but the fascia Ripa notes as her familiar emblem, with, also, a heart dependent on a chain.[4]

Eunomia we have already met as Honour's virgin priest; this person, according to Hesiod, was one of the Horæ or Hours, her sisters being Dike and Eirene—a trio of Law, Justice, and Peace. As such the three entered in *The Triumph of Peace*. First, Eirene "in a flowery vesture like the

Fig. 144. Peace in "La Mascherata della Genealogia degli Dei" (Florence, 1565)

Giorgio Vasari. Uffizi, Florence (copy of original).

---

[1] *Middle Temple.*   [2] Her other entries were in *The Golden Age*, *The World tost at Tennis*, and *Tempe Restored.*
[3] *Albion's Triumph*, *Cælum Britannicum*, and *Salmacida Spolia.*
[4] P. 80.   She had a basket of flowers and fruit at Florence in 1565 (Follini MS., p. 58 *verso*).

spring, a Garland of Olives on her head, a branch of Palme in her hand, Buskins of greene Taffata, great puffs about her necke and shoulders." This description, showing Irene both as Peace personified and as one of the original Horæ, spirits of the seasons, seems based on two descriptions in Ripa [1] and one in Cartari.[2] The latter speaks of the flowers, while Ripa gives one of his figures "a garland of olive on her head" and the other "a branch of palm in her right hand." Still a third figure of Peace in

Fig. 145. MERCURY, APOLLO, JOVE, AND ASTRÆA IN "LA PELLEGRINA" (FLORENCE, 1589)
Bernardo Buontalenti. Biblioteca Nazionale, Florence (C. B. 3. 53; ii, 32 *verso*).

Ripa has "a carnation dress," and that is taken for her colour in *Albion's Triumph*—"a woman in a carnation Robe richly adorned, a vale of silver and on it a Garland of Olive and in her hand a branch of Palme" (Fig. 144). What variation might on occasion be permitted is seen when we note that in 1604 at the *Arches of Triumph* the "Hours" were "in loose robes of light colours, painted with flowers," [3] Irene being "richly attired," "her upper garment of carnation hanging loose, a robe of white under it powdered with stars and girt to her." Here she held a caduceus and some ears of corn. These latter occur in Cartari's account, and "a fascia of ears of corn" is mentioned by Ripa on the authority of Pausanius.

Eunomia is recorded with two garments. The first, showing her as the virgin priest,

[1] Pp. 375–377. [2] P. 409.
[3] There is reference here to Ovid's "Conveniunt pictis incinctæ vestibus Horæ."

was a Robe of white silke, gathered about the necke; a pentacle of silvered ſtuffe about her shoulders, hanging foldedly downe, both before and behind. A veſtall vaile on her head of Tiffany, ſtrip't with silver, hanging with a trayne, to the earth;

the second, in *The Triumph of Peace*, was "a purple Sattin Robe, adorn'd with golden Starres, a mantle of carnation Lac'd and Fring'd with Gold, a Coronet of light upon her head, Buskins of

Fig. 146. Virtue in "La Fenice rinovata" (Fossano, 1644)
Biblioteca Nazionale, Turin.

Fig. 147. Virtue in "La Mascherata della genealogia degli dei" (Florence, 1565)
Giorgio Vasari. Uffizi, Florence (copy of original).

Purple drawn with Yellow." For the laſt of the Horæ, Dike, there was "a white Robe and mantle of Sattin, a faire long haire circled with a Coronet of Silver Pikes, white Wings and Buskins, a Crowne imperiall in her hand."[1]

Dike is Juſtice, but for that virtue there were other allegorical personifications. Immediately following Concordia in *The Vision of the Twelve Goddesses* came Aſtræa, the ſtar-goddess, daughter of Zeus and Themis, a further symbol of eternal law:

> Cleare-eyde *Aſtrea* next, with reverend brow,
> Clad in Cæleſtiall hue, which beſt she likes,
> Comes with her Ballance and her sword to shew
> That firſt her judgement weighs before it ſtrikes.

[1] The three Hours appeared also in Jonson's *Entertainment* of 1604; there Law carried a sundial, Juſtice a clock, and Peace an hourglass.

By some error, apparently, the text declares that her mantle was "Crimson with a silver imbrodery" (Fig. 145). The celestial hue, azure, was the one proper for her,[1] and her attributes the balance and the sword. It may be noted that she figured as Justice also in the *Arches of Triumph*, where "all her garments" were "thickly strowed with stars; a crown of stars on her head; a silver veil covering her eyes." Justice in her own name appeared in *Albion's Triumph*, "a woman in a yallow garment richly adorned, her mantle white, and on her head golden rayes, in her right hand a sword and in the middest thereof an Emperiall Crowne," somewhat like Ripa's "Guistitia," "a fair virgin, crowned and clad in gold . . . with a necklace in which is a carved eye."[2]

With her, naturally, go Wisdom and Truth, both of whom are introduced in *Cælum Britannicum*. The former had "a mantle wrought with eyes and hands, golden rayes about her head and *Apollo's* Cithere in her hand," the latter "a Watchet Robe, a Sunne upon her fore-head and bearing in her hand a palme."[3]

The active virtues too lend their aid. Affection to the Country, what now we name Patriotism, in *Albion's Triumph* is "a young man in a Coat armour of yallow, with a purple Mantle, his buskins adorned, his plumed Helme of silver, and in his hand a Garland of long grasse." Close to him are Reputation and Religion, the former "a young man in purple robe wrought with gold and wearing a laurell wreath on his head,"[4] the latter in *Albion's Triumph*

> a woman in a short Surplusse of lawne full gathered about the neck, and under it a garment of watchet with a short vale of silver and about her head beames of gold like the Sunne and in her left hand shee held a booke open.

Fig. 148. BELLONA
Inigo Jones. Chatsworth (*Designs*, No. 413).
Copyright of the Duke of Devonshire.

The same person in *Cælum Britannicum* was "in white and part of her face was covered with a light vaile, in one hand a booke and in the other a flame of fire."[5]

Reputation might be gained by Action, who in *Britannia Triumphans* was not unlike him—"a young man in a rich habit downe to his knees with a large gard of purple about the skirt wherein was written with silver letters MEDIO TUTISSIMA; on his head a girland of Laurell and in one hand a branch of willow." In the same masque Arms was represented "with a cuirass and plum'd helm and a broken lance in his hand." Of his troop were Admiration [6] and Wonder.[7] With these went, as a guiding spirit, Bellona, goddess of war (Fig. 148).[8] Maybe, although it looks as if it were

---

[1] See *Descrittione dell' intermedii fatti nel felicissimo palazo del Gran Duca Cosimo* (Florence, 1569), sig. B2 recto.

[2] P. 187: "Donna in forma di bella vergine, coronata & vestita d' oro . . . con un monile al collo nel quale sia un' occhio scolpito."

[3] See also *The Triumphs of Truth*, where Truth is clad "in a close garment of white sattin, which makes her appear thin and naked, . . . a roabe of white silk cast over it, fill'd with the eies of eagles, . . . over her thrice-sanctified head a milke-white dove, . . . under her feete serpents, . . . her forehead empal'd with a diadem of stars, . . . on her breast a pure round cristall, . . . a sun in her right hand, . . . a fan filled with starres in her left."

[4] *Cælum Britannicum*.

[5] C. F. Ménestrier, in *Des Ballets anciennes et modernes* (Paris, 1682), p. 256, remarks on the difficulty of finding suitable costumes for imaginative characters. As for Religion, he says, he would dress him "de couleur rouge semée de croix d'or qui sont la marque du sang répandu des Martyrs," putting "en tête la couronne de laurier, et en main la palme et le *labarum* de Constantin."

[6] *The Triumph of Peace*.

[7] *The Vision of Delight*.

[8] *Albion's Triumph*.

intended for a statue, one of Inigo Jones's designs gives us her appearance. With shield and lance she stands, noble-helmeted. Her lorica is Roman, with a short kilt falling over a longer skirt.[1]

THE WORLD OF ORDER

Since these masques were court affairs, we need not wonder that Reason, Order, and Government accompanied the private virtues. The first, in *Hymenæi*, was

figur'd in a venerable *personage*, her haire white, and trayling to her waste, crowned with lights, her garments blue and semined with starres, girded unto her with a white bend fill'd with *Arithmeticall* figures, in one hand bearing a Lampe, in the other a bright Sword.

The English edition of the *Iconologia* explains that "the Crown teaches that Reason alone can bring valiant Men upon the *Stage*, and into *Credit*," while the arithmetical figures demonstrate "that as by

Fig. 149. APOLLO IN "LA PELLEGRINA"
(FLORENCE, 1589)
Bernardo Buontalenti. Biblioteca Nazionale,
Florence (C. B. 3, 53; ii, 12).

Fig. 150. ENTHEUS, OR POETIC
FURY, IN "THE MASQUE OF
LORDS" (1613)
Inigo Jones. Chatsworth (*Designs*, No. 56).
Copyright of his Grace the Duke of Devonshire.

them real Things are prov'd, so by *Reason*, we acquire those that relate to the Common Welfare."[2] In the same masque Order appeared. "His under Garment was blue, his upper white and painted full of *Arithmeticall* and *Geometricall* Figures; his Hayre and Beard long, a Starre on his forehead and in his hand a *Geometricall Staffe*." Government, in *Cælum Britannicum*, was more martial, "in a

---

[1] Here too belong some of the 'heroes,' such as Hercules (*Pleasure reconciled to Virtue*) and Ulysses (*Browne's Masque*).
[2] P. 64 (Fig. 255).

coat of Armour, bearing a shield and on it a *Medusa's* head; upon her head a plumed helme and in her right hand a Lance."

Next came the Arts and Sciences, flourishing under these happy omens. Science herself in *Britannia Triumphans* was "a woman in a watchet robe trim'd with silver, on her head a Bend, with little wings like those of *Mercury* and a scrowle of parchment in her hand"—a conception derived, in all probability, from Ripa's "Inventione," who was "a lovely woman with a pair of wings on her

Fig. 151. ENTHEUS, OR POETIC FURY (1603)

Woodcut in Cesare Ripa, *Iconologia* (Rome, 1603).

Fig. 152. ORPHEUS IN "THE TEMPLE OF LOVE" (1635)

Inigo Jones. Chatsworth (*Designs*, No. 233). Copyright of his Grace the Duke of Devonshire.

head like those of Mercury." [1] Poetry soared into *Chloridia* and *The Temple of Love*; in the latter, a milk-white swan by her side, she is shown as "a beautiful woman; her garment was Sky-colour set all with Stars of Gold; her head was crowned with Laurel, with a spangled vaile hanging down behind and her hair in artificial curles graciously dress'd." This clearly is inspired directly from Ripa's account: "A lovely young girl, dressed in sky-blue upon which are many stars; she is crowned with laurel." [2] This figure of Poetry too had a swan by her side. "The Sky-colours," explains the English *Iconologia*, [3]

> signifie that none can excel in this Art, if he be not endowed with extraordinary Talents from *Heaven*.
> . . . The Crown shews that the Poets Design is to be *renown'd*. The Swan is the Emblem of *Music*;
> the Starry Robe, *Divinity*, as having her Original from *Heaven*.

[1] P. 321: "una bella donna, che tiene in capo un par d'ale come quello di Mercurio." The wings are also given to Science in the English *Iconologia*, where they denote "*Elevation* of the Spirit to the Things that are to be learnt" (p. 67, Fig. 269). The "bend," a "dischetto d'oro," appeared in the *Mascherata della genealogia degli dei* in 1565 (Follini MS., f. 98 *verso*).

[2] P. 406: "Giovane bella, vestita d'azzurro celeste, sopra il qual vestimento vi saranno molte stelle; sarà coronata d'alloro."

[3] P. 61, Fig. 243.

184

COURT HIEROGLYPHICKS

Putting forth in his emblems the "Insignia Pœtarium," Alciati emphasizes the importance of this swan image:

> Gentiles clypeos sunt qui in Iouis alite gestant,
> Sunt quibus aut Serpens, aut Leo signa ferunt.
> Dira sed hæc Vatum fugiant animalia ceras,
> Doctaque sustineat stemmata pulcher Olor.
> Hic Phœbo sacer, et nostræ regionis alumnus:
> Rex, olim veteres seruat adhuc titulos.[1]

Entheus, Poetic Fury, is a character in *Lords*,

attired in a close Curace of the Anticke fashion, Bases with labels, a Roabe fastned to his shoulders and hanging downe behind; on his head a wreath of Lawrell, out of which grew a paire of wings; in the one hand he held a booke, and in the other a pen.

"The Wings," we are informed by the English *Iconologia*,[2] "declare the *Quickness* of his Phansie, which soars aloft, and carries an Encomium with it, which still remains *fresh* and *green*, as the Laurel

Fig. 153. ONE OF THE MUSES IN "LA MASCHERATA DELLA GENEALOGIA DEGLI DEI" (FLORENCE, 1565)
Giorgio Vasari. Uffizi, Florence (copy of original).

Fig. 154. ONE OF THE MUSES IN "LA MASCHERATA DELLA GENEALOGIA DEGLI DEI" (FLORENCE, 1565)
Giorgio Vasari. Biblioteca Nazionale, Florence (C. B. 3. 53; i, 36).

and Ivy intimate." A comparison of Ripa's cut with the design by Inigo Jones (Figs. 150, 151) will show immediately how closely the former is followed by the latter. Sculpture, Architecture, and History, all of whom grace the production of *Chloridia*, belong here too, and we may be reasonably

[1] *Emblemata* (Amsterdam, 1551), p. 197. [2] P. 33, Fig. 132. See C. Ripa, p. 178.

sure that their habiliments differed not overmuch from those presented by Ripa—Sculpture, a young girl with a laurel wreath, holding the instruments of her art; Architecture, an older woman with bare arms, holding a compass; and History, a winged woman dressed in white, holding a book and turning her gaze backward.[1]

Over these arts and sciences Apollo is lord.[2] No design showing his appearance in any English masque is extant, but he can have been clad in no dress other than that in which the Renaissance imagination habitually conceived him (*cf.* Figs. 145, 149). Closely associated with him is Mercury, Mercury of many *rôles*, now messenger of Jove and now patron of light and learning. In no

Fig. 155. ONE OF THE MUSES IN "LA PELLEGRINA" (FLORENCE, 1589)

Bernardo Buontalenti. Biblioteca Nazionale, Florence (C. B. 3. 53; ii, 8).

Fig. 156. HERCULES, FAME, AND MERCURY

Inigo Jones. Chatsworth (*Designs*, No. 415). Copyright of his Grace the Duke of Devonshire.

less than nine recorded masques does he figure.[3] At the *Inner Temple* in 1613 he was "in doublet and hose of white Taffita, a white hat, wings on his shoulders and feet, his Caduceus in his hand"; in 1634 that habit had altered slightly into "a Coat of Flame colour girt to him, and a white mantle trimm'd with gold and silver; upon his head a wreath with smal fals of white Feathers, a Caduceus in his hand and wings at his heels."[4] Invariably he descended floating in air, "most artificially and in an exquisite posture,"[5] or else more decorously seated in his chariot.[6] Orpheus too was a popular figure, in *The Lords' Masque* "attired after the old Greeke manner, his haire curled and long, a lawrell wreath on his head, and in his hand hee bare a silver bird." A design by Inigo Jones shows him in a later masque, *The Temple of Love*, where "he wore a white Robe

[1] Pp. 445, 23, 118.
[2] *The Masque of Augurs, Neptune's Triumph, The Fortunate Isles.*
[3] *Penates, Entertainment at Theobalds, Tethys' Festival, Chester's Triumph, Inner Temple, Mercury Vindicated, Lethe, Albion's Triumph, Cælum Britannicum.* The accompanying *Muses* were characters in *The World tost at Tennis, Neptune's Triumph,* and *Love's Triumph.*
[4] *Cf.* C. Ripa, p. 50.
[5] *Tethys' Festival.*
[6] *Cælum Britannicum.*

girt, on his shoulders was tyed with a knot a Mantle of Carnation, and his head crown'd with a Laurel Garland."

From the pursuit of art and science and war springs Fame, that Fame which, partly after Vergil, Ripa described as a woman with a thin-girdled veil, ornamented with feathers, eyes, and ears, bearing a trumpet in her right hand,[1] or else Good Fame, also bearing a trumpet, but adding to that a branch of olive in her left hand and on her neck a golden chain with a heart hanging

Fig. 157. Fortune in "La Mascherata della Genealogia degli Dei" (Florence, 1565)

Giorgio Vasari. Biblioteca Nazionale, Florence (C. B. 3. 53; i, 51).

Fig. 158. One of the Parcæ in "La Mascherata della Genealogia degli Dei" (Florence, 1565)

Giorgio Vasari. Uffizi, Florence (copy of original).

from it.[2]   It was the latter which the masques, for the most part, presented.   Jonson's description in *The Masque of Queens* follows Ripa exactly—a woman "attyr'd in white, with white wings, having a collar of gold about her neck and a heart hanging at it. . . . In her right hand shee bore a trumpet, in her left an olive branch."   The eyes referred to by Ripa appeared in the *Arches of Triumph*, when her robe was "watchet . . . thickly set with open eyes and tongues, a payre of large golden winges at her backe, a trumpet in her hand, a mantle of sundry collours traversing her body."[3]   In *Chloridia*[4] she was set on her familiar globe "standing with her Trumpet in her hand," while in *Britannia Triumphans* her dress was "a Carnation garment trimd with gold, with white wings and flaxen haire; in one hand a golden Trumpet and in the other an Olive Garland" (Fig. 156).

[1] Pp. 142–143.   [2] P. 143.
[3] The "watchet" here corresponds to the "raso turchino" in which she was clad at Florence in 1569 (*Descrittione dell' intermedii fatti nel felicissimo palazo del Gran Duca Cosimo* (Florence, 1569), sig. A3 recto.   [4] *Designs*, Nos. 104–106 (Pls. XX, A; XX, B).

With Fame are closely associated Occasion and Fortune (Fig. 157), both of whom appear in *Cupid's Banishment*, the former "in a rich garment embroderd with silver, a crimson mantle and a shorte cloake of rich tinsie, with a white wand . . . with a longe locke before and bald behind," the latter in mixed colours, holding her familiar wheel.[1]   Of Fortune Tiche was the goddess, and as such she entered in *Cælum Britannicum*,

> her head bald behind and one great lock before, wings at her shoulders and in her hand a wheel, her upper parts naked and the skirt of her Garment wrought all over with Crowns, Scepters, Books and such other things as express both her greatest and smallest gifts.

Since Fame and Fortune look to the future, with them may be linked the Sibylla of *The Vision of the Twelve Goddesses* and of *Lords*.   The former, somewhat incongruously, was "deckt as a

Fig. 159. Imposture in "Britannia Triumphans" (1638)
Inigo Jones. Chatsworth (*Designs*, No. 259 *verso*).
Copyright of his Grace the Duke of Devonshire.

Fig. 160.   Discord
Stefano della Bella.   British Museum.

Nunne in blacke upon White," while the latter had "a Roabe of gold tuckt up before to her girdle, a Kirtle gathered full and of silver, with a vaile on her head, being bare neckt, and bearing in her hand a scrole of Parchment."   Near by are the Fates (Destinies or Parcæ),[2] "in long robes of white Taffata like aged women, with Garlands of Narcissus Flowers on their heads; and in their left hands they carried distaffes" (Fig. 158).   Prognostication in *Twelve Months* and Good Event in the *Entertainment at Theobalds* were of their company.

[1] Here again Ripa (pp. 169–170) was followed.   [2] *Entertainment at Theobalds, Somerset's Masque, Lovers made Men.*

COURT HIEROGLYPHICKS

The World of Discord

All the good and virtuous forces looked back longingly to that Golden Age which, personified, came forth in a masque to which his name was given and which found a glowing description in Ripa's volume.[1] So, too, they gazed sadly on the Iron Age, full of vices. Closely associated with such figures was Plutus, god of riches, who in 1613[2] made a gorgeous show, wearing "a short robe of gould, frindg'd; his wide sleeves turn'd up and out-showd his naked armes; his Head and Beard sprinckl'd with showrs of gould; his Buskins clinckant as his other attire." Here he was the companion of princes; twenty years later[3] he had turned into an aged miser with wrinkled face, bald head, thin white beard, and a hunchback. His opposite was, of course, Pœnia, goddess of poverty,

Fig. 161. The Curious in "Time Vindicated" (1623)
Inigo Jones. Chatsworth (*Designs*, No. 64). Copyright of his Grace the Duke of Devonshire.

Fig. 162. Capriccio (1603)
Woodcut in Cesare Ripa, *Iconologia*
(Rome, 1603).

a woman of a pale colour, large brims of a hat upon her head, through which her hair started up like a fury; her Robe was of a dark color, full of patches; about one of her hands was tyed a chaine of Iron, to which was fastned a weighty stone which she bore up under her arm.

The Iron Age brought with him a medley of distorted humours. Here, for instance, is Opinion, shown in *The Triumph of Peace* "in an old fashioned Doublet of blacke Velvet and truncke Hose, a short Cloake of the same with an antique Cape, a blacke Velvet cap, pinch'd up, with a white fall [and] a staffe in his hand," companioned by Confidence,

[1] Pp. 136–138. See also *Descrizione delle pompe e delle feste* (Florence, 1584), sig. 4, i, ii.
[2] *Middle Temple.*
[3] *Cælum Britannicum.*

189

in a slash'd Doublet, parti-coloured, Breeches sutable with poynts at knees, favours upon his breast and arme, a broad-brim'd Hat, tied up on one side, banded with a Feather, a long Locke of Hair, trim'd with severall coloured Ribbands, wide Boots and great Spurres with Bels for Rowels.

Here, too, are the Oblivion of *Luminalia*, "a young man naked and a greene mantle tucked about his shoulders, and upon his head a cuckoe," the Novelty of *The Triumph of Peace*, Mania of *Lords*,

Fig. 163. A Fury
Stefano della Bella. British Museum.

with a habit "confused and strange, but yet gracefull," and the Jealousy of *Chloridia*,[1] whom Ripa [2] described as a "woman in a blue dress with wavy design covered over with eyes and ears; wings on her shoulders; a cock on her left arm and in her right hand a bunch of thorns." With them goes Capriccio of *Middle Temple*—"a strange person and as strangely habited, halfe French, halfe Swizz, . . . wearing on his head a paire of golden Bellowes, a guilt spurre in one hand and with the other managing the reigns." He has been taken directly from Ripa (Fig. 162) [3] or from Henry Peacham's *Minerva Britanna*, where the same figure, called Capriccio in the motto, is headed "Levitas." [4]

Of this crew are the Imperfect Creatures who flock confusedly into *Mercury*. Imposture in *Britannia Triumphans* has

a coat with hanging sleeves and great skirts, little breeches, a high crownd hat, one side pinned up, a little ruffe and a formall beard, and an angling rod in his hand with a fish at the hooke, with a bag and a horne at his girdle—

a nice jibe at the devotees of Izaac Walton's craft (Fig. 159). Both in *Luminalia* and in *Salmacida Spolia* appears a Fury, ever a popular figure (Fig. 163).[5] Fear enters in *Chloridia* [6] and Doubt in *Love's Welcome*.[7] *Chloridia* also introduces Disdain and Dissimulation, the "Simulatione" of Ripa,[8] "a woman with a mask so placed that she shows two faces, dressed in changeable stuff, holding a magpie in her right hand." [9] The Curious in *Time Vindicated* are the Eared, the Eyed, and the Nosed (Fig. 161).[10] Close comrades of these are Milton's "rowt of Monsters headed like sundry sorts of wilde Beasts, . . . their apparell glistring, . . . with Torches in their hands."

[1] *Designs*, No. 90 (Pl. XVI, C).

[2] P. 181: "Donna con una veste di torchino à onde, dipinta tutta d' occhi e d' orecchie, con l' ali alle spalle, con un gallo nel braccio sinistro & nella destra mano con un mazo di spine."

[3] P. 48: "Giovinetto vestito di varij colori, in capo porterà un cappelletto simile al vestimento, sopra il quale vi saranno penne diverse; nella destra mano terrà un mantice & nella sinistra un sperone. . . . Lo sperone & il mantice mostrano il capriccioso pronto all' adulare l' altrui virtu ò al pungere i vitij."

[4] P. 149.   [5] *Designs*, No. 324–326 (Pls. XLIII, A; XLIII, B).

[6] *Id.*, No. 92 (Pl. XVI, A). See C. Ripa, p. 382: "Donna con faccia picciola, & smorta . . . haverà i capelli drizzati per l' effetto della paura."   [7] See C. Ripa, p. 118.

[8] P. 455: "Donna con una Maschera sopra al viso, in modo che mostri due faccie; sarà vestita di cangiante & nella destra mano terra una Pica."

[9] *Designs*, No. 91 (Pl. XVI, D).

[10] See C. Ripa, p. 99, on Curiosity: "Donna di vestimento rosso & azurro, sopr' il quale vi siano sparse molt' orecchie."

COURT HIEROGLYPHICKS

These creatures of imperfect shape are served by stormy and treacherous elements—the Thunder, Tempest, Lightning, Snow, and Rain [1] of *Chloridia* or the Ignis Fatuus of *Luminalia*. The contrast serves to make Virtue and her train the more eminent. Night brings many strange, crawling, and deformed things to life, but the glittering array of torches and candles, sparkling like so many jewels, acts as a charm to drive them in disorder back to their cavernous haunts. Opinion and Imposture are defeated by Innocence and Honour, surrounded by the Stars of Night. The cavalier's philosophy has come full circle, in the symbol of eternity.

[1] The last was "presented by five persons, all swolne and clouded over, their hayre flagging as if they were wet, and in their hands balls full of sweet water which, as they dance, sprinkle all the roome."

VII

OMNIUM FERE GENTIUM . . .

ALL the world is here, for the masque is a kind of microcosm, an image of the universe. The Continents themselves come upon the stage in *Somerset's Masque*: "*Asia* in a Persian Ladies habit, with a Crowne on her head";[1] "*Africa* like a Queene of the Moores, with a crown";[2] "*America* in a skin coate of the colour of the iuyce of Mulberies, on her head large round brims of many coloured feathers and in the midst of it a small Crowne";[3] "*Europe* in the habit of an Empresse, with an Imperiall Crowne on her head" (Fig. 164).[4] So, too, were shown the Kingdoms of Britain in *Cælum Britannicum*, with the river Thames,[5] "crowned with flowers, with a blue cloth of silver robe about him."

Into this strange array of allegorical figures come, bravely clad or in rags, a motley crowd of persons, ancient and modern, high-born and low, from Western lands and from the Orient. The world walks in these masques.

ROME AND GREECE

On the deities are attendant their priests and temple officers. Flamens (Fig. 165), Auspices, and Augurs move solemnly before us, and Priests in rich robes lend dignity to many a masque. In *Hue and Cry after Cupid* they serve Hymen, "attir'd in yellow, with wreathes of *marioram*, and veiles," in *Love freed from Ignorance* the Muses, in *Inner Temple* Jupiter, in *The Triumphs of the Prince d'Amour* Mars. The last were "cloathed in Crimson Robes of the Antick shape, girt to the wast and, being tucked up, fall in a fold; on their heads, Mitres of a Helmet form, with a Ponyard advanc'd on the top." With gold mitres and red gowns they appear in *Pleasure reconciled to Virtue* and Roman-clad in *Albion's Triumph*. The ancient poets accompany them in four masques.[6]

The patrician life of Rome reveals itself before our eyes. Albanactus (Fig. 166) enters in *Albion's Triumph*, "triumphing attended like a Roman Emperor," clad

> in a Curase of yellow Sattin embroidered with silver, his gorget clincant, cut round, and on his breast an Angels head imbost of gold, the Labells of the sleeves and short Bases of watchet embroidered with the same, the under sleeves and long stockings of white; on his head a Burgonet richly enchast with silver, turn'd up before in a scrowle, with an artificiall wreath of Lawrell, out of which sprang rayes like a piked Crowne.[7]

His Consuls are dressed in similar fashion, and Patricians walk by his side. Before him come the Plebeians, Gladiators, Pugilists, and Tumblers.[8]

Ancient Barbarians are figured in *Tempe Restored* (Fig. 167), Bœotians and Thebans in *Pan's*

---

[1] C. Ripa, p. 334.
[2] *Id.*, p. 335: "Una donna mora, quasi nuda."
[3] *Id.*, p. 338: "Donna ignuda, di carnagione fosca, di giallo color mista," with an "artificioso ornamento di penne di varij colori."
[4] *Id.*, p. 333.
[5] *Beauty*.
[6] *Neptune's Triumph, Albion's Triumph, The Temple of Love, Britannia Triumphans.* See *Designs*, Nos. 128, 129.
[7] A note inscribed in *Designs*, No. 123, reads, "The boddis yellow and imbrodered with siller   The labels of yᵉ sleeves and short bases wauchet   The puff sleeves and long bases whight   The girdell and gorgett clincant silver   The head pease and buskines sillur on yellow   The featherrs whight the cronett goulde   the laurell greene and goulde   The round hose carnation at the bottom imbrodered silver   A ruff white tiffony."
[8] *Designs*, Nos. 113–118.

Anniversary. In *Salmacida Spolia* the masquers are Amazons, clad in "habits of carnation, embroidered with silver, with plumed Helmes, Bandrickes with Antique swords hanging by their sides, all as rich as might be" (Fig. 169). Another Amazon was Penthesileia, of *Queens*, a masque

Fig. 164. THE CONTINENTS (1603)
Woodcuts in Cesare Ripa, *Iconologia* (Rome, 1603).

which introduced an array of empresses famous for their beauty and heroic virtues—Zenobia of Palmira, Valasca of Bohemia, Thomyris of Scythia, Hypsicratea of Pontus, Candace of Ethiopia, Camilla the Volscian, Boadicea of Britain, Berenice of Egypt, Carian Artemisia, and Atalanta the Ætolian (Fig. 168).[1] Each of these was carefully distinguished by contrasted colouring. Thus

[1] *Designs*, Nos. 18–34. The most important of these designs are reproduced in *Shakespeare's England* (Oxford, 1916), ii, 312, 316, 318, 322, 324, 326, 328, 330. The editors of *Designs*, p. 41, state that Atalanta did not appear in the masque, but she is included in the manuscript account of the performance printed in P. Reyher, p. 507. The libretto lists Boadicea and Hypsicratea, their places being taken in the manuscript account by Bundrica (Bonduca) and Atalanta.

Penthesileia had "Depe pink coler, Deep morrey," and "Skie coler," while to Camilla was granted "Wyllowe colord Carnation Whit." Peach colour, watchet, and carnation graced the dress of Thomyris; orange-tawny, ash-colour, and yellow that of Artemisia; green, carnation, and white

Fig. 165. A Flamen in
"Albion's Triumph" (1632)

Inigo Jones. Chatsworth (*Designs*, No. 127).
Copyright of his Grace the Duke of Devonshire.

Fig. 166. The Emperor Albanactus
in "Albion's Triumph" (1632)

Inigo Jones. Chatsworth (*Designs*, No. 122).
Copyright of his Grace the Duke of Devonshire.

that of Berenice; deep flame-colour, peach, and pale watchet that of Candace; watchet, carnation, and white that of Zenobia; and crimson, yellow, and white that of Atalanta.

The East and the West

The various races of the world are freely represented in this crowding mass of types. The Renaissance was an age of travel and discovery, so that we need feel no surprise when we discover that Indians, both of the Orient and of America, were popular figures.[1] In *Middle Temple* comes a set of musicians "attir'd like Virginean Priests. . . . Their Robes were tuckt up before; strang Hoods of feathers and scallops about their neckes, and on their heads turbants, stucke with severall

---

[1] With the Indians noted below should be compared the "Brasilianus" in Johannes Sluper, *Omnium fere gentium, nostræque ætatis Nationum, Habitus & Effigies* (Antwerp, 1572). C. F. Ménestrier, *Des Ballets anciens et modernes* (Paris, 1682), p. 252, notes that "Les Americains ont un bonnet de plumes de diverses couleurs, une ceinture de même façon qui couvre leur nudité; ils ont encore un collier de cesmê mes plumes dont ils portent un bouquet de chaque main quand ils dansent."

colour'd feathers, spotted with wings of flies of extraordinary bignesse, like those of their countrie" (Fig. 170). The chief masquers here were also

in Indian habits, the ground, cloath of silver richly embroidered with golden Sunnes, and about every Sunne ran a traile of gold, imitating Indian worke; their bases of the same ſtuffe and worke, but betwixt every pane of embroidery went a rowe of white Eſtridge feathers, mingled with sprigs of golde plate; under their breaſts they wore bawdricks of golde, embroidered high with purle, and about their neckes Ruffes

Fig. 167. A Barbarian in "Tempe Restored" (1632)

Inigo Jones. Chatsworth (*Designs*, No. 150). Copyright of his Grace the Duke of Devonshire.

Fig. 168. A Queen in "The Masque of Queens" (1609)

Inigo Jones. Chatsworth (*Designs*, No. 31). Copyright of his Grace the Duke of Devonshire.

of feathers spangled with pearle and silver. On their heads high sprigg'd feathers, compaſt in Coronets, like the Virginian Princes they presented. Betwixt every set of feathers and about their browes, in the under-part of their Coronets shin'd Sunnes of golde plate, sprinkled with pearle; from whence sprung rayes of the like plate, that mixing with the motion of the feathers, shew'd exceedingly delightfull and gracious. Their legges were adorn'd with close long white silke-ſtockings, curiously embroidered with golde to the Midde-legge.

And over these (being on horsebacke) they drew greaves, or buskins, embroidered with gould and enterlaƈt with rowes of feathers, altogether eſtrangeful and *Indian* like.

In their Hands . . . they brandisht cane-darts of the fineſt gould. Their vizards of olive collour, but pleasingly visag'd; their hayre blacke and lardge, waving downe to their shoulders.

In *Flowers* Kawasha and his Floridans play a considerable part. The leader sported

a Night-cap of red cloth of gold, close to his skull, tied under his chin, two holes cut in the toppe, out of which his eares appeared, hung with two great Pendants, on the crowne of his Cappe a Chimney,

Fig. 169. An Amazon in "Salmacida Spolia" (1640)

Inigo Jones. Chatsworth (*Designs*, No. 354).
Copyright of his Grace the Duke of Devonshire.

Fig. 170. An Indian in "The
Middle Temple Masque" (1613)

Inigo Jones. Chatsworth (*Designs*, No. 60).
Copyright of his Grace the Duke of Devonshire.

Fig. 171. A Group of Indians in "La Douairière de
Billebahaut" (1626)

Bibliothèque Nationale, Paris.

a glasse chaine about his necke, his body and legges of Olive-colour stuffe, made close like the skinne, bases of Tobacco-colour stuffe cut like Tobacco leaves, sprinkled with orcedure, in his hand an *Indian* Bow and Arrowes.

His Sergeant "carried on his shoulder a great Tobacco Pipe, as bigge as a Calvier."

The English masques were by no means alone in thus introducing to the stage those figures which, from travellers' tales, had so seized upon popular and courtly imagination.   Groups of

Fig. 172. Two Indians in "Il Tobacco" (Turin, 1650)
Biblioteca Nazionale, Turin.

"Ameriquains" graced the Parisian *Douairière de Billebahaut* in 1626 (Fig. 171), and later in the century Indians of fantastic sort made colourful the production of *Il Tobacco*, one of the Turin ballets (Fig. 172).[1]

The true Indians of *Tempe Restored* and *The Temple of Love* were not far different in appearance. Fig. 173 shows the former, clad, as a note on the design states, in "a scincote [skin-coat] of olive fleshcollor," with "feathers on a bend" and "a collor of tin[s]ell of gould in s[c]allopes about the neck," the feathers being red, white, green, yellow, and brown.   What seems to be the costume of Indamora has also been preserved [2] (Fig. 174), and several of her attendants are shown in two other sketches [3] (Fig. 175).   The former of these presents costumes for some Indian priests; the latter delineates two Brachmani (Brahmins).   A long inscription notes that the hat of one was like "ye persia[n] mitter," while the second wore "a roabe of russet Girt low w[ith] a great belley like a swoln ma[n]."   He had "long mistchahoes," and on his head was "a capp coming fou[r]th before like a peake . . . and a hood gatherd behinde."   Altogether his appearance, according to Inigo Jones, was "like a Sr Jon fall staff."   All we know of the Indian knights of 1604 is that their attire was rich with "loose robes of crimson sattin embroidered with gold and bordered with broad silver laces, dublets and bases of cloth of silver. . . . In theyr hats ech of them" had "an Indian bird for a fether with some jewells." [4]

---

[1] See Marcel Paquot, *Les Étrangers dans le ballet de cour* (*Revue du seizième siècle*, xv (1928), 43–55) and *Les Étrangers dans le ballet de cour au temps de Henri IV* (*id.*, xvi (1929), 21–39).

[2] Details of this sketch appear in *Designs*, No. 236.

[3] *Designs*, Nos. 213, 214.

[4] Sir E. K. Chambers, *The Elizabethan Stage*, iii, 279.

The Chinese knights and magician of the same masque are undescribed.   Moors, slaves to the Indians, occur in *Middle Temple*, and Gipsies appear both in the masque of that name and in *Cælum Britannicum*.   Some Persian nobles are figured in *The Temple of Love* (Fig. 176),

> apparelled in Asian Coats of Sea-green embroidered that reached down above their knees, with buttons and loops before, and cut up square to their hips, and returned down with two short skirts; the sleeves of this Coat were large without seam, and cut short to the bending of the Arm, and hanging down long

Fig. 173. AN INDIAN IN "TEMPE
RESTORED" (1632)

Inigo Jones.   Chatsworth (*Designs*, No. 144).
Copyright of his Grace the Duke of Devonshire.

Fig. 174. INDAMORA, QUEEN OF
NARSINGA, IN "THE TEMPLE
OF LOVE" (1635)

Inigo Jones.   Chatsworth (*Designs*, No. 236).
Copyright of his Grace the Duke of Devonshire.

> behind, trimm'd with buttons as those of the breast; out of this came a sleeve of white Sattin embroydered, and the Basis answerable to the sleeve hung down in gathering underneath the shortest part of their Coat; on their heads they wore Persian Turbants, silver'd underneath, and wound about with white Cypress, and one fall of a white feather before.

Many other attempts were made to show national dress, the artists taking full advantage of the opportunities thus offered for the introduction of diversity in styles and colourings.   Here is a Jewess of Portugal, a Pole (Fig. 177),[1] a native of Switzerland.   Particular attention, naturally, was paid to the local costumes of Britain.   Welshmen with harps appeared in *Pleasure reconciled to Virtue*, an old-fashioned Englishman and Englishwoman[2] in *Salmacida Spolia*, together with—no doubt to please the Stuarts—several early Picts and Britons.   A Druid is shown in *Richmond*, in which he wears a "Robe of crimson Taffita and a garland on his head," and in *The Passionate Lovers* (Fig. 178).

[1] See also *Designs*, Nos. 448, 449.   [2] *Id.*, Nos. 334, 335.

198

Ancient Scots appear in *Cælum Britannicum* and in *Salmacida Spolia* (Fig. 179). With them, in the latter masque, are several ancient Irishmen.[1]

FROM COURTIERS TO COOKS

Courtiers and cavaliers find a natural place in these living pictures. In old-fashioned armour a Knight steps forth in *Britannia Triumphans*,[2] a figure akin to the Antique Cavaliers in *Salmacida Spolia* [3] and to the Old-fashioned Courtiers of *Britannia Triumphans*.[4] Close companions of the last

Fig. 175. MAGICIANS IN "THE TEMPLE OF
LOVE" (1635)

Inigo Jones. Chatsworth (*Designs*, No. 213).
Copyright of his Grace the Duke of Devonshire.

Fig. 176. A NOBLE PERSIAN
YOUTH IN "THE TEMPLE OF
LOVE" (1635)

Inigo Jones. Chatsworth (*Designs*, No. 225).
Copyright of his Grace the Duke of Devonshire.

are several historical persons, Cade,[5] Kett,[6] or Jack Straw (Fig. 181). Of such historical representations the masque in general made but little use, although Skogan, Skelton, Long Meg of Westminster, and Mary Ambree appeared in *The Fortunate Isles*, and Madge Hewlett in *Twelve Months*. A fat, debauched Cavalier rolls into *The Triumphs of the Prince d'Amour*, and another into *Luminalia*. *Salmacida Spolia* has its Amorous Courtier, and *Tempe Restored* its Favourite Fugitive.[7]

[1] Probably through masque influence four "*Scotch* Antickes" and four "*wilde Irish*" were introduced in Ford's *Perkin Warbeck* (printed 1634).

[2] *Designs*, Nos. 292 (Pl. XXXV), 297.   [3] *Id.*, No. 338 *verso*.   [4] *Id.*, No. 279.   [5] *Id.*, Nos. 280, 281.

[6] *Id.*, Nos. 282 (Pl. XXXIV, D), 283.   [7] For details of his costume see P. Reyher, p. 511.

The courtier's life was dominated largely by love, and accordingly in several masques we are given the spectacle of this emotion in contorted forms. *Love's Triumph* brings forward no less than a dozen such types — lovers who are Glorious Boasting, Whining Ballading, Romantic, Umbrageous, Bribing, Jealous, Illiberal, Scornful, Angry, Melancholic, Envious, and Sensual, a series of grotesques inspired by *commedia dell' arte* figures as viewed by Jacques Callot.[1] *The Triumphs of the Prince d'Amour* introduces a group of kindred persons—a Formal Spanish Lover, a

Fig. 177. A Noble Polish Youth

Inigo Jones. Chatsworth (*Designs*, No. 9).
Copyright of his Grace the Duke of Devonshire.

Fig. 178. A Druid in "The Passionate Lovers" (1638)

Inigo Jones. Chatsworth (*Designs*, No. 320). Inscribed, "Druide Mr Carliles Play 1638." Copyright of his Grace the Duke of Devonshire.

Jealous Italian, a Fantastic French, a Dull Dutch, and a Debauched English—and these in turn are closely associated with the four mad lovers of *Salmacida Spolia* and with the Frantics (a Self-Lover, a Melancholic, a Schoolman, and a Usurer) in *Lords*.

From these we pass to the current figures taken from London's streets, thence to be set on Whitehall's courtly stage. *Hymenæi* presents a Bride,

> her hayre flowing and loose, sprinckled with grey; on her head a *gyrland* of *Roses*, like a turret; her garments white; and on her back a weather's fleece hanging downe; her *zone* or girdle about her waste of white wooll, fastned with the *Herculean* knot.

With her was the Bridegroom, "his haire short and bound with partie-coloured ribbands and gold twist; his garments purple and white." Stub, the Bridegroom in *Love's Welcome*, was "apparelled in a yellow Canvas Doublet, cut, a green Jerkin and Hose, like a Ranger. A Monmouth Cap, with a yellow Feather, yellow Stockings, and Shoes."

[1] *Designs*, Nos. 68–78.

OMNIUM FERE GENTIUM...

Flowers introduces a representative Citizen, and *Love's Welcome* two allegorically clad Men of Business. Some typical Old Men enter in *Salmacida Spolia*.[1] A Puritan, "a Modern Devil," is a character in *The Temple of Love*, akin to the Wolfgangus Vandergoose of *Salmacida Spolia*.[2]

The soldiers of that age and of earlier times were familiar characters. There were Fencers in *Flowers, Cupid's Banishment*, and *Pan's Anniversary*. Ancient British Soldiers marched into *Richmond*, their Captain clad in "a short Coat reaching almost to his knees, made in scales, and on his head a Petasus; Buskins or short Bootes on his legs." During the same year, in *The Triumphs of the Prince d'Amour*, appeared "swaggering Souldiers, and of the cheaper quality, . . . their Beards mishapen, with long Whiskers of the Stilletto cut." Sailors too were popular —Slug the Lighterman, Skippers, Dutch Seamen, and Londoners.

Fig. 179. Scots and Irishmen in "Salmacida Spolia" (1640)

Inigo Jones. Chatsworth (*Designs*, No. 333). Copyright of his Grace the Duke of Devonshire.

From London's streets too come a Constable, a Watchman, and a Bellman. The Roaring Boys roister away, companions of the Drunkard. The underworld of seventeenth-century England spawns here—Knaves and Ruffians, Thieves, Tinkers, Beggars, Coiners, Bawds, Midwives, and Courtesans, Mountebanks, Jugglers, Ballad-singers, Fiddlers, Mock-musicians, and Morescoes. A Bearward leads forward his performing animal; a Pedlar sells his wares; while a Seller of Tinderboxes and a Crier of Mousetraps announce their goods (Fig. 180).[3]

Mine Host and Hostess are characters in *Inner Temple*, and several other persons readily associate themselves with them —a Brewer and his Clerk, a Vintner's Boy, a Wine Cooper, a Waferman, and Lady Alewife. With these crowd in other familiar types—a Miller, a Pedant, a Melancholic Student, a Philosopher, a Physician, a Spagyrick, or chemist, and several Alchemists—the flocking and migrant persons of this universal caravanserai. The country folk, too, are not without representation. A Country Gentleman and his Wife lead this group, followed by the Country Fellow who was one of the Projectors in *The Triumph of Peace* and a Country Wench. Shepherds are common characters, and their appropriate companions are Farmers and Dairymaids.

Alongside the aristocrats, the tradesmen, the rogues, and the country people all degrees of servants make their entries. Here are Woodmen and Heralds and attendants at the hunt, Lacqueys and Keepers, the last

> formally attired in green Perpetuana, with ierkins and long hose, . . . having either of them a horne hanging formally at their backes, and on their heads they had greene Mommoth-caps with greene feathers, the one of them in his hand bearing a hooke-bill and the other a long pike-staffe, both painted greene.[4]

Jockeys, Gardeners, Porters, Barbers, Nurses, Chambermaids, Kitchenmaids, Charwomen, and Cooks complete this array of motley types—a microcosm of the teeming world around them.

[1] *Designs*, No. 304 *verso*.   [2] *Id.*, Nos. 330–332.
[3] *Id.*, Nos. 186, 451 (reproduced in E. Welsford, p. 216), 261, 263–268, 272–276. For coiners in *Le Château de Bicêtre* (1632) see Henri Prunières, *Le Ballet de cour en France avant Benserade et Lully* (Paris, 1914), Pl. 11.
[4] *Caversham Masque*.

WIZARDS AND WITCHES

Nor was that realm forgotten which peasants' tales and kitchenmaids' gossip loved to people with denizens of another kind.   Fairies, acted by children and captained by Oberon, found physical embodiment on this imaginative stage.   Various designs by Inigo Jones [1] apparently show us their

Fig. 180.   A Mountebank and other Antimasque Characters in "Britannia Triumphans" (1638)

Inigo Jones.   Chatsworth (*Designs*, No. 261).
Copyright of his Grace the Duke of Devonshire.

Fig. 181. Antimasque Characters in "Britannia Triumphans" (1638)

Inigo Jones.   Chatsworth (*Designs*, No. 263).
Copyright of his Grace the Duke of Devonshire.

appearance in *Oberon*, although they by no means confined their presence to that one masque.[2] Presumably Fig. 182 presents some of Jonson's Nation of Faies,[3] while Fig. 183 may quite possibly contain the picture of fantastic Oberon.   Another fairy-like creature is Thelema in *The Temple of Love* (Fig. 184).   This lady is described in the printed text as

> a young woman in a Robe of changeable silke, girt with severall tuckes under her breast and beneath her wast, and great leaves of silver about her shoulders hanging downe to the midst of her Arm; upon her head a garland of great Marigolds and puffs of silver'd Lawne between, and at her shoulders Angels wings.

[1] *Designs*, Nos. 46–53.
[2] They appeared also in *Althorpe*, *Twelve Months*, and *Luminalia*.   Robin Goodfellow was a character in the last-mentioned masque and in *Love Restored*.   [3] See also *Designs*, No. 48.

She is, as D'Avenant notes, the symbol of will. On one design Jones has written "Gnome garland of marigould and puffs of tin[s]el beetweene," and on his finished sketch he has repeated "Gnome," no doubt a variant character name.[1] Her companion is Sunesis, symbolic of understanding :

> a man of noble Aspect and richly attir'd; his garment of Cloth of gold reaching downe below his knees and girt with a tucke at the Wast, with wide sleeves turn'd up; his mantle of Watchet fastned on both shoulders and hanging long down behind, a garland of Sinope on his head, with a flame of fire issuing out of it; his Buskins were yellow, wrought with gold.[2]

Tempe Restored brings in a set of Magicians; these are not described for us, but the Enchanters of *Somerset's Masque* were clearly allegorical figures, Error and Rumour—the first "in a skin coate

Fig. 182. THREE FAIES IN "OBERON" (1611)
Inigo Jones. Chatsworth (*Designs*, No. 49).
Copyright of his Grace the Duke of Devonshire.

scaled like a Serpent and an antick habit painted with Snakes, a haire of curled Snakes and a deformed visard"; the second "in a skin coate full of winged Tongues and over it an antick robe; on his head a Cap like a tongue, with a large paire of wings to it." Their companion Enchantresses were Curiosity and Credulity—one "in a skin coate full of eyes and an antick habit over it, a fantastick Cap full of Eyes," and the other "in a like habit painted with eares and an antick Cap full of eares." Merlin of *Britannia Triumphans* wore "a gowne of light purple, downe to his ankles, slackly girt, with wide sleeves turned up with powdred Ermines" and carried "in his hand a silvered rod."

The old Enchantress of *Huntingdon Masque*, "in crimson velvet, with pale face, black haire and dislyking countenance," seems to have been a kind of witch, akin to the Hags of *Queens*, with their emblems of rats, ointment-pots, spindles, rattles, and "other veneficall instruments." Their Dame was "naked-arm'd, bare-footed, her frock tuck'd, her hayre knotted and folded with vipers; in her hand a torch made of a dead mans arme, lighted, girded with a snake." [3]

What the ghosts in *Lovers made Men* looked like we are not informed, but no doubt this familiar figure appeared much in the same shape it assumed on the professional stage, and possibly there may have been some agreement between both and the ghosts of the Italian theatre. Of the supernatural

---

[1] *Designs*, Nos. 237 *verso*, 239.   [2] See also *id.*, No. 237.
[3] There were witches also in *The Temple of Love* and *Luminalia*.

vision in general Angelo Ingegnieri [1] showed himself not a trifle contemptuous: "I have never yet," he assures us, "seen a ghost on the stage that did not appear ridiculous." The frequency with which such apparitions were brought into current plays, however, forces him to discuss the best methods of achieving a desired result. For various reasons, he opines, the ghost had best be made to stand fairly far up-stage, partly because there, set in juxtaposition to the smaller perspective side-wings, he gained in stature and thus became more horrifying, particularly

because the front of this perspective set, diminishing in size and finally becoming very small, may be the more conveniently covered (and also, when the proper time comes, uncovered) with a dark veil.

Fig. 183. OBERON IN
"OBERON" (1611)

Inigo Jones. Chatsworth (*Designs*, No. 52).
Copyright of his Grace the Duke of Devonshire.

Fig. 184. THELEMA IN "THE TEMPLE
OF LOVE" (1635)

Inigo Jones. Chatsworth (*Designs*, No. 239).
Copyright of his Grace the Duke of Devonshire.

This I deem necessary for two reasons. The first is that behind it—and particularly if it be moderately thick—one sees somewhat indistinctly all that happens in the rear of the stage; the second is that it provides greater realistic effect to the appearance of the ghost, which, as an infernal thing, ought to darken the air around it. . . . This veil, then, ought to be placed so far from the front of the set that the ghost may appear and move easily in the open space beyond. The ghost should be all draped, rather than dressed, in black silk or some similar light material. Its hands and feet should not show: it ought to look like some shapeless thing, moving rather on small wheels than taking formal steps and walking like a human being. As to its speech, it ought to have a high and resonant voice, but at the same time one that is rough, harsh, and horrible, inhuman in its tones. Always this same tone is to be preserved even when the subject-matter would ordinarily demand change of accent and varying emphasis. While it speaks, it should ever be restless, stopping in no one place, moving continually in the manner described above, by means of wheels or else with the aid of a similar machine. The

[1] *Op. cit.*, pp. 488, 533-534.

same device may be used to make it disappear of a sudden, immediately it has finished its speech. At this moment of disappearance the veil must be consumed by fire. Beforehand it is to be soaked in aqua-vita or the like and so placed that there is no danger of causing injury to anything. This flaming of fire adds to the horror of the situation and combines to dazzle the spectators' eyes, concealing the action on the stage. For that reason it is best to carry these things out at the extreme end of the set, farthest removed from the eyes of the spectators.

In some such way, we may believe, appeared the masque ghosts, and, recalling the rapid movements of Hamlet's father, we might even suggest a connexion between it and Ingegnieri's vision; that spirit worked "i' the earth so fast" that it became "hic et ubique."

WILD MEN AND GROTESQUES

Among the earliest-mentioned stage types in Italy were "wild men,"[1] and these, in various guises, find scope for their clumsy amblings in the masque. The Wild Men in *The Triumphs of the Prince d'Amour* had "Wastcoats of Flesh colour," making them seem naked, "their heads cover'd with green leaves, their wasts girt with the like, and a green Basis fring'd reach'd to their knees."[2] So, no doubt, were clad the Green Men of *Chester's Triumph* and closely akin were the Sylvans. These, "attired in changeable Taffatie, with wreaths of flowers on their heads," appeared in *Lord Hay's Masque* and, menacing with clubs, in *Oberon*. Sylvanus was a character in *Caversham*, where he was

> shapt after the description of the ancient Writers, his lower parts like a Goate and his upper parts in an anticke habit of rich Taffatie cut into Leaves; and on his head he had a false Haire, with a wreath of long Boughes and Lillies that hung dangling about his necke, and in his hand a Cypresse branch.

Caversham also brought forward a group of Robin Hood Men,

> in sutes of greene striped with blacke, drest in doublets with great bellies and wide sleeves, shaped fardingale-wise at the shoulders, without wings; their hose were round, with long greene stockings; on their heads they wore broad flat caps with greene feathers crosse quite over them, carrying greene Bowes in their hands and greene Arrowes by their sides.

Fig. 185. A Lion in "Tempe Restored" (1632)

Inigo Jones. Chatsworth (*Designs*, No. 146). Copyright of his Grace the Duke of Devonshire.

A May Lady appears in *Inner Temple* and *Love's Welcome*; the former also has a May Lord.

Fantastic animals gambolled round. *Tempe Restored* introduced Hare and Hounds, Lions, Apes, an Ass, and Hogs (Fig. 185). An Ape appeared also in *Cupid's Banishment* and in *Britannia Triumphans*, while Baboons sported in *Inner Temple*.[3] Birds, notably a Magpie, a Crow, a Jay, a Kite, and an Owl, were characters in *The Triumph of Peace*, and several animal-shaped and bird-shaped men came into *News from the New World*, *Browne's Masque*, and *Luminalia*. How the Cat and Fiddle of *Time Vindicated* was dressed we cannot tell.[4] With the human actors disguised

---

[1] See F. Neri, *La Maschera del selvaggio* (*Giornale storico della letteratura italiana*, lix (1912), 47–68). A picture of such a "Vir Sylvestris" appears in Johannes Sluper, p. 133, No. 118.

[2] *Designs*, Nos. 460, 461.

[3] See also *Britannia Triumphans* and *Middle Temple*; *Designs*, Nos. 147, 148, 151, 152, 448, 464, 466.

[4] See also *Designs*, No. 455.

came numbers of artificial animals. There were moving bats and owls (controlled by wire) in *Lord Hay's Masque*. Round about Orpheus in *Lords* were "tamely placed severall wild beasts." "An artificiall Asse" figured in *Flowers*, so constructed that, "being taken with straine of the Musicke," it "did bowe downe his eares and listen with great attention." Whether the sea-horses and sea-monsters which appeared in maritime scenes were always actors in disguise is uncertain, but artificial creatures assuredly accompanied the deities—the swan with Diana, the

Fig. 186. Animal-headed Servants at Florence, *c.* 1580
Biblioteca Nazionale, Florence (C. B. 3. 53; ii, 77).

peacock with Juno, and the eagle with Jove. Moving trees formed a special attraction in *Lord Hay's Masque*.

These animals and similar figures were grotesques, and grotesques of other kinds aided them by their presence. Fools of both sexes joined hands with Dwarfs and Pigmies (Fig. 187).[1] The Dwarfs in *Richmond* were squires "attir'd in short coates of Taffita, bonnets of the same, with feathers round about them, bearing in their hands every one their Knights or Masters sheild, with their Impressa, or device." In contrast to them are the Giants of *Albion's Triumph* and *Britannia Triumphans*, the latter

> in a Coat of Mayle, his bases red and silver, with a Fauchion hanging in a Chaine; and in his hand an iron mace; a great roll of black and white on his head; a Saracens face with great black moustachoes.[2]

Finally may we note a group of fantastic persons from the *commedia dell' arte*. A Zany and a "Harlekin" have been recorded, together with several other types which, although not named after the stock figures, clearly were inspired by those. With them are to be associated the Tartaglia, Doctor, and Pedants of Francolin who appear in *Salmacida Spolia*[3] and the John

[1] For the figures in the "Mock Romansa" of *Britannia Triumphans* see *Designs*, No. 292 (Pl. XXXV). Various grotesques are shown in No. 338 (Pl. XLV, A); *cf.* also Nos. 87 (Pl. XV, A), 88 (Pl. XV, B), 293, 453, 454.
[2] See *Designs*, No. 295.
[3] See *id.*, No. 337 (Pl. XLV, B).

Farino of *Britannia Triumphans*.[1] Six Pantaloons dance an entry in *The Vision of Delight*, and there is another in *Flowers*. Francischina has a *rôle* in *Love's Triumph*,[2] and Fritellino ("Fretelyne") in *Flowers*, while the "Burratines" of *The Vision of Delight* are clearly Burratini.

In these characters all the grotesqueries of the age are revealed. Here in essence is the spirit of the 'antimasque,' by comparison with which the main masque and its gorgeously dignified figures became richer and more splendid. Sometimes the grotesqueries went even further. There were dancers disguised as Bottles, Tuns, and Barrels in *Pleasure reconciled to Virtue*; a Windmill appeared in *The Triumph of Peace*, a Hobbyhorse in *Owls*. There was a She-monster in *The Vision of Delight*, while *Althorpe* introduced Nobody, "attyred in a paire of breeches which were made to come up to his neck, with his armes out at his pockets and a cap drowning his face."

With all such marvels and oddities the directors of these shows delighted courtly audiences, seeking to give to the masque's gorgeous and bizarre settings costumes equally bizarre and gorgeous.

---

[1] *Designs*, No. 285. [2] *Id.*, No. 80 (representing "Fransiskina").

Fig. 187. A Polish Page leading a Dog
Inigo Jones.   Chatsworth (*Designs*, No. 449).
Copyright of his Grace the Duke of Devonshire.

VIII

KNIGHTS OF APOLLO

IN the performance of any masque by far the most thrilling moment came when the masquers, men or women as the theme demanded, were discovered in all their glory. Sometimes these masquers were clad to resemble particular figures, historical or mythological, and several of these have already been recorded above. Generally, however, the particular character of the masquing troop mattered less than the magnificence of their appearance, so that the costumes worn, albeit varied in shape and adornment, rarely attempted to reproduce historical forms or adapt themselves closely to allegorical requirements. A basic masquing dress is familiar from the earliest entertainments of this kind down to the final lavishness of *Salmacida Spolia*.

THE MASQUERS

The women masquers of *The Vision of the Twelve Goddesses* pretended to be deities, and as such have been dealt with among their peers. For *Blackness* Jonson, to gratify a queen's whim, created a plot which permitted the ladies to come forth as negro nymphs—"a very lothsome sight," according to a contemporary, who also took occasion to criticize the dresses as "too light and curtizan-like for such great ones."[1] An extant design by Inigo Jones[2] hardly gives evidence for the second jibe; the dress is among the fullest and most reserved of the entire series. According to Jonson, the colours were "*Azure* and *silver*" with neck and ear ornaments "of the most choise and orient pearle, best setting off from the black."

The chief masquers in *Hymenæi* were men, clad in costumes which professed to follow the Greek,[3] deliberately, according to Jonson, "taken from the *antique Greeke* statues, mixed with some *moderne* additions, which made it both gracefull and strange."

> On their heads they wore *Persick* crownes that were with scroles of *gold-plate* turn'd outward and wreath'd about with a *carnation* and *silver* net-lawne, the one end of which hung carelesly on the left shoulder; the other was trick'd up before in severall degrees of foulds betweene the plates and set with rich iewels and great pearle. Their bodies were of *carnation* cloth of silver, richly wrought and cut to expresse the *naked*, in manner of the *Greeke Thorax*, girt under the brests with a broad *belt* of cloth of gold, imbrodered, and fastened before with iewels. Their Labels were of *white* cloth of silver, lac'd and wrought curiously betweene, sutable to the upper halfe of their sleeves, whose nether parts with their bases were of *watchet* cloth of silver, chev'rond all over with lace. Their Mantills were of severall colour'd silkes, distinguishing their qualities, as they were coupled in payres; the first *skie colour*, the second *pearle colour*, the third *flame colour*, the fourth *tawnie*; and these cut in leaves, which were subtilly tack'd up and imbrodered with Oo's, and betweene every ranke of leaves a broad silver lace. They were fastened on the right shoulder and fell compasse downe the back in gracious folds and were againe tyed with a round knot to the fastning of their swords. Upon their legges they wore *silver* Greaves, answering in worke to their Labels.

"Partaking of the best both ancient and later figure," too, was "the attire of the *masquers*" in *Hue and Cry after Cupid*. The colours here were carnation and silver, "enrich'd both with

[1] Sir E. K. Chambers, *The Elizabethan Stage*, iii, 376. [2] *Designs*, No. 1 (Pl. I, A). [3] See also *id.*, Nos. 11–13.

embrodery and lace." On their heads were feathers and jewells. To what strange lengths the blending of ancient and modern could be carried is revealed in the print which accompanies Campion's *Lord Hay's Masque*, wherein the masquers were feigned to be Knights of Apollo (Fig. 190). Extravagantly habited also must have been the eight heroes of *Huntingdon Masque*, with "wisards like starres, their helmes like Mercurye's, with the addition of fayre plumes of carnation and white, their antique doublets and other furniture sutable to those colours." *Beauty*,

Fig. 188. A Knight Masquer
Inigo Jones. Chatsworth (*Designs*, No. 11).
Copyright of his Grace the Duke of Devonshire.

Fig. 189. A Knight Masquer
Inigo Jones. Chatsworth (*Designs*, No. 430).
Copyright of his Grace the Duke of Devonshire.

which immediately followed this, was a woman's masque, composed, as Jonson declared, in order to provide a sequel to *Blackness*; here the sixteen masquers were divided into two groups, the one clad in orange-tawny and silver, the other in silver and sea-green. In *Queens* the ladies were supposed to represent famous historical heroines, while in *Tethys' Festival* they became nymphs of the ocean. The fairy world, strangely mingled with the antique and the modern, intruded into *Oberon*. His knights are presumably pictured in Fig. 183.[1]

Especially glorious seem to have been the costumes in *Lords*. They are described as "infinitly rich."

The ground of their attires was massie Cloth of Silver, embossed with flames of Embroidery; on their heads they had Crownes, Flames made all of Gold-plate Enameled, and on the top a Feather of Silke, representing a cloude of smoake.

Possibly Fig. 191 shows a sketch for one of these dresses.[2] As "Olympian knights"

[1] For another graceful design which may have been executed for *Oberon* (*Designs*, No. 54) see E. Welsford, frontispiece.
[2] For a finished study see *Designs*, No. 58 (Pl. VI, A).

appeared the masquers in *Inner Temple*, disguised first by large veils or capes, but later revealed wearing

> Arming doublets of Carnation satten, embrodered with Blazing Starres of silver maile, with powderings of smaller Starres betwixt, gorgets of silver maile, long hose of the same, with the doublets laide with silver lace spangled and enricht with embroderie betweene the lace; Carnation silke stockins, imbrodered all over, garters and roses sutable; Pumpes of Carnation satten imbrodered as the doublets; hats of

Fig. 190. A KNIGHT OF APOLLO
IN "LORD HAY'S MASQUE" (1607)
Etching in the original quarto (1607).

Fig. 191. A KNIGHT MASQUER
IN "THE LORDS' MASQUE" (1613)
Inigo Jones. Chatsworth (*Designs*, No. 57).
Copyright of his Grace the Duke of Devonshire.

> the same stuffe and embroderie, cut like a helmet before, the hinder part cut into Scallops answering the skirts of their doublets; the bands of the hats were wreathes of silver in forme of garlands of wilde Olives; white feathers with one fall of Carnation; Belts of the same stuffe and embroidered with the doublet; Silver swords; little Italian bands and cuffes embroidered with silver; faire long Tresses of haire.

All we know of those in *Caversham* is that they wore "rich imbrodered sutes of greene Satten, with high hats of the same," but fuller description remains concerning *Flowers*. Doublets and hose of white satin, stockings of white silk, and pumps of white satin must have given them a vivid appearance on the stage. The doublet was

> richly imbrodered in curious panes with imbossed flowers of silver, the panes bordered with imbrodery of carnation silke and silver. The hose cut in panes answerable to the embroderie of the doublets. The skirtes of the doublets embroidered and cut into Lillies flowers and the wings set forth with flowers of severall colours, made in silke and frosted with silver, ruffe bands edged with a lace of carnation silke & silver, spangled very thicke and stucke full of flowers of severall kindes, faire vizards and tresses, delicate Cappes of silke and silver flowers of sundry kindes, with plumes of the same, in the

210

toppe whereof ſtucke a great bunch of Egrets. Every Maskers pump faſtned with a flower sutable to his cappe; on their left armes a white skarfe fairely embrodered . . . and on their hands a rich paire of embrodered gloves.

Perhaps the masquers in *The Vision of Delight*, representing the Glories of the Spring, were not unlike these. Something, too, of the same ſtyle seems to have appeared in *Browne's Masque*, when the lords wore

> doublets of greene taffita, cut like oaken leaves as upon cloth of silver, their skirtes and winges cut into leaves; deepe round hose of yͤ same; both lin'd with sprigge lace spangled; long white sylke ſtockings; greene pumps and roses done over with sylver leaves; hattes of yͤ same ſtuffe and cut narrowe-brim'd and risinge smaller compasse at yͤ crowne; white wreath hat bandes, white plumes, egrettes with a greene fall, ruffe bands and cuffes.

For three masquing suits in *Pleasure reconciled to Virtue* an extant account informs us that the coſt was over £249. In these were tinsel and silver lace, crimson satin and watchet satin, white taffeta and "silver spangled sprigg lace," silver points and ornamented buttons. One performer wore "a fayre white plume . . . with ffiftie dozen of Egretts"; his ruff and cuffs were "edged with a fayre peake purle."

"Mixt, betweene the Ancient and moderne," were the habits of the masquers in *The Triumph of Peace*:

Fig. 192. A KNIGHT MASQUER
Inigo Jones. Chatsworth (*Designs*, No. 431).
Copyright of his Grace the Duke of Devonshire.

> their bodies Carnation, the shoulders trim'd with Knots of pure silver and scallops of White and Carnation; under them the Labels of the same, the under-sleeves white, and a puft sleeve full of gathering falling downe to the elbow; about their waſte was a small scallop and a slender Girdle; their under Bases were Carnation and White, with Labels as at their shoulders, and all this in every part was richly Embroydered with pure silver; their Hats Carnation low croun'd, the brimme double and cut into severall quarters lined with white and all over richly Embroydered as the reſt; about their Hats were wreathes of Olive and plumes of white Feathers with severall falls, the longeſt toward the backe; their long ſtockings were white, with white shooes and Roses.

The "ancient hero" motive again appeared in *Cælum Britannicum*, "the Colours yellow embroydered with Silver, their antique Helmes curiously wrought and great plumes on the top" (Fig. 193).

In *The Temple of Love* the ladies again took the lead, the masquers surrounding Indamora, Queen of Narsinga. Their dresses were "of *Isabella* Colour and Watchet, with Bases in large panes cut through, all over richly embroidered with silver, and the dressing of their heads was of silver, with small falls of white feathers tipp'd with Watchet."

As Knights Templars the men ſtepped forth in *The Triumphs of the Prince d'Amour*, their habits "Martial and richly imbroider'd, inclining near the old Roman shape; their Helmets Triumphantly plum'd, whiles the Bevir falling o're the face serv'd for a disguise and supply'd to each the office of a Vizard." And "Roman" too was their coſtume in *Britannia Triumphans* (Fig. 194):

> The habit of the Masquers was close bodies of Carnation, embroydered with silver, their arming sleeves of the same; about their waſte two rowes of severall fashioned leaves and under this their bases of white, reaching to the middle of their thigh; on this was an under basis with labels of Carnation

embroidered with silver and betwixt every paine were pufts of silver, faſtned in knots to the labels; the trimming of the shoulders was as that of the Basis; their long ſtockins set up were Carnation with white shooes and roses; their bands and cuffes made of purles of Cutworke; upon their heads little carnation caps embroydered as the reſt, with a slit turned up before; out of the midſt came severall falls of white feathers diminishing upward in a Pyramidall forme.

Fig. 193. A KNIGHT MASQUER
IN "CŒLUM BRITANNICUM"
(1634)

Inigo Jones. Chatsworth (*Designs*, No. 201). Copyright of his Grace the Duke of Devonshire.

Fig. 194. A KNIGHT MASQUER
IN "BRITANNIA TRIUMPHANS"
(1638)

Inigo Jones. Chatsworth (*Designs*, No. 304). Copyright of his Grace the Duke of Devonshire.

Lady Masquers once more appear in *Luminalia*, amply illuſtrated in designs by Inigo Jones.[1] Here they had

close bodies, open before the breaſts, of *Aurora* colour, richly embroidered with silver; about the waſte ran a short Basis, cut in ſtarre-like beames of white and under these were lower labels, large at the bottome and cut in a Trefoile, tacked together with small twiſts of gold; the ornament at the shoulders comming down to the bowing of the arme was of the same colour and forme as the Basis, their arming-sleeves and skirts of their gownes as that of the bodies; they wore well-proportioned ruffes and on their haire ſtood a small bend or diadem of jewels and ſtarres betweene, which in the hinder part had a scrowle, large at the bottome and narrow toward the top, to which their fals of white feathers were faſtned.

Fit companions were they for King Charles and his courtiers when they were discovered gloriously in *Salmacida Spolia*, clad in coſtumes of "watchet, richly embroydered with silver," with white ſtockings and silver caps "with scrowles of gold." The details of these dresses have been

[1] *Designs*, Nos. 312–318 (Pl. XLI, A; XLI, B).

happily preserved. One, specifically marked "for yᵉ kinge 1640,"[1] shows us Charles's own array, and others indicate the appearance of his troop.[2]

THE TORCH-BEARERS

In a blaze of light these masquers flashed into sight, their resplendent silver and gold, carnation and white, taking on an additional glory because of the comparative darkness of earlier scenes and

their majestic richness set off by contrast with the bizarre eccentricities of the immediately preceding antimasques. The vivid illumination which revealed their costumes came from two sources. Partly it was provided by the nature of the setting with the concealed lamps reflecting the scintillating stuffs of which their dresses were composed; partly it was introduced by the torch-bearers who almost invariably attended their masters. The sole business of the torch-bearer was to add glory to others. "He is just like a Torch-bearer to Maskers," says a character in *Westward Hoe*; "he wears good cloathes and is rankt in good company, but he doth nothing."

Usually the "good clothes" of these attendants were wrought in harmony with the masquing clothes. "Betweene every ranke of Goddesses," we read of *The Vision of the Twelve Goddesses*, "marched three Torch-bearers in the like severall colours, their heads and Robes all deᵍt with Starres"; and this principle, thus established in the first great masque of James's reign, was continued through the others that followed. As Oceaniæ, riding on sea-monsters and with torches made of shells, they attended the ladies in *Blackness*. Clad as pages in white, they appeared in *Hymenæi*, and as "Pages in blew satten robes, imbrodered with starres," in *Huntingdon Masque*. Green satin graced them in *Caversham*, where they wore "high hats of the same." "Like fierie spirits, all their attires being alike composed of flames, with fierie Wings and Bases," they burst into *Lords*;[3] in *Middle Temple* their dress was the

Fig. 195. A TORCH-BEARER IN "CŒLUM BRITANNICUM" (1634)

Inigo Jones. Chatsworth (*Designs*, No. 204).
Copyright of his Grace the Duke of Devonshire.

Indian garb, but more stravagant then those of the Maskers, all showfully garnisht with several-hewd feathers. The humble variety whereof stucke off the more amplie the Maskers high beauties, shining in the habits of themselves, and reflected in their kinde a new and delightfully varied radiance on the beholders [Fig. 170].

Most elaborate were their costumes in *Cœlum Britannicum*. There, impersonated by "a troop of young Lords and Noblemens Sons," they "were apparelled after the old British fashion in white Coats, embroydered with silver, girt and full gathered, cut square coller'd, and round caps on their heads, with a white feather wreathen about them." This dress is shown in Fig. 195.[4]

[1] *Designs*, No. 341 (Pl. XLVII, B).   [2] *Id.*, Nos. 342–348 (Pl. XLVI, A; XLVI, B).
[3] See *id.*, No. 59 (frontispiece).   [4] See also *id.*, Nos. 205, 206.

While adding splendour, one may imagine that quite frequently the presence of this group of attendants, with flaming torches, may have defeated its own object. The direct light might easily have negated the concealed illumination which was designed to shed bright rays on the masquers. Perhaps Daniel felt this when in *Tethys' Festival* he boldly dispensed with their services, although the explanation he advanced suggests another cause. "The introducing of Pages with torches," he informs us, "might have added more splendor, but yet they would have pestered the roome, which the season [the month of June] would not well permit." His procedure, however, seems not to have been followed by others, and in our mental reconstruction of a masque performance we must include this troop of "young Lords" whose torches flashed radiance upon the settings and upon the newly discovered assemblage of knights or heroes, impersonated by the highest lords of the land.

Fig. 196. MASKS WITH HEADDRESSES
Inigo Jones. Chatsworth (*Designs*, No. 463).
Copyright of his Grace the Duke of Devonshire.

For this discovery the entire masque was conceived; all the rest—the changing prospects, the descents of deities, the eccentric measures of the antimasque—was merely a framework and a preparation for the true masquing display when the noble courtiers, suddenly revealed in their glory, doffed their vizards and descended in solemn state from their thrones or triumphal chariots. Far removed is this from the spirit of the public theatre, yet the masque, intimately related to the Italian *intermezzi*, played no unimportant part in bringing the theatre to the condition in which it now is. Through the experimentation of an Inigo Jones, theatrical machinery and standard methods of scenic display became established; in the masque the proscenium arch and the attendant conception of living pictures upon the stage were definitely made familiar; from the costumes, mixed antique and modern, of the masquers the tragic heroes of nearly two centuries took their model.

The candles and lamps are gone from Whitehall, and the masquing entertainment is a thing of a distant and colourful past; but the theatre, with its long memory and sense of tradition, has never quite forgotten the days when a king in state, surrounded by his courtiers, sat in dignified isolation to hear Ben Jonson's words and watch the scenic marvels created by Inigo Jones. "Thus," says Whitelocke, "was this earthly pomp and glory, if not vanity, soon passed over and gone, as if it had never been," [1] yet the air still trembles with the echoes of Sabrina's song and the coarse laughter of Comus, nor has the theatre of another age been able quite to forget the canvas oceans and the flimsy forests of this vanished stage.

[1] Bulstrode Whitelocke, *Memorials* (Oxford, 1853), i, 61.

APPENDIX

LIST OF MASQUES (1603–41)

[The first titles given in italics are those by which the various masques are referred to in the text of this work. Only a few 'entertainments' are noted here. The figures after the author's name indicate the day and month of production: 25/6 is June 25.]

1603. *Althorpe*

    Ben Jonson. 25/6. *A particular Entertainment of the Queene and Prince their Highnesse to Althrope* (4to, 1604 (in *B. Jon: his part of King James his Royall and Magnificent Entertainement*)).

1604. *The Vision of the Twelve Goddesses*

    Samuel Daniel. 8/1, Hampton Court. *The Vision of the 12. Goddesses* (8vo, 1604).

    Penates

    Ben Jonson. 1/5, house of Sir William Cornwallis. *A Private Entertainment . . . At Sir William Cornwalleis his house* (folio, 1616).

1605. *Blackness*

    Ben Jonson. 6/1, Banqueting House. *The Characters of Two royall Masques. The one of Blacknesse, The other of Beautie* (4to, [1608]; folio, 1616).

1606. *Hymenæi*

    Ben Jonson. 5/1, Banqueting House. *Hymenæi: or the Solemnities of Masque, and Barriers* (4to, 1606; folio, 1616).

1607. *Lord Hay's Masque*

    Thomas Campion. 6/1, Great Hall. *The Discription of a Maske . . . in honour of the Lord Hayes* (4to, 1607).

    Entertainment at Theobalds

    Ben Jonson. 22/5, Theobalds. *An Entertainment . . . at Theobalds* (folio, 1616).

    Huntingdon Masque

    John Marston. /8, Ashby Castle. *The Masque presented . . . at the right noble Earle of Huntingdons house of Ashebie* (manuscript, printed in J. Nichols, *The Progresses of James the First*, ii, 145–150).

1608. *Beauty*

    Ben Jonson. 10/1, Banqueting House. See under *Blackness*, above.

    Hue and Cry after Cupid

    Ben Jonson. 9/2, Whitehall. *The Description of the Masque . . . Celebrating the happy Marriage of Iohn, Lord Ramsey, Viscount Hadington* (4to, [1608]; folio, 1616).

1609. *Queens*

    Ben Jonson. 2/2, Banqueting House. *The Masque of Queenes Celebrated from the House of Fame* (4to, 1609; folio, 1616).

1610. *Tethys' Festival*

    Samuel Daniel. 5/6, Whitehall. *Tethys Festival: or The Queenes Wake* (4to, 1610).

1611. *Oberon*

    Ben Jonson. 1/1, Banqueting House. *Oberon, the Faery Prince* (folio, 1616).

    Love freed from Ignorance

    Ben Jonson. /2. *A Masque of Her Maiesties. Love freed from Ignorance and Folly* (folio, 1616).

1612. *Twelve Months*

    Unknown. 1/1 (?). *The Masque of the Twelve Months* (manuscript, first printed by J. P. Collier, *Inigo Jones . . . And five Court Masques* (1848), pp. 131–142).

    Love Restored

    Ben Jonson. 6/1. *Love Restored. In a Masque at Court* (folio, 1616).

1613. *Lords*

Thomas Campion. 14/2, Banqueting House. *Description of the Lords Maske . . . on the Mariage Night of the . . . Count Palatine* (in *A Relation Of The Late Royall Entertainment . . . At Cawsome-House* (4to, 1613)).

Middle Temple

George Chapman. 15/2, Great Hall. *The Memorable Masque of the two Honourable Houses or Innes of Court: the Middle Temple, and Lyncolnes Inne* (4to, [1613]).

Inner Temple

Francis Beaumont. 20/2, Banqueting House. *The Masque of the Inner Temple and Grayes Inne* (4to, [1613]).

Caversham Masque

Thomas Campion. 27/4, Caversham House. See *Lords*, above.

Somerset's Masque

Thomas Campion. 26/12, Banqueting House. *The description of a Maske: presented . . . At the Mariage of the Right Honourable the Earle of Somerset* (4to, 1614).

Irish Masque

Ben Jonson. 29/12 and 3/1/1614, Whitehall. *The Irish Masque at Court* (folio, 1616).

1614. *Flowers*

Unknown. 6/1, Banqueting House. *The Maske of Flowers* (4to, 1614).

1615. *Mercury Vindicated*

Ben Jonson. 6/1 and 8/1. *Mercury vindicated from the Alchemists* (folio, 1616).

Browne's Masque

William Browne. 13/1. *The Inner Temple Masque* (manuscript, printed in *The Whole Works of William Browne* (ed. W. C. Hazlitt, 1868), ii, 239–259).

1616. *The Golden Age Restored*

Ben Jonson. 1/1 and 6/1. *The Golden Age restor'd* (folio, 1616).

Christmas

Ben Jonson. December (?). *Christmas, his Masque* (folio, 1640).

1617. *The Vision of Delight*

Ben Jonson. 6/1 and 19/1, Whitehall. *The Vision of Delight* (folio, 1640).

Lovers made Men

Ben Jonson. 22/2, Essex House. *Lovers made Men* (4to, 1617; folio, 1640.) (This is sometimes called *The Masque of Lethe*.)

Cupid's Banishment

Robert White. 4/5, Deptford. *Cupid's Banishment* (manuscript, printed in J. Nichols, *The Progresses of James the First*, iii, 283–296).

1618. *Pleasure reconciled to Virtue*

Ben Jonson. 6/1 and 17/2, Banqueting House. *Pleasure reconciled to Vertue* (folio, 1640).

Mountebanks

John Marston (?). 19/2, Banqueting House. *The Masque of Grayes Inne; with the Antimasques of Mountebanks* (manuscript, printed in J. P. Collier, *Inigo Jones*, pp. 111–130).

1619. *Heroes*

Thomas Middleton. /1. *The Inner-Temple Masque. Or Masque of Heroes* (4to, 1619).

1620. *World tost at Tennis*

Thomas Middleton and William Rowley. Denmark House (?). *A Courtly Masque: The Device Called The World tost at Tennis* (4to, 1620).

Pan's Anniversary

Ben Jonson. 19/1 (?), Salisbury (?). *Pan's Anniversarie; or, the Shepherds Holy-Day* (folio, 1640). The date given by Jonson is 1625; perhaps this masque did not appear until 1624.

1621. *News from the New World*

Ben Jonson. 6/1 and 11/2. *Newes from the New World discover'd in the Moone* (folio, 1640).

Gipsies

Ben Jonson. 3/8, Burleigh; 5/8, Belvoir; and 9/9, Windsor. *The Masque of the Gypsies* (12mo, 1640 (with *Q. Horatius Flaccus: His Art of Poetry*); folio, 1640 (as *A Masque of the Metamorphos'd Gypsies*)).

APPENDIX

1622. *Augurs*
  Ben Jonson. 6/1 and 5/5 or 6/5, Banqueting House. *The Masque of Augures* (4to, 1621; folio, 1640).
1623. *Time Vindicated*
  Ben Jonson. 19/1, Banqueting House. *Time vindicated to himselfe, and to his Honors* (folio, 1640).
1624. *Neptune's Triumph*
  Ben Jonson. Planned for 6/1. *Neptunes Triumph for the returne of Albion* (4to, [1624]; folio, 1640).
  Owls
  Ben Jonson. 19/8, Kenilworth. *The Masque of Owles* (folio, 1640).
1625. *The Fortunate Isles*
  Ben Jonson. 9/1. *The Fortunate Isles and their Union* (4to, [1625]; folio, 1640).
1631. *Love's Triumph*
  Ben Jonson. 9/1. *Loves Triumph through Callipolis* (4to, 1630; folio, 1640).
  Chloridia
  Ben Jonson. 22/2. *Chloridia. Rites to Chloris and her Nymphs* (4to, 1630; folio, 1640).
1632. *Albion's Triumph*
  Aurelian Townsend. 8/1, Banqueting House. *Albions Triumph* (4to, 1631).
  Tempe Restored
  Aurelian Townsend. 14/2, Great Hall. *Tempe restord* (4to, 1631).
1634. *The Triumph of Peace*
  James Shirley. 3/2, Banqueting House; 11/2 or 13/2, Merchant Tailors' Hall. *The Triumph of Peace* (4to, 1633).
  Cœlum Britannicum
  Thomas Carew. 18/2, Banqueting House. *Cœlum Britanicum* (4to, 1634; also in the *Works* (1673) of Sir William D'Avenant).
  Love's Welcome (Bolsover)
  Ben Jonson. 30/7. *Loves Welcome. The King and Queenes Entertainment at Bolsover* (folio, 1640).
  Comus
  John Milton. 29/9, Ludlow. *A Maske presented at Ludlow Castle* (4to, 1637).
1635. *The Temple of Love*
  Sir William D'Avenant. 10/2, Banqueting House. *The Temple of Love* (4to, 1634; *Works*, 1673).
1636. *The Triumphs of the Prince d'Amour*
  Sir William D'Avenant. 23/2 or 24/2, Middle Temple. *The Triumphs of the Prince D'Amour* (4to, 1635; *Works*, 1673).
  Richmond
  Unknown. 12/9, Richmond. *The King and Queenes Entertainement at Richmond* (4to, 1636).
1638. *Britannia Triumphans*
  Sir William D'Avenant. 7/1, Masquing House. *Britannia Triumphans* (4to, 1637).
  Luminalia
  Sir William D'Avenant. 6/2, Masquing House. *Luminalia, or The Festivall of Light* (4to, 1637).
1639. *Brethbie*
  Sir Aston Cockayne. 6/1, Brethbie. *A Masque, presented at Bretbie* (in *A Chain of Poems* (8vo, 1658)).
1640. *Salmacida Spolia*
  Sir William D'Avenant. 21/1, Masquing House. *Salmacida Spolia* (4to, 1639).
1641. *Knowsley Masque*
  Sir John Salusbury. 6/1, Knowsley Hall. *A Masque at Knowsley* (*Transactions of the Historic Society of Lancashire and Cheshire*, lxxvii (1925), 1–16).

[*The Masque of the Four Seasons*, printed by J. P. Collier, *Inigo Jones*, pp. 103–110, has no certain dating. For further particulars concerning the masques produced at court see P. Reyher, pp. 516–532. The most important pageants were *The Arches of Triumph*, designed by Jonson and Dekker in 1604, and Middleton's *The Triumphs of Truth* (1613). These are printed in J. Nichols, *The Progresses of James the First*, i, 339–399, and ii, 683–688.]

INDEX

INDEX

INDEX

INDEX